Your Life Can Be Better

Your Life Can Be Better
Using strategies for adult ADD/ADHD

Dedicated to the disorganized, distracted and demoralized.

Douglas A. Puryear, MD

"Most men live lives of quiet desperation."
Thoreau

Illustrations by Juan Antonio Villalobos

Mill City Press

Mill City Press, Inc.
212 3ʳᵈ Avenue North, Suite 290
Minneapolis, MN 55401
612.455.2294
www.millcitypublishing.com

ISBN-13: 978-1-937600-43-3
LCCN: 2011942055

Cover Design and Typeset by Nate Meyers
Illustrations by Juan Antonio Villalobos
Cover Photo © 2011. All rights reserved - used with permission.

Printed in the United States of America

Acknowledgments

With gratitude to:

My wife, Martha, who has chosen to tolerate me, my ADD, and my writing, with varying degrees of patience but with constant affection.

All those family, friends and patients who have contributed to this book and allowed me to tell part of their stories.

All those who struggled to review some of the terrible early drafts, and those who reviewed and proofread the last ones, which were somewhat better.

Those few hardy souls who both contributed and reviewed.

And Juan, the illustrator.

Thank you!
Doug Puryear

Table of Contents

Your Life Can Be Better

Life can be hard sometimes. If we have Attention Deficit Disorder, a.k.a ADD, it makes life much harder. Despite our best intentions, we're always messing up, and people are frustrated with us. ADD causes us a lot of problems, and we've all devised ways to cope with them, ways that work more or less well.

I am a psychiatrist who has ADD. I'm going to share with you some of the ways I've learned to cope with my ADD problems. I'll also share with you some coping strategies from my friends, Tom, Richard and Harry, and some from my patients with ADD. I will also share some of the ways that we all are still not coping so well.

Unlike most books on ADD, the focus of this book is on strategies: strategies that will make your life easier.

Section I

The basics: problems and strategies

Life with ADD is hard. Strategies make life much easier. Let me give you an example of a basic strategy and how this works.

Chapter 1

"Where are my keys?"

I was losing my keys about three times a week. I'm not good at looking for things. Actually, I'm pretty good at looking for things; I can do it for a long time. I'm just not good at finding things. If something is not where I expect it to be, or isn't looking like I expect it to look, I can't find it. In the refrigerator, unless the ketchup bottle is the color and shape I expect, and in approximately the place I expect be it to be, I can look right at it and just not see it. I can easily spend fifteen minutes or more looking for my keys. When I can't find them, I usually have to ask my wife to help me. I'll often be in a rush and a panic, and always frustrated. My wife does not have ADD, but neither does she have unlimited patience, and she gets tired of this. She figured out the solution:

The strategy is to put my keys on the table by the front door. I always put my keys on the front table. I don't allow myself to put them anywhere else, not "just for now," not "just this time," not "because I'm busy." No. On the front table. I do not leave them in my jacket pocket. I do not lay them on my desk or on the bureau top. I put them on the table by the front door. Right now. Always.

Now that is a strategy that becomes a rule. And the rule helps me make it a habit. And a habit means that I don't have to think about it anymore.

Strategy.... Rule.... Habit....

I have a lot of rules, and I'm grateful for them, because my life is so much easier now. So that rule about the keys is a strategy, which was made into a rule, which became a habit. But to be honest, occasionally this has to work as a rule again. If I hear myself saying, "Oh, it will be alright just this once," my rule says, "Oh, no, it won't." That not only saves me trouble that one time, but it keeps the habit strong.

It took a while to make that a habit. I slipped up a number of times, but I kept at it and it did become a habit. Now I don't have to think about it, I don't have to remember it, I just do it. Keys on table. The truth is, I lose my keys still, but maybe twice a year instead of three times a week, and even that's getting better.

Summary:
- Identify a problem.
- Pick a strategy.
- Make a rule.
- Stick with it.
- It becomes a habit.
- Life is easier.

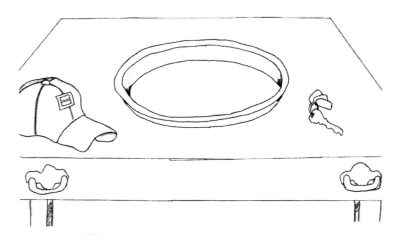

Illustration 1.   The table by the front door
The keys go here!

Chapter 2

About the book

This chapter tells you about the book. This ordinarily would be the introduction, but when I pick up a book, I often skip the introduction and maybe you would, too. I wanted to give you a real example of what this book can offer right off the bat, rather than beginning by telling you what I was going to tell you. If you've gotten this far you probably have some idea what it's about anyway, but I want to share a little more information with you. It's probably worth your reading, but it's up to you.

There are many books on ADD out there, many of them good, many of them similar. This book aims to be different:

1. It doesn't go much into the history of ADD, the definition, causes, diagnosis, medications; it focuses on using strategies to make your life better.

2. It gives specific real life examples of people struggling with ADD rather than general tools or made up cases.
3. It's personal; it could be subtitled "my life with ADD". I hope this will make it light reading rather than hard work or study, and will make it more interesting so that you will get more out of it.

This book focuses on strategies, tried and true ways to deal with your ADD and to make your life much easier. I know they work, because they work for me and have made my life easier.

The strategies in this book deal with some specific problems that ADD causes. I've given you one example: my habit of losing my keys. Some of these problems are big and important, and some of them are seemingly trivial, but a day filled with minor frustrations is usually not a good day; even minor frustrations add up.

The book may help you recognize which problems and frustrations in your life are related to ADD, and you may identify some of the things you do that are your way of coping with ADD. You may congratulate yourself for having come up with these ways, or you may realize that there might be better ways. We are all different: my problems may not be the same as your problems, and my solutions may not be the ones that will work best for you. But if we both have ADD we will have a lot in common.

When we have ADD, we're trying to live daily life with at least one hand tied behind our back. Our life will be harder than it has to be. We can use strategies and tools to make our life better. That is my hope for you. Even small changes can make a big difference. I told you how one small change, a rule about my keys, made a significant difference in my life.

This book is written mostly from my own experience. I don't intend to push spiritual beliefs on anyone, but since the examples are real and largely from my own life, some of them will be about spiritual things. But you can apply the strategies and principles to anything you want.

I want to tip you off in advance; there's a lot of information here and some readers have said they found it overwhelming. Just take it easy, see what clicks for you: "Oh, I know about that!" or "Hey, that makes sense; maybe I could try that." Pick one or two things you want to work on. It will take time to master them. Then pick another. It's taken me well over fifty years to create the strategies I use and to make the habits I need, and I'm still working on it, as you will see.

I've mostly written in the first person, "I," because I thought that would make it more interesting, and maybe less threatening. You can say, "Oh, that poor devil. Thank God I'm not like him" (like many alcoholics say at their first AA meeting). And the "I" stories might be more likely to turn your focus center on. That's the place in our brain where our problem lives, in our hardwiring, which causes us to have trouble focusing. It can also be called the "attention center."

I also use "we", because we're in the same boat, and "we" might make it easier for you to pick up the similarities. But I also like the "you" approach, because I'm addressing you and hoping you will get the ideas. But then people with ADD, like me and maybe like you, don't necessarily like having our problems and flaws pointed out to us, and don't like being told what we "should" do. So I lean towards the "I" mode, hoping you'll catch the points that apply to you or the strategies that will be useful to you. But I did some of each, and probably not in any organized fashion. This could be an example of my difficulty making decisions, which we who have ADD often have. Don't you?

I want to be clear that I do not have all the answers. Some of my many ADD problems are solved by the strategies, some I am still working on, and some I don't have a clue about. And we can only work on one or two things at a time, so it's a long term ongoing project. I didn't want to tell you that it's easy.

There's a list of typical ADD problems on page 15; you might want to glance at that and see if any of it seems familiar. Or you might not; it could look pretty demoralizing. Fortunately, there's also an outline of coping strategies on page 18, and you might want to glance at that and see which ones you are already using.

About the term itself, ADD, attention deficit disorder: the official term is ADHD, attention–deficit/ hyperactivity disorder. I prefer ADD; it's shorter and it best fits what I personally struggle with. So from now on, I will use ADHD only when I want to emphasize the hyperactivity aspect.

Maybe you don't have ADD yourself, but you're reading this because someone else does: a partner, friend or relative, a colleague or employee, a student, or even a boss. This book will help you understand them, which will help you cope with them and decrease the frustration you both share.

The symptoms and problems of ADD are pretty common in humans; many people have some of them some of the time. The difference is that those of us with ADD have most of them most of the time, and they cause lots of problems for us, both large and small problems. If you have not been diagnosed, you may find yourself wondering if you have ADD.

If it's a strong enough suspicion, you don't need to diagnose yourself; you can get some professional help with this. Diagnosis is discussed on page 360.

Summary:

This book is written to help you make your life better by using strategies to cope with your ADD. It can also help non-ADDers understand ADD problems.

Chapter 3

Our focus center

Our focus center is different. This is the hypothetical spot in our brain that has to be turned on in order for us to focus our attention on something. Our focus centers simply don't turn on like people's without ADD.

Our lack of focus is our primary problem and the source of many of our difficulties, like procrastination, trouble setting priorities, trouble dealing with time, trouble finishing projects, perfectionism, and the inevitable demoralization. We have trouble starting something, staying with it and not getting distracted. We drift into dead ends and into unnecessary and fruitless pursuits and time wasters. All of this is due to our focus center not being turned on when we need it.

Paradoxically, sometimes we have extreme focus. If our focus center is turned on, we can focus - we can really focus! This can be good; we can really accomplish something if our focus center is turned on. But we can have trouble shifting to something else when we need to. Maybe I have finally gotten around to starting work on the dripping faucet, which I procrastinated about because I wasn't quite sure I could fix it. Now at last I'm working on it. I'm focused on what I'm doing, and my wife innocently enough says, "Doug, when you've finished that would you please take a look at my computer?" That drives me up the wall. I'm focused, totally focused, on the faucet. I cannot deal with anything else right now.

Or sometimes when I can get started on an ongoing project, like this book, I become, as my wife unhappily says, "preoccupied" with it, obsessed. This is the opposite of the inability to focus; it's hyper focus.

So, as a model, we say that there is a problem with the focus center in our brain. Most people's focus center is turned on by the fact that something is important. But not ours. We understand "important." We can acknowledge "important", but "important" does nothing for us. "Important" does not turn on our focus center and we can be nearly helpless to try to get something done without our focus center on.

But our focus center does get turned on at times.

It gets turned on by :

1. Things that happen to be of **personal interest** to us. I have no interest in taxes and bookkeeping. It's very hard for me to get the taxes done. But I'm interested in writing, and I can do that, at least once I can get started.

2. Something that is **novel** to us. So I get excited when someone takes me bowling for the first time and shows me how to do it. I want to go out and buy a ball and some good bowling shoes, and I'm bowling every night for a month, and then I'm done. The expensive ball and shoes go in the back of the closet, and I'm off on some other new obsessive interest, probably also temporary, because nothing can stay new, novel, for very long.

3. Something that is a **challenge**. When I take something as personally challenging, I want to master it, or I want to show that I can do it better than someone else. And of course, once I've mastered it, it not only is no longer novel but it's no longer a challenge. So then I lose interest, and the focus is gone.

4. Something with an immediate **deadline**, with heavy consequences. That's why we can finally get around to doing the assignment the night before it's due. We stay up all night and very likely we even do a good job. And if it doesn't go so well, still we can protect our self esteem by saying, "Well, I only got to it at the last moment."

It's useful to remember these four focus center turn ons: personal interest, novelty, challenge, deadline. Then we can use them to help ourselves focus and get some things done. Sometimes I use them to play mind games with myself, which I'll discuss later. There are ways to trick my brain into focusing.

Summary:

We have trouble with focusing. Sometimes we hyperfocus. Four things will turn on our focus center:

1. personal interest
2. novelty
3. challenge
4. immediate and heavy deadline

Chapter 4

Effects of having ADD

What are the effects of having ADD? Our life is difficult, often frustrating, often pressured, and sometimes miserable. It's no fun spending fifteen minutes searching for my car keys, and not finding them, and then having to ask my wife to find them and then having her aggravated with me because I've lost them again. And that's only a trivial problem. We have trouble with keeping appointments, being on time, meeting deadlines, organizing, getting things done, losing things. As a consequence we have trouble holding jobs or staying married. We tend to feel depressed and we have a high tendency to develop alcohol and drug problems. My personal addiction happens to be food. It used to also be computer games.

List of Problems

These are some of the ADD problems that will covered in this book. You might use them as a check list, to note which problems you have. We have problems with:
- focusing our attention
- being able to shift our attention
- getting distracted
- finishing things
- setting priorities
- going off on tangents and dead end projects
- impulsiveness
- being socially inappropriate
- blurting things out
- irritability
- judging time
- organization
- sloppiness
- losing things
- finding things
- learning disabilities
- fine motor skills
- reading
- relationships
- jobs
- and the resulting demoralization

That does seem like an overwhelming list; it's a wonder we survive at all, let alone function. Where would we be without strategies?

Summary:
There are many problems associated with ADD. Most basically stem from the difficulty with the focus center. But don't despair! Life can be better with strategies. Read on.

Chapter 5

Strategies

This book is about strategies, rules, and habits. Strategies are tools to help us deal with problems and thus make our life go smoother and easier. When we identify a problem, something that makes our lives more difficult and less productive, or that adds to the pile of minor irritations, like my always losing my keys, for example, then we come up with a strategy to help. Then we keep applying that strategy and make it a rule (except that we keep forgetting to apply it, of course, because we have ADD). But we just keep applying the strategy when we can remember, and eventually it becomes a habit. That means we don't have to remember it or think about it anymore; it's just a habit. Then we can pick another problem to work on. We can only work on one or two problems at a time, though.

Here is a list of the strategies that are most important to me. They will be discussed and explained as we go on. You may find that you are already using some of them.

List of strategies:
- Most important tools:
  - appointment book
  - to do list
  - small steps
  - positive self-talk
  - reframing, attitude
- Most important rules:
  - keys on front table
  - check gasoline hose before driving off
  - look behind me before backing down the driveway
- Most important slogans:
  - Do it now, do it right, do the hard part first.
  - I have as much time as anyone else.
- Most important red flags:
  - "Oh, it'll be ok."
  - "Oh, I have plenty of time."

All of these will be explained as we go on.

Summary:
ADD causes us lots of problems, small and large. Strategies help, especially once we make them hab-

its. We can deliberately choose problems to work on, one or two at a time, and overcome the difficulty.

The formula is: identify the problem, make a strategy, make the strategy a rule, stick with it, make the rule a habit.

Strategy....Rule....Habit....

Chapter 6

I learn that I have ADD

I was sixty-four years old when I first learned that I had ADD. Suddenly, a lot of things made sense: Why I carry a pocket full of index cards. Why I couldn't make model airplanes like the other guys when I was a kid. Why I killed a pregnant guppy fish. Why I made a "C" in engineering drawing in high school. Why I couldn't study in college. Why I kept losing my car keys. And on and on.

About the model airplanes: in those days, you got a kit with instructions, some plans on tissue paper, more tissue paper, and some very light soft wood, balsa. You laid the plans on the wood and cut it, carefully and precisely, with a sharp Xacto knife. Then you glued it together precisely and carefully according to the instructions and waited patiently for it to dry. Then you carefully stretched the thin paper over it, wet it so it would shrink, and you waited patiently for that to dry. Then you put on a rubber band motor or a small gas motor and it would fly!

I could buy the kit, but what I was lacking was the "carefully", the "precisely", the ability to follow the directions, and above all, the "patiently". Just couldn't do it. So I bought ship kits and made ships instead. Guess what? They had blocks of harder wood that you had to patiently sand to the precise shape of the hull. Then you had to patiently sand the smaller parts, precisely glue them together according to the directions and then paint the ship. But it was easier than the airplanes. Since I didn't have the patience for sanding the hull, my ships usually had a deck that was sloping up in front instead of flat. Still, some of them looked pretty good.

The guppy was about patience too. She was beautiful and pregnant, brought home from the pet store in a plastic bag of water. I was putting new water in the aquarium for her and the water had to be boiled to drive the chlorine out. I boiled it, waited a while and felt the water. It was still too hot, but I said "Oh, it'll be alright" - and put her in. She came to the top belly up and died. "It'll be alright." - dangerous words.

This was my ADD in childhood. Like for many of us, it continues into adulthood.

Summary:

When I finally learned I had ADD, a lot of things suddenly made sense. I could understand many of the difficulties I'd had all my life, and also many of the habits I had developed which, it turns out, were strategies to cope with my ADD.

Chapter 7

First, the appointment book and the to-do list

I've read a number of books on ADD. They vary significantly but all agree on one thing: when you find out you have ADD the first thing you need to do is actually two things: get an appointment book and make a to-do list. Maybe you make a to-do list first, and then the first thing on it is to get an appointment book! But you need to do both. Of course, just doing that isn't enough; then you need to learn how to use them.

Appointment book

All of my shirts have a pocket, and my appointment book fits in there. It has a celluloid cover; in the front is a religious picture and on the back a photo of my grandsons. The inside covers have flaps where I keep photos of all my grandkids (so that I can easily share them with anyone who might have the slightest interest), a copy of my weekly standing appointment schedule, a list of principles of living that I need to review regularly, and my favorite poem. But the main thing in the appointment book is the monthly appointment schedule. I need a month at a glance type, so I can look at it and orient myself in time. Otherwise, I become lost and confused, and things come up that I should have known about but was thinking were way way off; if you don't have ADD you may not know what I'm talking about here.

I've made a habit of recording every appointment, carefully and correctly and legibly. I've made a habit of looking at the book about six times a day, like whenever I'm not actually doing something. When I'm sitting with my wife, this bothers her. I explain that I need to see what's going on, but she doesn't have ADD so she doesn't understand and she feels neglected. I don't just look at the book, I study it. Sometimes I just orient myself. Sometimes I find a mistake that I've made (I have ADD, you see), or I see something that's coming that I need to prepare for. And I need to fix a pattern in my mind of what tomorrow will look like, and what needs to be done and when. So it's not just a glance, it's a real look, and it's at least six times a day. My life has gone much better since I started to do this, and now it's a habit. I never hear myself saying, "Oh, I forgot to look at my appointment book." It doesn't happen.

I keep my appointment book with me everywhere I go, even if it doesn't seem to make sense. I'd feel naked without it. Ok, I don't sleep with it or take it into the shower, but everywhere else. Have I made it clear that the appointment book is vitally important and that you not only need to have it, you need to use it, and it needs to become a habit?

To-do list

And my to-do list. Very necessary to have it, but there are tricks I need to do to make it work. I'll tell you about the whole system later, but right now let's focus on the red card. It has the major things to do that I'm working on right now. Like the appointment book, it is always with me.

These to-do's are the major, non-routine things that really need to get done, probably today or tomorrow. They may be steps that are part of a larger project. For example, right now I'm working on my taxes for the year. That is a major project and will take me over a month to complete. I don't have "taxes" on my red card; I have "get charity info," which is the step of the taxes that I need to do next.

In order to make the red card work, I need to look at it as often as the appointment book, at least six times a day. Second, an important rule: I cannot have more than five things on my to-do list. I call this "The Power of Five." If I have more than five things there, what happens? I start to feel overwhelmed and confused. I don't know where to start. I wind up not doing anything. If that sounds familiar, you may have ADD. But there are a lot of things I need to do. Every time I turn around a new one pops up. So it's just natural that I would quickly pull out the card and add the new thing to my to-do list. Then before I know it, there are twelve things on there. Then I feel overwhelmed and confused, get stalled and I'm not doing anything. So I've been trying to learn to actually keep the list down to five. And I'm getting better at that.

Summary:
     The foundation for coping with ADD is to have an appointment book and a to-do list, to have them with you at all times, and to learn how to use them. I need to review my appointment book and my main to-do list frequently, about six times a day. And I need to keep my to-do list down to five items or I will get overwhelmed and stalled.

Chapter 8

Other cards and lists

Three to-do cards

I keep three to-do cards in my pocket: red, orange, and yellow. The red is the five things, priority. On the orange card I put the other to-do things that have any priority or urgency, that I need to get to reasonably soon. On the yellow card I put anything that I might get to someday. I don't use this system perfectly; it requires some self discipline, which is something I don't have a lot of (I have ADD, remember?). But I'm getting better at it. It helped a lot to add the orange card. When I only had the red and the yellow, I always tended to write everything on the red, because everything seemed urgent, because I'm not good at setting priorities.

When I can cross something off on the red card, it makes me feel good, increases my morale. I feel like I have some control and like I'm on top of things. Then I can move something off the orange card to the red, as long as there are no more than five things there. It helps to number things on the card in the order I plan to do them, and to keep it neat and easily readable.

The red card, with the list of five, is the key. The three colored cards are always in my pocket. When something comes up or pops into my mind I can put it on the appropriate colored card. But things are not that simple. I have a whole card system in my pocket, and I have other lists.

The working list

I live with my appointment book and cards in my pocket, and I'm surrounded by lists. Most of my work is done in my office, at my desk. There I keep another list, the working list, on the back of an envelope, right in front of me.

I get a lot of mail: bills, of course, ads, even payments sometimes. I save the envelopes that have blank backs for scratch paper. They're in a stack under one corner of my computer monitor, out of the way, but handy. I use envelopes for the working list, but I also use them for other things: Spanish conjugation I'm trying to learn, ideas for this book, new guitar chords to use, random thoughts, whatever. These other envelopes sit in a stack to the right of the working list, so they're handy and I can find what I'm looking for.

Illustration 2. The Desk

From left to right: Top - stack of papers I'm working on, envelopes under monitor, to-do list, other envelopes: finances, Spanish, book ideas, etc. Bottom – stack of papers I refer to sometimes, keyboard and mouse.

Using the lists

The to-do cards are always in my pocket, but in the office I work more from the working list. This list has the list of five on it, but also all the routine and less important things I need to get to today or perhaps tomorrow or the next day. These might include routine phone calls, or other routine tasks, like typing up my patient notes. If I've gotten behind on a routine or non-urgent task, it might wind up on the list of five because then it has become more urgent, but those are usually just on the working list. I keep redoing this list throughout the day, as I get some things finished and other things come up. If this list gets long, I'll underline the few things I want to focus on next or I'll just make a new and shorter list.

For example, today in the kitchen my wife said her knives need sharpening. She was clear that there's nothing urgent about it, so I put it on the orange card. I could do it today or tomorrow or the next day. Later I also put it on the envelope working list, so if I find some down time, I might get to it. But if I don't have it done in three days, then she's waiting too long. Then it becomes urgent and I will put "knives" on the red card. However, since it's on the working list, I probably will get to it without it ever reaching the red card.

The list of five has priority, but I don't always do the things on it immediately. Some things take preparation; sometimes something needs to be done before I can do something. Some things can only be done at certain times; I can have "call the insurance company yet again" on my red card, but I won't be able to do it on a weekend. Or sometimes there's suddenly a very convenient time open to do something else that's only on the bigger working list.

Right now on my red card I have "organize taxes." I started working on the taxes, but then I got stalled, so now I need to stop and write out the steps that I need to do for the task. That's what "organize taxes" means. Once I organize and have all the steps written down, I can pick one to start on. Maybe first I'll choose to collect all the information on charitable giving for the year. That step will go onto the red card. Thus I will be moving forward on the taxes. Only one step at a time will make it to the prestigious heights of the red card. The others will be on the working list.

The power of lists

I make lists over and over, all day long. It's not just about having the list; there is also benefit in making them. Writing down what I need to do is somehow calming and organizing, and therefore motivating. When I write things down, it's as though I'm on top of them. Then I can make another shorter list and it seems doable, and I don't have to think about any of the things on the long list. This is related to the rule of five. When I get a few things crossed off of one to-do list I throw it way and make another one. This gives me a sense of accomplishment, which help me stay motivated and keep going.

The time used making lists is well spent, because it keeps me focused, organized and motivated. I can stay aware of what the day needs to be looking like, and I'm not keeping all these things in my head. They're right in front of me within reach of my hand. When I'm in my office, the red card is in my pocket, but I'm relying more on the envelope list. Everywhere else, I keep looking at the red card.

Summary:

Since the red card to-do list needs to be limited to the five top priority things, I need auxiliary cards for other to-do's. The cards are available wherever I am. In the office I also have an evolving working list. The act of making the lists is a helpful organizing activity. It's helpful to break tasks into small steps, and then a step can be one of the list of five.

Chapter 9

Small steps and staying on top

Riddle: How do you eat an elephant?
Answer: One bite at a time.
(Courtesy of Jim Bracken, educator and proofreader)

Small steps

Small steps is a major coping strategy for dealing with ADD. It has many uses; it helps deal with inertia, procrastination, distractions and with getting things finished. Let's talk about the to-do list and small steps; this will apply to all the difficulties I just mentioned.

After "The Power of Five", the next biggest trick for using the to-do list is to write down only small steps. I would never write " Do taxes" on the red card . That would be overwhelming and it offers no organization. I would just never get started.

No, I would write down:

1. Get last year's checks.
2. Call accountant for appt.
3. Buy paint for porch
   (Note: not- "3. Paint porch.")

See, I can't "Do my taxes." That's an impossible job, totally overwhelming. I would just stall. But I can find the checks. Actually, I might have needed my wife's help, but that's old history. Now I know exactly where the checks are, because I have one place for them and I always and only put them there. Like the car keys. When I retrieve the checks, I can cross that item off with a sense of accomplishment, control, and relief. That's a reinforcing reward. Then I can write the next small step on my to-do list: "1. Sort checks".

If there's a big task coming up, but it's not time to work on it yet, I might put the whole task on the orange card –"paint the fence." But when the time comes, I will break it down into steps – "buy paint."

Occasionally, I can't see the small steps ahead of time; I may need to get into a project first. But that's OK. I can just start on the first small step – "What is the first thing I need to do to get started on this project? Well, I can turn on the computer for starters"- and then break it into small steps as I go.

So, it's small steps, and no more than five. One or two steps might relate to the taxes, but no more. There are things beside taxes that need my attention, too, and if all five things are about taxes, it will start to look overwhelming again. I pick one step and focus on that for the moment, on what I need to do now. I forget about the other things I need to do in that project until I get that one done. It's kind of like the Buddhist thing of "living in the moment." One thing at a time.

Summary:
Break tasks into small steps. Limit the to-do list to five things. Focus on one at a time. You never have more than that one thing that you need to do at any given moment.

Staying on top - the dog poop principle
It's my job to clean up the dog poop in the yard. I perform this moderately unpleasant chore every week. (Everybody has to be good at something.) Actually, more recently I've started performing it about three times a week, and it really isn't that unpleasant anymore. It may take a little more time than before, but not much anyway. I haven't let things pile up.

This is a three part principle:

1. Don't let things pile up. If they pile up, they become overwhelming and harder to do. Stay on top of them.
2. Break tasks into small parts.
3. If somehow you still get behind (and like me, you probably will), then break the task into manageable small steps. If I've let the poop pile up, so to speak, I might clean one half of the yard today and the other half tomorrow.

Staying on top of things means not letting them pile up to the point that the prospect of dealing with them seems overwhelming. This can apply to paying bills, or to keeping up with my patient notes, to homework or studying, or dog poop. So we're not letting things build up or hang over our heads. Who wants dog poop hanging over their head? Ugh!

The strategies, rules and habits I describe contribute to making my life go better. They are ways of coping with problems, like the dog poop problem. But they also eliminate some problems entirely so that I don't need to deal with them at all. Like losing the keys.

Summary:
A major tool for dealing with many ADD problems is to break every task into small steps. Then the task doesn't seem so overwhelming or difficult or unpleasant, and it's easier to get myself to start

on it. If I don't fall behind and let things pile up then they don't seem so overwhelming either. But if I've let something pile up then small steps is the key to getting started on it. And again, if I can identify something as a problem, like the dog poop task being unpleasant, then I can come up with strategies to cope with it, and my life gets better. Yours can too.

Chapter 10

The list of three

There is yet another important list. One of the ADD books says that we ADDers are creative, right brain creatures with good visualization skills. It recommends starting each day by visualizing ourselves actually doing all the things we need to do that day. That's a good tool, but it doesn't work for me. Instead, I do the list of three, which is kind of related to that and does work for me. This is a schedule made from the to-do list, of the next three things I'm going to do. It includes the one I'm doing right now. I say these three things in my head: "OK, right now, I'm writing about the list of three, and then I'm going to check my e-mails, and then I'll catch up on my patient notebooks." Next, "OK, finished the writing; now I'm checking my e-mails, and then the notebooks, and then I'll go get the mail." And so on, through the day. This is the list of three. This process helps me keep on track and keep organized as I work down through the written list of five on my red card. It helps me to avoid suddenly and impulsively starting off on another track that just popped into my head and isn't on the red card. It helps me remember, as I walk down the hall, the reason why I'm walking down the hall, where I'm going and what I need to do when I get there. In other word, it helps me stay focused.

This sounds like it violates the rule of focusing on one thing at a time and not worrying about the rest, but it doesn't seem to. I say the list of three to myself, start working on the first thing, and I do forget the rest until I've finished the first. But then I'm able to recall the list of three, update it, and start anew, without having been thinking about it while I was working. I know what I'm going to do next.

My friend, Tom, has a similar tool, a list of one. He calls it the "What's next?" tool. When he starts a project, and while he's doing it, he asks, "What's next?" Then when he finishes the project, he knows what to do next. He's not going to wander off into a timewaster, get captured by a distraction, or become bogged down in indecision; he already knows "what's next". You'll read more about Tom and his story and his strategies in section X.

Summary:

We can have a plan for what we are going to do next, to help us avoid distractions and stay on track.

Somehow we can file this in the back of our mind so we're not thinking about it until we need it.

Chapter 11

The card system

All my shirts have pockets, which always contain my appointment book and my index cards. You might develop a different system; this is what works for me. I had developed these strategies and habits years before I realized that I had ADD. I didn't know that I was coping with ADD; I just knew that these things made my life go better.

My index cards are colored and there is a system. I am still training myself to follow it better, so that it will be even more effective.

The red, orange and yellow cards are for to-do. The blue card is "memory", with information that I need available: phone numbers, names I forget, bible verses, sayings, etc. The white cards have everything else: a song I'm memorizing, some music theory I'm learning, some Spanish conjugation and vocabulary that I can pull out and study, etc. It's a collection of things in general, usually things I'm working on. I just added a new card, purple, so that at any moment I can jot down an idea for the book and won't be tempted to clutter up the red card with it.

Illustration 3.   The cards
The red cards on top, then the orange, the yellow, the white, and the blue.

Summary:
    The red card with the list of five is one of the most important tools I have for helping me cope with my ADD. The other cards substitute for the memory that I don't have. But wait! There's more!

Chapter 12

Other tools

White boards

On my desk to the right are two erasable white boards, a large one and a small one. They're actually not important, but I like them. I have no real system for using them. I can write in something I want to remember, like to do my Spanish course first before I start something else, or else I will procrastinate on it - "Sp 1st!" I can put down things I need to do, maybe large things not broken down into steps yet -"Taxes coming!", or something I want to do fairly soon but not urgent enough for the red card – "clean desk". That's something I might do when there's a bit of time free and I see it on the white board. On the back of the white boards I put a list of my most needed numbers and computer passwords, so they're handy. As I said, I have no real system for using the white boards. They're in my view there on my desk and just useful for anything at all that I might want to put there to catch my attention. I can use all the help I can get.

So I'm surrounded by lists in my office. They're right there, in my face and under my hand; that's the way I like it. The red card is the master list, the one that overrules the others, but it's good to have the more flexible working list handy when I'm in my office, which is where I do most of the work that is on the lists. Other lists serve as memory and reminders. Works for me.

Electronic devices

I love books, newspapers, and medical/psychiatric journals. I enjoy holding them and reading them, and I like owning books. It's hard for me to read things on the computer or on an electronic book. On my cell phone I have many of the documents from my computer, and some great programs, especially Spanish and the Bible. I take the occasional photograph with it. But I don't use those things very much. I don't take my phone with me everywhere I go, and I don't have the internet on it. Maybe I'm getting old and hopelessly out of date.

But I can imagine how you can use these new electronic marvels to be part of your strategies. Someone, maybe you, is going to get rich designing some applications specifically for people with ADD. There's a lot of technology available already just waiting for someone, someone smarter and less technologically challenged than me, to figure out ways to apply it for coping with ADD. You will read about my friend Tom's Personal Information Manager. It's a program for scheduling and for handling all kinds of personal information. It sounds like a step towards helping with ADD, but it may not work too well the way it's designed right now. Clearly it was designed for just regular people, without ADD. You will also read about my friend Richard's FOFA gadget with tags and a buzzer for finding lost items. Amazing!

For various reasons my wife and I seem to buy new phones frequently. After we bring one home it often don't have all the features we want, so we exchange it, again. I've just realized how important it is to me to have a phone with a screen that shows the number I just dialed, before I push the 'talk' button, so I can check what I dialed and cut down on the wrong numbers.

If you have ADD, and you've gotten this far in the book, please take a deep breath and congratulate yourself. It's a challenge to stick with things like this. I'm hoping that as you read you're thinking about some of the problems that make your life frustrating and difficult. I hope that you will consider some of the strategies that I bring up, and think about how you might use them or modify them so that they'll work for you. Then you can try them out and if they don't work for you, adjust them so that they will. You can certainly come up with your own strategies. You can find creative ways to use electronics to do some of this. Depending on your age, for one thing.

Summary:

My cards and envelopes work well for me, but there are wonderful new options for people with ADD. I predict that new devices and programs will become increasingly popular and will be even more effective in helping people cope with ADD. Each one of us is different, although we share many of the same problems. I hope you will find what works for you.

Section II

Simplify, organize, take charge of your life

Your first reaction to reading this title - simplify, organize, take charge of your life - might be that that is exactly what you are unable to do. Maybe you're saying, "Yeah. Right. Sure."

Trust me, you can do it. I have, so I know that you can. But we need the strategies and the tools. That's what's coming. Let's assume you already have the appointment book and the to-do list, which are the foundations for coping. Here I want to give you some more tools to help manage things and stay out of messes. We don't have to feel overwhelmed, which just makes it harder to function, which makes us feel even more overwhelmed. We need to set goals, stay out of traps, be aware of the red flags that warn us we are about to get into a mess, focus on one thing at a time, and learn to simplify. We can be in control of our life.

Chapter 13

Simplify

Avoid over committing

I've learned to be very careful about agreeing to do anything. I try hard to stay off committees and boards. I've been to too many meetings in my life. They are giant time absorbers. I don't go to any meetings if I can help it. I still do things that contribute to the community, but I can usually find ways that don't involve meetings, and I'm extremely selective about the things that do. I also used to do more extra things for my patients – "Oh, I'll just give your doctor a call." I've learned that some of those things aren't actually necessary, and if they are, often the patient can do them at least as well as I can. So I think twice before volunteering to do something extra.

My wife pointed out that I had signed up for a lot of e-mail programs - for Word of the Day in Spanish and in English, free guitar lessons, news, political movements, and more. My inbox was quite crowded every morning. So I kept the ones I really like and use, but I was able to eliminate many of them and save time and simplify.

I've also learned not to make promises. Now it's "OK, I'll try," or "OK, I'll do my best." No promises.

Learn to say No

In order to avoid committees and boards and other projects, I needed to learn to do a better job of saying "No". That's hard for many of us, especially those of us that tend to be "people pleasers." We want everyone to like and admire us. That is not a healthy condition. It partly comes from low self-esteem, which can often come from having ADD. Fortunately, therapy can help with the "people pleasing" problem. Willpower, if we have any, helps too. I'll tell you later on about Ms. M, a patient who learned how to say "No". I will also tell you about my famous colleague, Dr. John Rush, who has no problem at all in saying "No", and who became a role model for me. Hang around.

"Is this a good use of my time?"

I need to pause occasionally in the middle of whatever I'm doing and ask this question. This is a form of "awareness", which I'll also discuss later. This is also a good approach when I'm being asked to do something. Will the benefits justify the use of my time? For example, occasionally I'm asked to volunteer for a good cause. Sometimes it's clear that it would be more effective to just give money. Someone else can be hired to do the work; that will benefit them, benefit the cause, and save my time. I do put a dollar value on my time and that helps me make some decisions, such as when to hire someone to do some work in or around the house and when to do it myself.

Minimize decisions

I'm not great at making decisions. I can ruminate for a long time over the pros and cons and still wind up on the fence. Part of the reason is that with ADD, I have trouble prioritizing. Everything looks important. One strategy for this problem is to realize that if the decision is that hard to make there must not be a "right" answer, or else it would be obvious. So it is a guess, a coin flip. We can't know how something will come out, so we can only play the odds, and sometimes they're about fifty-fifty.

Strategies for decision making help, but if I can minimize decisions it simplifies my life even more. One way to do that is to have rules. My grandson, Michael, is nine years old. He lives here in Santa Fe and spends a lot of time with us. He likes me to play games with him. As part of my grandfatherly responsibilities I've taught him to play poker and chess; he can't beat me at chess yet. Michael's growing up fast. About six years ago I paused and thought about my priorities and I was blessed with a great revelation. I had not been a great dad. They grow up fast. Before long they won't be wanting you to do things with them; they will be out on their own. I work a lot at home: record keeping, book writing, repair projects, etc. But I made a rule: if Michael asks me to play with him, I will stop whatever I'm doing and play with him. If Michael asks me to do something with him, I do it. Not "later," not "in a little while," or "wait 'til I finish this." Just, "OK. Let's go." My priority is playing with Michael. What can I be doing that is more important than spending time with my grandson? So the rule eliminates the need for decisions, and in this example, gives a better result, too.

This is an example of thinking through priorities, but it also illustrates the value of rules in simplifying our lives and in keeping them on track. This rule saves me from making decisions. I made this decision one time, a long time ago. I wish I had figured this out earlier, when my kids were young. Of course, the downside is that before long he will probably be beating me not only at poker but also at chess.

Habits avoid decisions. Just for example: I don't have to decide every morning whether or not I am going to brush my teeth. I just do it. And I don't have to decide where to put my keys.

Summary:

We tend to feel overloaded and overwhelmed. We tend to get distracted and not accomplish the things we need to. Simplifying and organizing are ways to deal with these problems, or even better, to avoid them. Focusing on doing one thing and forgetting about the rest simplifies the moment. I try to avoid over-committing or over-volunteering. I learned to say "No". I ask myself, "Is this the best use of my time?" Rules and habits help me to minimize the number of decisions I need to make.

Chapter 14

Problem solve and simplify your life

We need to make life as easy and simple for ourselves as possible. There are a lot of little things that are minor inconveniences or annoyances, and often these are also time wasters. If we can identify these problems as problems, instead of just accepting them as a normal part of life, something to be put up with, we can devise strategies and make our life better. Often, when I finally recognize a problem and then a solution, it's so obvious that all I can say is "Of course!" (You may picture me slapping my forehead.) Here are some examples of problems that are trivial, but add up and make life more frustrating than it has to be.

I arise before my wife, and try to dress quietly in the dark. I put on yesterday's clothes; I will exercise and shower later. At night I get into bed, then take off my socks and throw them towards the chair where my clothes are. So the next morning, I start my day with the small hassle of trying to find the other sock in the dark. Except I didn't identify it as a hassle; I didn't really think about it. I just kept searching for the sock. Then one morning, I had a brilliant idea. Now I put one sock into the other (Of course! Duh!). I also aim, so now the socks are always to the right side of the chair. Of course there are many alternative solutions to this problem. I could put the socks down by the side of the bed instead of throwing them, or I could put a small flashlight on my bedside table. You can probably think of others, but I'm very happy with this one. Just put one sock inside the other before I throw them! And aim. It works! The point here isn't to tell you what to do with your socks, or to say that this is the right solution to this minor problem; it's about learning to recognize that something is a problem. Then you can think of a solution.

We have two stamps for putting the return address on envelopes. One is for us and one is for my office. They are identical in appearance (the outside of the stamper, not the message) and we keep them next to each other in the desk drawer. So every time I wanted to use one, I would have to stop and figure out which one was which by looking at the stamped end, which wasn't so easy to see. Again, there are many obvious solutions to this minor frustration: keep one on the left and one on the right, or on opposite sides of the drawer, or even in different drawers. Again - Duh! But once I realized it was A Problem, I found the magic marker and wrote my initials on the side of mine and always place it with that side up. Saves ten seconds of minor frustration twice a week. Those seconds add up and we certainly don't need any more frustration in our lives, thank you.

Once we recognize and identify something as a problem, we can make a strategy. Life can get simpler and simpler.

Let's take a short break. Here's a little story:

Back in the old days two friends enlisted in the cavalry. They each were assigned their own horse and they were trying to figure out how to tell them apart. They decided to put a ribbon in the mane of Joe's horse. That worked for a while but soon the ribbon was pulled off as they rode through the brush. So they decided to cut the tail of Mike's horse short. That worked for a while, but then they saw that the poor horse couldn't brush the flies away and the tail grew back in pretty soon anyway. So they decided to measure the heights of the horses. And sure enough, the black horse was two inches taller than the white one.

Oh, well.

With persistence, we can come up with a solution.

I like berries on my cereal in the morning. Usually we have several plastic containers of different kinds of berries. I would take them out of the refrigerator, set them on the counter, and get ready to rinse the berries and put them on my cereal. I'd open one container and get out some berries, but I'd have trouble opening the next container while holding the berries in one hand. I'd get the next one open and then I'd have more berries in my hand. It's pretty hard to close those plastic containers with one hand. Then I really hate it when I knock over a container and the berries roll off the counter and go all over the floor. Blueberries - now those suckers can roll!

I bet you're saying "Duh!" right now. But I finally figured it out. Put the containers on the counter. Open all of them. Take out the berries and rinse them. Put them in the bowl and then, with both hands free, close the containers. Duh! But it was a triumphant moment when the light dawned and I figured out the solution to the problem, after finally realizing that it was a problem. I don't think people without ADD realize what life is like for us.

This next example is a little complicated. I have an answering machine in my office. When someone calls I don't want a session interrupted or to have my patient overhear something that might be confidential, so I turn the volume all the way down when I'm seeing a patient. Later, I turn the volume up to listen to my messages, but I often forget to turn it back down again. Then when my next patient is in the middle of something we hear, "Hello, Dr. Puryear, ---", and I have to leap out of my chair and turn the volume down fast. Very disruptive, kind of embarrassing and not fair to the patients. So I kept telling myself to remember to turn the volume down, and to check that it's down before I start a session. Do you think that worked? Did I mention that I have ADD?

So I found a new solution. I have a rhinoceros doll in the office (that's another story). I started putting it on top of the answering machine when it was turned down and moving it off when it was turned up. Then I could just glance at the machine and see if the volume was up or down. That should've worked, but I often forgot to move the doll. So that was an improvement, but not good enough.

Then I made a rule: I'm not allowed to turn the volume up to listen until after I move the doll to the very end of the desk, where it really sticks out. If the rhino is at the end of the desk, then I know that I need to turn the volume down and move him back before I start a session. I glance at the desk to check before each session but I don't really have to because the rhino sticks out; he's hard to miss. That has solved the problem ninety-nine per cent.

Illustration 4. The rhino
Turn down the volume!

I have some heroes in life. One of them is the match book cover person. Most of you are too young to remember when every matchbook cover had printed on it, "Close cover before striking." This was because the striking plate was on the front, where the bottom of the cover hooked in; occasionally someone would strike a match with the cover open and the whole packet would blow up in their hand. That was not a good thing. Therefore, "Close cover before striking." I have researched this, but I couldn't find out when matchbooks were first invented, when they started printing "Close cover before striking" on them, or the name of my hero. But, who figured out to put the striker plate on the back instead of on the front? Wow! Now that is a great example of recognizing that there's a problem, and that things don't just have to be that way, and then coming up with a solution. Then everyone goes, "Duh!' but it was brilliant.

Summary:

We tend to think things are just the way they are. Once recognized as A Problem, problems can be solved. Problems can be large or small. Small frustrations take their toll on us and we can figure out strategies to deal with them. Life will be better.

Chapter 15

Goals

We all have goals, but we may not stop and think about them. Maybe the closest we'll get are the ill fated New Year's resolutions. Knowing our goals helps us have an organized approach to our life. There are short term goals and long term goals. The short term goals mostly need to be steps to help us progress towards the long term ones.

I worked with John Rush, a psychiatrist who has become prestigious, and I assume prosperous, by doing research on depression. When John and I were working together, he was not nearly so prestigious yet, but he was impressive and I learned from him. John always impressed me as being clear about what his goals were. In general, if something didn't further his progress towards his goals he didn't do it. John was excellent at saying "No", and his inspiring model has been helpful to me. John knew much more about pharmacology than I did, and he often gave me help, information and good advice. But when he didn't, it was striking:

I would see him in the hall – "John, do you have a minute?"

"No" - and he would move on (or, rush on, you might say).

No excuse, no apology, no arrangement to see me later, just "No". A man with his eye on his goals, which were very clear to him, and he has been successful at achieving them.

I wouldn't necessarily want to do it in John's style, but watching John really helped me learn to say "No" and become better at keeping my eye on my own goals. Of course to do that, I need to know what my goals are, both short term and long term. At least once a year I sit down with a yellow pad and ask myself, "What are my long term goals?" and "What are my short term goals?" which will mostly be the things I need to do to move towards my long term goals. "How am I doing on my goals? How am I spending my time? What might I need to do differently?" Asking these questions is a very useful exercise. If my short term goals don't seem to lead towards my long term goals, or if what I am doing now doesn't fit in with my goals, then I need to rethink. I keep the yellow pad with my long term goals on it on my desk and review it occasionally.

This helps me to stay out of the time-waster dead-end traps.

One of my long term goals is to achieve financial security (if such a thing exists). Therefore, I try to keep my stock portfolio balanced; this is a short term goal. Thus my investments are spread between stocks, bonds, mutual funds and certificates of deposit, with a target of a certain percentage of the whole for each type of investment. The idea (illusion?) is that since each type of investment can lose money at different rates, and even can occasionally make money, or so I've been told, a balanced portfolio is the safest. I occasionally need to do some buying and selling to keep the percentages on target to meet my short term goal of keeping the portfolio balanced.

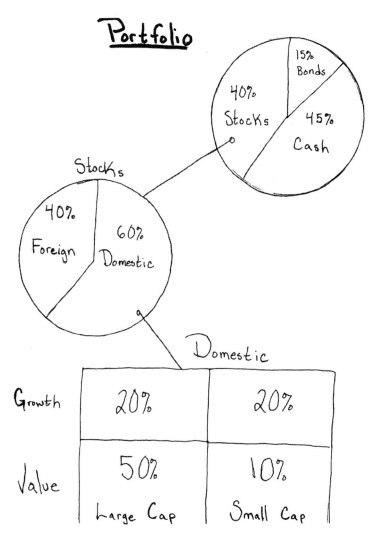

Illustration 5. Stock portfolio

Rebalancing is buying and selling to keep each group at its assigned percentage.

If we have ADD, we tend to set unrealistic goals. We especially do this regarding time, thinking we can get more done in a day than is possible, but we set unrealistic goals in other ways too.

I have a long term goal of keeping my weight down, so I have a short term goal of losing some of the weight that I'm carrying now. So I need to improve my eating habits and increase my exercise.

For a long time my goal was a weight of 168 pounds. Once I even reached it for a day. Finally I revised my goal to 170. I got closer to staying near that. But it's discouraging to have goals you just can't meet. So I changed it again, to 172. Does that seem like cheating? Taking the easy way out? I prefer to think that it's setting a goal I can achieve. Anyway, finally I am doing pretty well at staying about 172 pounds most of the time. The goal of 168 was just not realistic and it led to discouragement and demoralization, two emotions familiar to ADDers. Also, I have to realize that 172 pounds is more of a target than a goal that I might actually reach and maintain. I keep 172 in focus and keep shooting at it, but apparently it's a process rather than an end point.

It's useful to set goals, but the trick is to set small goals, low goals, goals that I can actually reach. When I do reach one, that's positive reinforcement, like crossing something off the to-do list is.

There are some traditional American values and sayings that I don't agree with. One is "A man's reach should exceed his grasp." Maybe that works sometimes, but it is a recipe for the rat race and for frustration. If we reach a goal, that's positive reinforcement and we can always set a new goal.

The same strategy of achievable goals works for planning my day and for my short to-do list. If I say I'm going to do all five things on my to-do list today, I may not succeed, and I'll wind up discouraged. Discouraged does not help me to start moving on the next task or to stick to it. So if I pick just one thing, then I'm likely to succeed, especially if I used the small steps principle. Then I can do another one. I can probably get those two things done and maybe even have some time left over to get another one or two things done, and then I'll really feel good at the end of the day. That kind of positive reinforcement helps me get off to a good start the next day. And I may get all five things done, or even more, which is great, but I don't set that as my goal.

So, it's setting small, manageable, realistic goals with a good chance of success. Life not only feels better but actually goes better, and I function better, when I'm achieving my goals than when I'm not.

Summary:
Knowing our goals helps us be organized, and we need to ask ourselves if the things we're do-

ing are leading us towards our goals. One way to help with our tendency to inertia is to thoughtfully set reasonable goals and to pay attention to them. Breaking things into small steps is one form of setting achievable goals. Reaching a goal gives positive reinforcement; it helps us to avoid demoralization and to keep going. Reachable realistic goals. Small steps. Do you see how they work together?

Chapter 16

Traps

Traps

I am prone to falling into traps, traps of time wasters and dead end projects. Dead end projects never have a payoff, don't lead towards one of my goals and thus are a waste of time. Many time waster are not big projects but just nonproductive, like watching TV, often to avoid something that I actually need to be doing.

For example, I will be in the middle of a productive project, like writing this book, and then it pops into my mind that I'd like to know about the six wives of King Henry the VIII. I'm already at the computer, so I just look that up on the internet. That's easy; there they are. That leads to the interesting puzzle of figuring out who the various Marys were, and that leads to looking up the dates of Queen Elizabeth's reign. I'm wasting time. Then the idea for a good short story about Elizabeth comes into my mind, and I begin to write it before it escapes me, but I have to do some more research to get the facts right. Now I'm totally off the track of writing this book and I'm suddenly involved in a project, perhaps a dead end project.

But then the questions are, "What is the value to me of knowing about Henry's wives?" and "What is the purpose of the short story? Will I be able to sell it? Or it is a dead end?" Well, I could argue, it is recreation; it's fun and interesting, and I enjoy doing it. But there are other recreational things I can do: practice the guitar, work on this book, go for a walk; things that might take less time and not only be recreational but productive in some way at the same time. And it's likely that I'm diving into this King Henry and short story side line as a way to avoid dealing with something else. At least something else isn't getting done while I'm pursuing the King Henry project. Which likely leads nowhere.

A neat free program, SpaceEd, showed up on the internet, offering courses in a number of medical topics. I chose cardiology, because I've always been interested in that. I used to know a lot about cardiology –used to. I do have some patients with heart trouble; sometimes I do medical missionary work where cardiology could be useful. I enjoy learning. So I took the course. The SpaceEd program e-mails you a problem every day and gives you test questions on it. It explains the questions you miss. It's a good learning process. I enjoyed it. It didn't really take much time. So the question is, was I wasting time? I was learning, but the course certainly wasn't necessary for me. So it could have been a dead end project; I'm not sure. Sometimes it's hard to tell. I stopped it because I need more time to work on this book. If only time was unlimited, I could do both the course and the book. If only money grew on trees, we could all be rich.

A few years ago an original tune popped into my head. I liked it and was afraid I would forget it. Fortunately, my computer has a recording program on it, so I hummed the tune into the mike. Now it's safe; I won't lose it. I also have a fancy program that lets me write music. I could transcribe my tune into that and come out with an actual music score, with the notes all written out. I started doing that. It isn't a user friendly program and I'm not used to it, so I was having to learn as I went. It went pretty slowly. After about an hour I had some of it done and was improving in using the program. Then I stopped and asked myself, "Why?".

Transcribing this tune was novel, a new process for me, and it was personally interesting, and it was certainly challenging. So my focus center was turned on, but what was the point? How was I going to use it? It became clear that I was wasting time. This was a dead-end project, going nowhere. Probably there was something else I needed to be doing, perhaps something difficult or unpleasant. I enjoyed transcribing the notes for a while, but when I recognized that it was a dead-end project, I was able to stop.

I've at times gotten into chat-rooms, and also into writing letters to the editor. I've enjoyed both of those, but they can easily be black holes sucking up my time. It's usually not clear what real benefit is going to come of that. I rarely do either anymore.

There must be thousands of traps. I can always find something to do, and spend a lot of time on it, only to realize afterwards that it really wasn't very important.

Another trap is when I say, "Well, I need to relax a while." which is a real red flag, because then I get started on something like a computer game. I got addicted to computer games, but that's another story. We ADDers do tend to addictions. Anyway, I'm talking now about telling myself I need a break and then getting caught up in some activity and then later realizing that I haven't gotten back to my original task.

Sometimes the trap involves preparing to do something. In college I had no idea how to study. Once before a big physics final, I made flash cards to help me memorize all the important formulas.

That made sense. But I saw that the cards were pretty sloppy (after all, I have ADD), and I decided they'd be easier to memorize if they were neater. So I copied them over onto another set of cards, more carefully. But by the time I'd finished copying them I didn't have time to memorize them all. So I picked the most important ones and wrote them neatly on new cards. I don't have a clue why I didn't just pull out the important ones from the cards I already had. By the time I had all my neatly written cards ready to memorize, I didn't have any more time left to memorize them; I'd spent it all on card making. I didn't do well on that test. Making the cards made sense, but it became a trap; I spent my time preparing to do rather than doing. And amazingly, I did this more than once.

Summary:
There are innumerable traps available for ADDers. We can learn to recognize and avoid the traps that we most often fall into. Projects can be useful or can be dead end traps, serving no purpose. Breaks can be a useful tool or a trap. I can easily find ways to just waste time. So I need to stay aware of what I'm doing, and whatever I'm doing, I try to ask: "Is this really the best use of this time?" and "Why am I doing this? What is the goal or purpose?" and "Is there something I'm avoiding?"

Chapter 17

Breaks

Taking a break can be a valuable tool, but it can also be a trap. Another time in college I had only one more final to go, and I was totally worn out. I needed some help. So I got an amphetamine pill to help me stay up all night and study. I didn't know then that I had ADD or that amphetamines are supposed to help us focus, just that it would keep me awake so that I could study. That's the only time I've ever taken an amphetamine. And it worked. Sort of. I did stay up all night and I did stay focused. But I decided that I needed a break before I started studying. I picked up a book, Of Human Bondage, by Somerset Maugham. That's a very good book. And also quite long. I did stay up all night and I did stay focused: I read all of Of Human Bondage. Beginning to end. I finally finished it in the early morning and had about fifteen minutes to study before I had to go take the final. Didn't do too well on that one either. So, breaks can be a trap.

We do need breaks if we're studying or working on any long project, but we also need a way to limit the breaks, so they don't become traps. I'm not good at this, and I don't have any great strategies for it. An alarm clock or timer can be helpful, if I can force myself to follow them. But it's easy to just turn them off or reset them. Sometimes I can enlist my wife to help me, "Please come call me in ten minutes and remind me to get back to work." Or sometimes I can set another kind of limit, "I will read one chapter and then get back to work". That didn't work with <u>Of Human Bondage</u> though, and it didn't work with computer games either – "Oh well, just one more game and then I'll go back to work." If you have a good strategy for controlling breaks I would be happy to hear from you.

If we're studying, or doing anything that requires concentration, at some point our efficiency starts to drop. For most of us, this is at about an hour. If we push beyond that, we start accomplishing less and less for the time we are putting in. At that point, we need a break. Then our efforts will be more efficient again when we come back. (If we come back.) We can accomplish more in two forty-five minute sessions than we can in one two hour long session. If my attention limit is forty-five minutes, and I try to push myself to study for two hours straight, I've probably wasted about half an hour.

We do need recreation and relaxation and breaks. We need to make sure that we get them. We also need to make sure that we aren't using the need for relaxation as an excuse to avoid doing something else that is difficult or unpleasant, or that we aren't sure we can do well. When I was addicted to computer games I spent many hours on them. I know it was an addiction. I would stay preoccupied with them in my mind even when I wasn't playing, and I would be doing them at times when there was something else I clearly needed to be doing instead. I had no control; I'd say, "OK, just one more game," or, "OK, but just for 45 minutes," but I couldn't hold it to that. That is addiction. I finally had to give up the games entirely, erase them all from my computer and throw away the CD discs.

The thing is, in those games you have some control. That is, I had some control in the game, but not of the time I spent on it. You can win or improve (and you can pick the games to ensure that). You get a sense of mastery as well as a challenge. Probably most importantly, it doesn't really matter how you do. No one needs to know if I did poorly and nothing bad will come of it anyway. I can just play it again and try to do better the next time. And again. And again. It was a safe escape. So if it's a personal interest and if it's a challenge, then my focus center will be turned on. And I really enjoyed those games, but they were interfering with my life. I had to get rid of them.

I always have many things to do. The lists on my orange to do cards are always long, and so I have to be careful what I choose to work on. I needed to ask myself if writing this book is a trap, when I could be working on other things on the list, especially since I know this book will take a lot of time.

So I asked myself about this book, "Why am I writing it; why am I spending all this time on it?" There is some chance I can get it published; then it might help people and I might even make some money. There is some benefit to me just in thinking about all these ADD things and becoming more clear about them in my mind, even if no one else reads the book. There is even a little recreational value in the writing, although it is also hard work. And I think that at worst I can print it out myself and give it to my patients with ADD, and it will be helpful to them. So it is a worthwhile project. I can't see anything I'm avoiding by doing it. If I wasn't writing on the book I could be using the time to study more Spanish, or to practice the guitar more, but I am doing those things fairly well enough as is. I also kind of ran the idea of the book by my wife to see what she thought. She maybe wasn't that enthusiastic, but she wasn't negative. And I decided it was a reasonable use of my time. But that is the question that needed to be asked.

The book could have been a trap, just swallowing large amounts of time into a deep black hole, while other things just slide. A real dead end project.

So it is with most anything I start to do. I need to ask myself, "Is this really useful? What is the purpose? Is this the best use of my time?"

Sometimes the purpose is recreation, which is useful. However, recreation is best when it's done with intent and awareness: "I'm doing this now because it's recreation and I need recreation and it's good for me." So the recreation has a purpose other than just avoiding or escaping things. Even computer games could be good for this if I could have any control over how much I play them.

Summary:

When I'm going to take a break, to do something for recreation, I can intentionally choose what I want to do instead of drifting into some time-passing pastime. Watching TV or just sitting doing nothing are fine if that is what I have chosen to do. I need strategies to keep the break limited to the time I chose for it.

Chapter 18

Red flags (and little bits of time)

Red flags can be warnings of danger or just a signal to alert us to something.

" I'll do that later."

When I hear myself saying that, it's a signal, a red flag. I need to stop and ask myself, "Could I just do it right now?" Often, I could. Then it's done. I don't have to put it on a card; I don't have to remember to do it. It's no longer hanging over my head. I don't have to put something - a bill to pay or a letter to respond to or an item to take out to my car - on the coffee table where I can see it, because otherwise I won't remember, because if I can't see it, it doesn't exist. But if I put the item where I can see it, then my wife, who likes things neat, will put it away neatly. So the coffee table will be neat, but then I won't see the item, and then I won't remember it and it will never get done. On the slim chance that I do remember I will have no idea where it is and will have to spend a lot of time looking for it. But if I heed the signal, the red flag, and ask myself, " Can I just do it right now?" often I can just do it in less time than it would take to pull the cards out of my pocket, and decide whether it belongs on the red or the orange, and see if I already have five things on the red card (I probably do), and write the note on the appropriate card, and check to make sure I wrote it legibly, and then put the cards back in my pocket. And I don't have to put something where I can see it. If I just do it, it's done, and my life is one step simpler. And it only took a little bit of time.

Little bits of time
     There are many little bits of time in a day. I may be waiting for a patient to arrive, or for the computer to finish turning on, or for my wife to get ready to go somewhere. I don't need to just wait: there's often a brief phone call I can make, or I can clean up some of the clutter on my desk, or I can update my to-do list. Something else has been taken care of, a small thing, but it's no longer hanging over my head.

Another red flag- "Oh, it'll be OK."
     No, it won't. Or there's at least a one in three chance it won't, that I will drop the too big stack of boxes, or spill the paint on the rug, or in the brief

time it will take me to just run into the store instead of going back and getting the keys that I forgot and left in the ignition someone will steal the car (OK, the car being stolen is less than a one in three chance, but on the other hand, it's a big one. For that matter, spilling the paint on the rug can be a big one, too.)

When I was young, often I had to work in my father's shoe store. Most of my work was restocking - unpacking big cartons of shoe boxes and taking them to the place for that particular style of shoe. First I had to move the boxes already in the shelf around in careful and precise order to make the holes for the new ones. Then I had to carefully and precisely shelve the new ones in the right holes, by style and size. This was all repetitive and uninteresting work that required concentration. I have ADD. I was not good at it. I hated it.

So I would carry a two-column load of shoe boxes from the back of the store to the shelves. Usually I'd try to carry too many at once and often they'd topple over. My father called this "a lazy man's load," meaning that I would try to carry too many so that I wouldn't have to make as many trips. In the time it would take me to pick up all the shoes and boxes I'd dropped, and to put the right shoes back properly in the right box, and to restack the boxes and start over, I could've made three trips, with much less frustration. But I'd straighten it all out and then I'd go back and pick up another too big stack, and say to myself, 'Oh, it'll be OK', and off I'd go. I eventually learned to recognize the red flag and that it doesn't apply only to shoes: "No, it won't be OK!"

And another - "Oh, I have plenty of time."
       When I hear myself say this –red flag! I'm not good at time. To me, "plenty" becomes like infinite. That means I can dawdle around, and do a little of this and a little of that, and I don't really have to start getting ready yet. It means I'm going to wind up rushing around at the last minute, probably frantically looking for my car keys (not anymore! front table) and then I'm going to be late. So right now is when I need to get ready to go. Now, it's good not to feel rushed, and to actually plan ahead so that I really do have plenty of time, but then I need to say, "I have enough time," not "plenty." That is, I have enough time if I stay focused and on track and get ready and go. No, I do not have time to look at this TV show. No, I do not have time to play just this one computer game. No, I do not have time right now to do that chore that I didn't get to last night. I have just enough time so that I do not have to feel rushed, as long as I plow ahead with getting ready and going.

       Once I am ready, I may have a few spare minutes, and I might be able to get some little thing done before I leave, which would be great. But I need to be sure that I actually am ready before I say I have a few minutes to spare and start in on something. And I need to be very careful that I don't get involved in something and wind up rushed and late anyway.

This same process applies on a larger scale to a project, "Oh, that isn't due 'til next week; I have plenty of time." or a trip, Oh, we're not going to Houston 'til June." I had better notice the red flag and start getting ready, right now.

Summary:

Flags alert us to something, usually to danger. We can learn what our red flags are and to recognize them when they pop-up. Then we can take appropriate action to save ourselves trouble, to avoid getting into a mess. We can be conscious of little bits of available time; using them decreases the pressure we feel. Some of my personal red flags are: "I'll do that later," and "Oh, it'll be OK," and "I have plenty of time."

Chapter 19

One thing

One thing at a time can be applied in many different ways. Focus on one thing off my red card of five; that's one way. Another way is in learning the guitar. Here, I'm struggling. I just signed up for another course on line, which looked very good and was very cheap (they're always on sale.). Couldn't pass it up. Now that I have it, it is indeed very good. A bargain. Problem is I haven't finished the blues guitar course DVD, nor the fretboard lessons book, nor the other on line course I recently signed up for. In fact, the DVD and the book and the first online course are on my list of things I'm avoiding. In each of them, I started and then ran into something difficult, and without really thinking about it I just let it go and started on something else. So what I need to do now is to sit down with my yellow legal pad and organize. That's the guitar courses.

I'm working on learning just one song, and that's going pretty well. The trick is to not be impatient but to break the song into very small parts, and learn one part at a time. Remember small steps? When I have all the small parts learned it is easy to start with the first one and add the next to it, and learn that, and then keep putting parts together into larger parts until I have the whole thing. So I know how to do that and it's working well, one song at a time. I just need to force myself to stick to one song at a time, not be trying to learn two or three at once.

But at the same time, I'm also trying to learn the different notes on the fretboard, like the notes on the piano keys, and the names of some chords. I'm not focused or organized. I need to pick the one online course and stay with it, while it's still available on the internet. All the other courses I can get to later. I need to break the fretboard into very small chunks (not literally, of course; that's silly!) and do a little at a time, and also one new chord at a time, plus focus on the one song and on the first online course. That still may be too much at once, but that's my current strategy; I hope I can stick to it. Similarly, if you're going to use the problem, strategy, rule, habit, approach from this book, and some of the tools, you need to start with just one, or at most two, until you get those down; then move to another one.

Otherwise you'll likely get into a mess, like I have with the guitar.

Someone is going to misunderstand what I explain to them, or they might misapply it. Of course, sometimes when they misapply it they do it in ways that make things turn out better than what I had originally intended. But that wasn't the case with a patient, Mr. B. He was feeling pretty overwhelmed; he had a lot of things to do. Mr. B may have ADD but we haven't actually considered that; we've had other things to deal with first. Anyway, he came in one day feeling overwhelmed, with too many things to do. I explained to him about to do-lists, the long one and the list of five. He thought that sounded good.

The next appointment he was still feeling overwhelmed, and after we discussed it, I asked him how many things he had to do now. He replied, "A lot!"

I said, "No, you just have one thing to do. Pick one off your list of five, and that is the one thing you have to do. When you finish that one, then you will have another one thing to do."

I explained to him how to pick priorities on his long list, using the questions: "Is it urgent? How soon does it need to be done? Is it important? What would happen if you didn't do it, or didn't do it soon?"

Important means there is a big consequence if you don't do it or a big reward if you do it. Urgent means that it is not only important but also has to be done right away; tomorrow will be too late. If it's neither important nor urgent, just cross it off the list. If it's both important and urgent, put it on your list of five. Part of feeling overwhelmed comes from regarding everything as important and urgent. You can underline the most important things on your list, or you can put numbers by them, classifying them each as priority 1, 2 or 3. Then when you complete something off your list of five, you can pick another high priority to move into its spot.

I asked Mr. B to bring in his lists the next time.

When he returned, he was still feeling overwhelmed, but less so. He showed me his to-do lists. He'd done a pretty good job. Instead of making one list of five he had made lists for each day, Sunday, Monday, Tuesday--. So it could still look somewhat overwhelming, but it was organized, and he didn't have to keep it all in his head. He hadn't crossed anything off. I asked him what he'd gotten done, and it turned out he had done almost all of the things on his lists. I explained the positive reinforcement, the good feeling, the reward each time you cross off something. But when he looked at his lists, with nothing crossed off even though he had done almost everything, it would add to his sense of being overwhelmed. I explained that I thought having a list for each day might be a good approach, but it didn't mean you had to get all of those things done that day. If you didn't finish your list of five today, you started the next day's list with the things that were left over. So it might work better if he just made a list of five for one day at a time. If carrying over some of today's five to tomorrow creates a long list, then you need to prioritize again and whittle that list down to five. If you get those done, you can always add more.

I asked to see his long list. Mr. B said he hadn't made one because he feared it would be so long that he would feel more overwhelmed looking at it. He said that was OK, because he knew all of the things he had to do; he was carrying them in his head! I explained that that was much of the problem; if he was carrying all that in his head, he was going to feel overwhelmed. I told him that if he would make the long list, prioritize it, and then make his list of five from that, then he could forget about the long list until he had crossed something off the list of five and created a space.

Then I asked Mr. B. how many things he had to do. He said, "A lot!" and I said, "No, you only have one." Then we looked at his list of five for the day and picked the one he could be working on. I suggested that after he made a list of five, then he needed to go a step further and make a list of one, to literally write it down.

So Mr. B had quickly picked up the general idea, and he was doing a good job making his lists of five, but it needed some fine tuning to truly become a helpful system for him.

The system:

Make a long list, in writing.

Set priorities. "What would happen if this doesn't get done? Is it urgent to do it now?"

Make a list of five, put the day on top of it if you wish. (It's probably best to not make the next day's though, because you need flexibility, and you don't know how many of today's list you will get done today.)

Pick the one you're going to work on.

Cross it off when it's done.

Add another high priority item to that list - either when you cross off one, or maybe better, when you cross off the last one.

You are doing one thing at a time. Make a list of one.

If you don't finish all five today, put the leftovers on the next day's list.

If that list grows to more than five, reprioritize and shorten it.

Although Mr. B and I are working on a number of issues in his therapy, what I have just described would be an illustration of coaching as it would be for ADD.

Summary:

We need to learn to focus on one thing at a time. One-to do. One guitar lesson. One song. If we make a long to-do list, then we don't have to carry a bunch of stuff in our head and feel overloaded. The long list has all the stuff on it and it's not going to go away; we can focus on the short list, and then on one thing off the short list. One thing at a time.

Chapter 20

Slogans

The Big Slogan

One of the most useful tools for me is a slogan, which I discovered years before I knew I had ADD -"Do it now, do it right, do the hard part first."

This slogan has become a habit. It pops into my head whenever I'm deciding whether or not I am actually going to go ahead and do something, or what to do next. It pops in automatically now, without having to think about it, or remember it. Then my rule is, when I think it, do it. Don't dismiss it or argue myself out of it, just do it. Now!

Do it now

Right now I'm thinking about it, it's on my mind. "Now" will get it done; it won't be hanging over my head and cluttering up my mind any more. I noticed that often I would think about something – "Oh, I need to do that. I will get to it. I better add that to my to do-list." I realized that sometimes the thing to do was small, and that I could probably do it in the time it would take me to list it on my card. If I do it now, then it's done. I don't have to think about it anymore, and if it's already on my list, I can cross it off. It might be a phone call, or putting something away in the right place, or any other small thing. These are the small bits of time. Many of the small to-do things can be done in those small intervals. It's good to get some of those small things done. But it also applies to big things - "do it now" means get started now; break it into small steps, pick one, and get going.

Do it right

I used to do a lot of things sloppily or half way: "Oh, that's good enough; it'll be alright." I did this partly because I assumed, unconsciously perhaps, that if I tried to do my best it wouldn't turn out right anyway. So why waste the time and effort? Plus I could protect my morale. When it didn't turn out- "Well, I didn't really try, and I didn't spend much time on it anyway." But there's an old saying, "If you don't have time to do it right the first time, when will you have time to do it over?" It's best to slow down, and just do it right.

Do the hard part first

This is the gem! First it means that I am breaking it down into small parts, which is the first step in actually getting started on actually doing it, a major tool against procrastination. And the hard part is the major source feeding the procrastination. Procrastination keeps it all hanging over my head, especially the hard part, and feeds the unpleasant sense of being overwhelmed, because there are many things hanging over my head. And this concept is an organizing principle; when I'm not doing anything because I can't decide where to start, this gives me a guideline. So to get started, I start with the hard part, and once I have that part done it is all downhill from there; now it is easy. And of course, once again, part of the trick is to make the hard part as small as possible so it may turn out not so hard after all, once I can finally get myself to actually start.

"Do it now, do it right, AND DO THE HARD PART FIRST."

Other slogans, sayings

We can use slogans or sayings as rules. I try to make "Do it now, do it right, do the hard part first." a rule and to make myself follow it, at least every time I think of it. I'm working on myself to become more assertive, so my slogan for that is-"Fearless."

When I'm vacillating about whether or not to do something or to speak up or not, then "Fearless" enters my mind and I proceed. Of course, nothing is ever simple. I want to also remember that having ADD, I need to think a moment before I impulsively act or blurt out something, but just for a moment. It doesn't help to just keep vacillating, and to let myself be controlled by fear instead of by judgment. Easy to say. I used to think, at whatever age I was at the moment, that once I was ten years older I would no longer care what other people thought. Then I would be fearless. So far, hasn't happened. But I am working on it.

AA uses lots of slogans, like "One day at a time" And "Easy does it" to help people stay on track, and we can use those, too. Slogans are quick and easy ways to remind of us something we need to remember, usually an attitude or a perspective.

Another slogan I use is "I have as much time as anyone else."

My friend Richard mentions a friend who uses the slogan, "Just get her done." That's a good slogan and a good example of using self-talk.

Summary:

Easily remembered slogans can become rules and help us follow our program for coping with ADD, and making our life better. The most helpful one for me is : "Do it now, do it right, AND DO THE HARD PART FIRST."

"Do it now, do it right, do the hard part first."

Chapter 21

Mind games, language, attitude

What turns our focus center on? Personal interest. Novelty. Challenge. Heavy immediate deadline. So when faced with a task that doesn't fit one of these, sometimes I can use mind games to fool my focus center into turning on. Sometimes this works. This gives me more control over my life.

Some of the mind games are tricks, some have to do with language, some with attitude.

Language

Language is powerful. It can strongly affect our emotions and our behavior. By being careful in our choice of language, we can have more control over how we feel and over our attitudes and our behavior.

For many of us, "I have to--" or "I should--" evokes an automatic resistance, mostly unconscious. These words bring up the picture of the principal standing over a kid and shaking his finger in the kid's face. "Have to"' or "should" automatically turns whatever needs to be done into a chore, an unpleasant prospect.

I have learned to eliminate "I should" and "I have to" from my internal vocabulary. Instead, I say to myself, "I need to--", or "It would be good if I--." This reduces the resistance and thus the procrastination.

I also don't say "I should have-- ." I might say "It would've been good to have --" but even better is, "Well, next time I will--" This reduces the self-critic, the beating up on myself, and thus reduces the demoralization that then makes it harder to complete something or to get started on the next thing up. These improvements in my vocabulary are fairly recent. I used to use lots of "should"s, and clearly they made it harder to get started on something, and the "should have"s were demoralizing. And remember, something being "important", or a "should", does not turn on our focus center.

Attitudes

One example of a mind game: if I need to rake the leaves (which fortunately I don't have to do in Santa Fe), I can tell myself I'm in a leaf raking contest, and racing against the clock. Or I can come up with a new way to rake the leaves; maybe I'll see if I can rake them all into one huge pile, or I can divide the lawn into sectors so that I'll make the perfect bag size pile in the middle of each sector. This not only makes the raking a challenge, but it gives me a novel way to do the job. Another great strategy is to use the new I-pod with ear plugs that my daughter gave me that I have my favorite music on. Then instead of saying I need to rake the leaves this afternoon (not "I have to" or "I should", but "I need to"), I'll say "Oh boy, this afternoon I have time to really listen to my music." (That is also an example of reframing, which I'll discuss soon.)

I do the same thing with exercise. I kind of enjoy the treadmill, partly because I've made it a challenge by setting goals - "Two miles last time, so can I do 2.25 this time?" But it's really the time I can watch a poker game or football game that I've taped. Also, watching those shows focuses my mind on them, and I can go much further than if I was just doing the treadmill by itself. So this isn't my exercise time, it's my poker or football time, and I look forward to it as a treat instead of dreading it as a chore.

I can use imagination to change my perception and attitude. Some years ago, back when we had four young children, I would put in a hard day's work and couldn't wait to get home so that I could relax. When I arrived home, my wife would meet me at the door with the latest stories of what the kids had done wrong today that I was going to have to take care of right now ("You just wait 'til your father gets home!"). I resented this and it caused a lot of conflict between us. So I decided to imagine that times were hard for us (not a stretch of the imagination) and that I'd had to take a second job to make ends meet. This imaginary second job was as the director of a residential treatment center for disturbed children. When I finished my first job, the day job, I would commute to my imaginary second job at the treatment center, where the nurse would meet me at the door and give me the day report, with the problems that I needed to address. As weird and silly as this sounds, it worked for me. I was able to let of go of the illusion that I was entitled to a restful evening and of my resentment about not getting it. Things went better.

Reframing

Another technique is 'reframing'. A while back I found that some mornings I was saying to myself, "Oh, I have to go to work today," or "Oh, I have a lot of patients to see today." Notice that those are have to's. It put a gloom on the day to start with, a sense of being tired, burdened and even somewhat misused. Fortunately, once I started seeing patients, I usually enjoyed it, and the negative feelings left, but it was a poor way to start the day. Then one day I realized that I was going to spend most of the day visiting with and having interesting conversation with a number of people that I liked and enjoyed, and further, that I was going to get paid for it. How blessed and lucky is that?

This strategy of saying "I get to see my patients today" is not the same as a mind game using my imagination to 'fool' myself, like the treatment center director job. This is an example of what therapist's call 'reframing', putting a different slant on something. The second view about my work, the privilege of seeing my patients, is actually more realistic, but that's not the point really; it's more useful to me. I can start the day in a better mood, with more energy and enthusiasm. The 'realistic' is in the eye of the beholder. We have some choice as to which way we choose to think about something, or to talk to ourselves about it. So now I don't say "have to" but "Today I get to-", and I don't call it "work".

"Today I get to visit with some nice interesting people that I like and enjoy talking with." Doesn't that sound better than "Today I have to go to work"?

Dr. Peter Goldblum gave another good example on my blog (That's ADDadultstrategies.wordpress. com - my blog advertising this book.) He suggested reframing "nagging" as "a loving effort to help." I really do have some choice in how I view things. This is partly a matter of self-talk. When my wife offers some unrequested advice for example, I can either say to myself, "There she goes, nagging and criticizing again. Does she think I can't do anything?" or I can say to myself, "She's trying to help me. It's one of the ways she expresses her love for me. She has a lot of good ideas."

Summary:

We can play mind games to trick our focus center into turning on. We have some ability to control our attitudes, and one way is to choose what kind of language we are going to use to ourselves. 'Should's and 'have to's tend to stall us even though they 'should' encourage us. Reframing means looking at something in a new and different way, and we can choose how to look at it.

Chapter 22

Checking

This chapter will wrap up the main points of this section: simplify, organize, take charge. We'll cover the tool of checking before we move on to the next section, issues of coping with time.

Twice in the past few years I've backed out of the garage and into the cars of visitors who had parked in our driveway. I just didn't see them. Twice was enough. It was expensive, embarrassing and it was inconvenient for our guests. So now, I look carefully behind and to both sides before I back out of the driveway. That is a rule which is becoming a habit. It has to be a rule, so that I do it every time, even if I know for sure that there are no cars parked in the driveway. If I don't do it every time, because sometimes I'm sure there is no car there, then sooner or later I'll be wrong, and I'll hit the car that I was sure wasn't there. Also, if I don't do it every time, it won't become a habit. I'll tend to forget to do it, and then of course sooner or later I'll hit another car.

Note: Yesterday, I was quite aware that we had guests. I was very careful backing out of the driveway, very careful. Made it out of the driveway safely. Then I backed into their car which they had parked at the curb near the driveway. Guess I need to expand my rule.

Similar problem at the gas station: twice I've driven off with the gas nozzle still stuck in my gas tank. Of course that pulled the hose loose and I dragged it along. Fortunately, I realized it right away and didn't go speeding down the highway with the hose flying out behind me. But it is embarrassing, and it's difficult to refit the hose onto the pump. Further, the gas station people don't seem to appreciate it. If you don't have ADD, you might find it hard to see how that could ever happen, let alone twice.

So I made the rule, "Check the hose." meaning that I take the hose out and put the cap on and check to see that I did it. Then I get in the car, and before I drive off, I look in the rear view mirror to check again, even though I may be absolutely sure I put it up correctly. Same reasoning, if I don't do it every time it won't become a habit and eventually I'll do it again.

When I was young we would pick my father up after work. We'd park in front of the store and wait for him. The lights would go out in the store and then he'd come out the door. He would lock the door, come out to the car, and then walk back and check the door again. This practice made an impression on me. Some degree of compulsiveness is not a bad thing if we have ADD. I don't always check to see that I've locked the door, but when I write a prescription for a patient, I always double check it before I hand it to them. Making a mistake on a prescription is one of the worst things I can do. So checking the prescription is a rule that has become a habit. I don't have to remember to do it, and I don't have to decide whether to do it or not; I just do it. When I fill up the car with gas, I always check to make sure I've put the nozzle back and closed my gas cap. When I get in the car, I always check the gas gauge before I start out. While I'm writing this book I stop every few pages to save what I've written. These are instances of checking which have become habit now. They are a little compulsive; that's good.

After I use a credit card, I put the card back in my billfold, and then I pull it out and check to make sure that the card is there before I leave. I didn't always have this habit. Once in France I ruined a day of vacation for us and our friends by losing my credit card. We turned the place upside down. We retraced our steps. We, not speaking French, got the desk clerk to, reluctantly, call where we had been last. Finally I got him to call the credit card company to cancel the card. Right after that I found the card in my shirt pocket, where it doesn't belong. I was brave enough to show it, rather than to hide it or throw it away at that point. I did not impress my wife nor our friends, nor the desk clerk, who was already pretty much not impressed. Time for a new rule.

All of these rules and habits and checking may sound kind of compulsive. They are. This may sound like a restrictive or constricting way to live, or that it takes a lot of time. It isn't and it doesn't. Once it becomes habit it really takes no time at all. It beats the heck out of not doing it, even when the mistakes don't occur too often. Talk about time consuming - have you ever lost your credit card? Or driven off with the gas nozzle? Or backed into another car? Now there's time consuming for you. I suspect that this rule, strategy, habit and checking approach won't sound so restrictive or time consuming to someone with ADD; you know what it's like if you're not using these tools.

The summer I was fifteen, I worked on a farm for Shady, my uncle's friend. One day he told me to get in the truck. His shot gun was in there. I was used to a gun that only held three shells; Shady's held eight. Shady drove me out to a field, and there were more starlings than I'd ever seen. He told me to shoot them and I let go. They were so thick in the trees that you thought one shot must kill twenty or thirty, but usually only four or five fell at a time. They would fly off and we would drive to the next tree and I'd shoot a bunch more. It wasn't very sporting but it was kind of fun (I can't explain why.). Finally Shady said, "Alright, let's go." I got back in the truck. I set the gun between us with the barrel pointing up. Although I was very well trained and responsible in gun safety, I hadn't pumped the gun to make sure it was empty as I should have, and I didn't have the safety on. In the back of my mind I thought we might run across another thick flock and he might stop again. Shady asked, "Is it empty?" and I said, "Yes, sir." because I had counted my eight shots and I knew that it was empty. He reached over and pulled the trigger and I about messed in my pants. I had counted the shots, and I knew it was empty, but I hadn't pumped it, and I didn't <u>know</u> that it was empty. I never expected a grown man to rely on my word for something serious. It's hard to explain what I learned that day, but it had something to do with growing up, being responsible, and standing behind your word. I saw myself, my relationship to other people and my place in the world differently after that. And I learned something about checking, not assuming.

I volunteer in the State Penitentiary about once a week. Twice I've walked into the prison with a pocket knife in my pocket, which is way way way against the rules. So now I have a check list for getting ready to go into the prison: check my pockets: no knife, no money; be sure I have my badge. This is a mental check list, though I've considered writing it down: knife, money, badge, the right shoes, pack lunch. Then when I reach the prison, another rule: check all my pockets again before I leave my car. This is like the check list pilots use before taking off.

For fishing, I use another principle: prepare ahead. This is related to checking, and it also eliminates rushing. Once I drove all the way to the river and found that I'd forgotten my rod. I also once leaned my rod against a tree while I was cleaning fish and I drove off and left it. When I got back it was gone. So I have yet another rule: when I drive off from the river, I check to make sure my rod is in the car. So anyway, I put my fishing gear in the car the night before. There's no rush, and I can make sure I have it all. Then in the morning I look again to see that it's all there. The way a rule works is, you always have to follow it or it will not become habit. So I don't say, "Oh, I checked it last night so I know it's in there, so I don't need to check it again". No, the rule is check it, so I do. I don't need to remember a check list for the fishing, I just need to remember "four." Rod, vest, boots, wading stick; four things.

I have a lot of rules built up by now: "My keys only go on the front table." "Check and make sure the hose is out of the gas tank before I drive off." "Check my pockets before I go to the prison." Eventually these rules become habits, which is the desired goal, so that I don't have to think about them or remember them. It takes time, repetition and consistency to make a rule a habit, and there will be slips. Just keep going. It's best to focus on only one, or at most two new rules at a time, until they become habit. Then you can begin to work on another problem.

I'm a little concerned about how all these rules, habits and compulsive behaviors might sound to you. Do they sound constricting, like I live in a straight jacket, and am always worried about everything? I still remember when I was in the second grade, quite a long time ago. I know what they're teaching in health these days; believe me, they weren't teaching those things back then. I remember one passage in our health book particularly, talking about the importance of trimming toenails. It admonished, "Many a stocking has been torn by an untrimmed toenail!" I laughed so hard that I got in trouble (ADHD?). A picture came into my head of this prim little old lady writing this in the 1800's. Nowadays we would say, "Get a life!" I never thought about my toenails. I guess if they needed trimming my mother did it for me. And the idea of having any concern at all about "a torn stocking" struck me as incredibly silly. I was eight years old and I had a lot more important things to worry about than torn socks; that was way down on my list of priorities. So I'm hoping that you don't have that kind of reaction to all these rules and sayings and habits. Of course, I'm not talking about torn stockings; I'm talking about driving off with the gas hose, or into the visitor's car. And if you have ADD, or live with someone who does, I'm guessing that you won't have that reaction.

Summary:

Because we have ADD, we need to simplify our lives. The basic approach is identify a problem, develop a strategy, make the strategy a rule, make the rule a habit. That process can make life less frustrating, improve our functioning, save us time, reduce pressure, and provide other benefits. Checking is one useful tool which we can make into a habit. These rules and habits contribute to making our life go better, and eliminate some mess-ups so that we don't have to deal with them. They will save a lot of time in the long run. They are tools to put us in charge of our own lives.

Section III

Time

Although the main problem in ADD is in the focus center, it's remarkable how many of our difficulties involve time in some way. So we need strategies to help us deal with time.

Chapter 23

Philosophizing about time

I may be indulging myself a little in this philoso-phizing piece. Maybe that's an author's prerogative, or maybe not. We both know that you don't have to read it. Feel free to skip this and go on to the next chapter. You'll save a little time.

Old Pennsylvania Dutch saying having to do with time:

"Ve get too soon oldt und too late schmart."

What I am going to say now you've heard before. I've often heard it before, too. It took many
years before I understood it. I always thought it was
just touchy-feely nonsense:
What is important?
Relationships. Health. Time.
It's nice to have money, but that's a distant fourth.
Security would go up there, but security is an illusion (except spiritually).

Modern physics is questioning the reality of the
concept of time; time may be an illusion too. Time
is subjective. It moves very fast when we are on
vacation; we can sit in the dentist's chair for an eter-
nity. When we're young, we have all the time in the
world and it moves very slowly. It takes forever for
Christmas to get here. As we get older, it speeds up.
The days and then the weeks and the months whiz
past.

"Zzzip!"
"What was that?"
"That was your life, mate."
*" Gor, that was quick. Can I have another
go?"*
"One's the lot, mate."
*Australian humor bit (I couldn't find the original
source)*

Summary:

Time is precious.

End of philosophy piece. Thank you.

Chapter 24

ADD and Time

Time is precious.

I have trouble with time in many ways:

- I can't judge time -How much time will this take? How much time has passed?
- I can't grasp time - "That's next month? Oh, I have plenty of time."
- I waste time - "Gee, why did I spend all that time on that when I have all these other important things to do?"
- I feel short of time - I'm always concerned that I don't have enough time and it's racing away from me. I have to do all these to-do's and I have more to do than I can possibly get done.
- I can't locate myself in time - This is hard to describe, but if you have ADD, you might know what I mean: "This is December; Christmas must be coming? How far off is it?

Is there something after that? What's happening next year? Is there anything I need to be doing to prepare for it?"

- I can't remember time - My brain records whatever is happening but doesn't attach the date to it. Was that last year, or three years ago? Was it in 1984 or 1994? Maybe because I'm not located in the time, as above?

I use calendars to help with some of these problems with time. They help me locate myself. I try to prioritize, to help avoid wasting time. And I focus on one thing, so I won't feel so rushed and pressured. I'll tell you about the fifty percent rule next chapter.

Summary:
Time is an important and difficult issue for us ADDers. It causes us a lot of trouble. An appointment book and lots of calendars are examples of strategies that can help us cope.

Chapter 25

Time and calendars

In addition to the appointment book in my pocket I'm surrounded by calendars. I have a small calendar of the month on my desk top. The large three months at a glance calendar is hanging on the wall. I can see it from anywhere in the room. A calendar hangs on the side of the bookcase next to my therapy chair. Next to my phone is a large monthly calendar, where I note my open appointment spaces and my out of office appointments, kind of as a supplement to my appointment book. Under that is the one sheet calendar for the next month. I print these one month calendars free from the internet.

I am not good at time, in many ways. I need to keep track of my appointments, both for my practice and out of the office. I need to keep track of where I am in the week and in the year and in time- hence the three months at a glance calendar. (You likely will not really grasp what I'm talking about here, unless perhaps you have ADD, too.) The three month calendar has the current month on the left, next month in the middle, and the next month on the right. So if something is planned for next month, or the month after, I can really see where it is, and how many days are between now and then. Telling me that something is two months away does not convey useful information to me. I have to see it.

JANUARY	FEBRUARY	MARCH

							2011								2011									2011				
						1		1	2	3	4	5				1	2	3	4	5
2	3	4	5	6	7	8	6	7	8	9	10	11	12	6	7	8	9	10	11	12
9	10	11	12	13	14	15	13	14	15	16	17	18	19	13	14	15	16	17	18	19
16	17	18	19	20	21	22	20	21	22	23	24	25	26	20	21	22	23	24	25	26
23	24	25	26	27	28	29	27	28						27	28	29	30	31		
30	31																			

Illustration 6.   The three months at a time calendar

I can see it all.

I need these calendars to stay on track with where I'm supposed to be and what I need to be doing. Otherwise, things sneak up on me. "I need to get my papers together for the taxes; oh, that's a long way off, I have plenty of time" or "That trip is coming up, but it's not 'til next month." When I say that, well, it might as well be next century because next month seems so far off, but the day is going to suddenly be here, and I'm not going to be ready, just surprised.

I don't seem to have trouble knowing where I am in space - I'm in my office, or the kitchen, or in Houston- but, if we're going to Houston next week, I have little concept of what "next week" really means, how much I can reasonably expect to get done before we leave, what are the things I need to do to get ready and when do I need to do them, when do I need to start packing, etc. You could have told me "We're going to Houston next month", or "next year", or "sometime", and it would all be about the same to me. So I need to keep checking the three month calendar where I have all these events written in and can see where they really are.

I'm poor at judging time. I can't tell how long I've been doing something. If I'm playing a computer game (I don't anymore) hours can pass and I'm not aware of it. I'm no good at estimating how long it will take to do something, or how long it will take to get somewhere. This uncertainty contributes to the sense of being rushed. If I'm about to start something, a project, or a trip, my strategy now is to guess how long it will take and add fifty

percent. Also now I'm aware that anytime I'm doing a project at home, it will require three trips to
the hardware store. I will never manage to pick up
everything I need on just the first two trips. I can
count this into my time estimate.

I just can't judge time well. If I have a day or a
weekend off, I get excited about all the things I'm
going to get done, some fun things and some "catch
up." So I make a list. But then I need to put some of
the things in parentheses or just cross some of them
off, because I'm never going to get all that done. Then
I'm just going to feel disappointed and down on myself. Part of the problem is, I start thinking, "Wow, I
have all day Thursday off!" Well, I do have all day
Thursday off, but I don't have all day Thursday to
get things done. By the time I have my prayer time
and eat breakfast and read the paper and shave and
do my exercise and shower and dress and check my
phone messages and my e-mail, half the morning is
gone. At least. And then, of course, it is expectable
that unexpected things will come up. And if I have
some extra time off, I want to spend some extra time
with my wife. So if I say, "I have a week off." or "I
have a day off." it gives an unrealistic picture of the
time available to accomplish things. So I've needed
to learn to be realistic in what I think I'm going to
accomplish. And to always make a short to-do list

off the long one, and then to focus on one thing on the list at a time.

Right now I'm starting on a week off, a wonderful thing. I don't mean vacation, going somewhere, but just off. I have a list of all the things I'd like to accomplish with this week of free time. It is a long list. Since I know from experience that I can't possibly get all those things done in this week, I will need to prioritize. If I don't do this, I'll feel lousy at the end of the week when I see all the things that I didn't get done. Unfortunately, prioritizing is not one of my strengths.

One strategy I'm using for this week off is scheduling. I have seven days. So I looked at my long impossible list and selected the seven things I really would like to get done, and I assigned one of them to each day. If I can do more than one of them on a day then I can always pull another one off the big list. And that can happen, because some of the things are hard and/or time consuming but some of them aren't. It's early in the week and already I'm a little ahead. That feels so much better than being behind. And by assigning one for each day I definitely will have all seven done by the end of the week.

Today I finally cleaned the dust out of my computer, and the fan is much quieter now. I've been avoiding doing this for a long time because I wasn't sure I could do it, so it was one of my seven scheduled tasks for this week. It felt very good to finally get it done. It didn't take as long as I'd expected (usually things take longer than expected) so now I can work on another listed item this afternoon. I'm having to keep revising my schedule, because I'm getting more done than I planned. That is a good feeling. By following this system, I'll be sure to finish at least the big seven things that I picked as priorities at the beginning of the week.

So usually I have the list of five and try to get as much of that done as I can in a day, but on special occasions I schedule one special task for each day for a while and focus on getting that one done each day.

Summary:

We need strategies to help us deal with time. Some strategies are: the three month at a glance calendar, add fifty percent to any estimate of how long something will take, don't plan to do more than you possibly can do, and sometimes make a schedule for the next few days to be sure to get things done.

Chapter 26

Choices

Time assay

Occasionally, maybe every four months or so, I do a time assay. I sit down and write out my typical daily schedule. Then I write down the things I'm doing that aren't on the routine schedule. Then I check to see if it makes sense, if there are things there that I don't need or want to be spending time on. I experience myself as being very busy but I need to remember that I spend much of my time doing things that are elective. When I'm feeling pressured, sorry for myself, and that I'm being over worked, I need to step back and see that most of what I do is actually voluntary. I go fishing a lot, volunteer in the prison, go to church, practice the guitar, study Spanish, have the daily cocktail hour and watch movies with my wife, and I write on this book. All of that is by choice, even though some of it is very important to my well being (although it's possible I go fishing a little more than is absolutely necessary). And yet I sometimes find myself thinking that I don't have any free time. Poor me. Well, I kind of don't have much 'free time', because I have so many things I want to do and I've scheduled them in; so I don't have much time that is unaccounted for. In a way, this is part of structure and that's good. But I need to adjust my attitude. All of those things are voluntary and therefore they actually are free time. I could drop any of them and I can have just about as much free time as I wish. The human mind is a strange thing.

Occasionally the time assay reveals that there is something I can cut down on or eliminate, and it always becomes clear that I'm trying to do more than is possible, but I guess that's what I'm choosing. Maybe I need to think about that some more, but there's nothing on my list that I want to give up. I do think I will do these weeks off more often though; it's been very good. Anyway, the time assay is a very useful exercise – if I can find time to do it, of course.

Choices

There are twenty-four hours in a day: my day, your day, every day. Some people get by on less sleep than others, but basically we each have the same twenty four hours. And we can only cram so much into twenty-four hours. We folks with ADD tend to try to do too much. So many things seem so appealing or so necessary. We have a hard time prioritizing and we tend to try to do them all. But on one of my time assays I realized I needed to give up chess. That doesn't mean I'll never play it again. I do still look at the daily chess problem in the paper, but I no longer play on the internet and I no longer subscribe to the daily chess problem. I'm no longer trying to learn the openings. I'm not very good at chess, and I realized that I never will be. Although I was enjoying chess, I saw that if I want to exercise and fish and do prison ministry and learn the guitar and study Spanish, something was going to have to go. So, goodbye to chess. We find so many things interesting and it's hard to accept that we can't do them all. It's hard to let go of something. So we have trouble making a choice or a decision. We procrastinate on doing anything. We have trouble choosing an occupation or which book to read today. Every choice made involves giving up some other options, and we have trouble doing that.

We want it all.

And that is part of our problem with time.

Summary:

With ADD, we can have many kinds of problems regarding time: wasting it, misjudging it, losing track of it, and being temporally disoriented. We tend to be interested in many things, and it's hard to accept that we have to make choices. Then we feel short of time. So we need strategies. These can involve various ways of using calendars and an appointment book, time assays, and attention to priorities. That's next.

Chapter 27

Priorities

Once I read of a business man complaining to his therapist that he didn't have enough time. It took them a while to arrive at the fact that this man subscribed to three newspapers and thought that he had to read all three front to back every day. We often don't clearly see ourselves and what we're doing. When I do the time assay, I usually don't find that I'm throwing away time; rather, I'm usually impressed by how much I'm actually getting done.

I try to make good use of time. When I'm driving I can do exercises or study a topic on a CD, or in my head I can review Spanish or recite Psalms. Those are good exercises. And if I'm standing in line or if I'm in a waiting room I can do the same. Often in a waiting room I'll go over my pocketful of cards and update and organize them. Maybe it would be nice if I could just relax or be comfortable doing nothing while I'm waiting somewhere, but I can't. I see the time being wasted. The clock is ticking and I'm not getting anything done and my big to-do list is really long. I get exasperated, frustrated and antsy if I feel like I'm wasting time. Some of this is just compulsiveness but I think most of it is ADD. One of the symptoms of ADD is impatience. We are not good at standing in line or waiting. We get fidgety. We tend to have road rage. By using these strategies I don't experience these problems anymore. If I'm stuck in traffic, or in a line, or in a waiting room I make good use of the time.

It is valuable to be able to just sit. I am not good at it, but over the years I've been getting better. I can sit and look at the ocean, or the trees or watch the birds. The key is that I'm doing it intentionally. I have deliberately chosen to just sit, and I recognize that it's not only enjoyable but also good for me and so it is not a waste of time and it doesn't feel like a waste of time.

I love to read and I read a lot. I try to pay attention to what I choose to read, to be intentional. I'm not going to be able to read it all, so I need to set priorities; I'm choosy. Will this be productive, help me towards my goals? Am I reading this for recreation? Is it something I'm interested in or that someone has recommended, not just something I happened to pick up? As I've grown older, I read more nonfiction. Sometimes it seems to me that all of the good novels have already been written and the current ones are just repetitions. But I enjoy an occasional good novel. Many of the novels that I read are on my wife's recommendation. She's pretty good at knowing what I would enjoy. Also, I've grown more flexible. I used to somehow think that if I started a book I was obligated to finish it. Nowadays I can say, "This just isn't working for me" and put it down. I can do this even if my wife really liked it. I also realize that I don't have to read all of every book. Sometimes I'll skip parts that don't catch my interest or that seem too difficult. Time is too precious to spend it reading something I don't really like.

After I learned about the man with three newspaper, I stopped to think. I really enjoy reading the newspaper, but I realized that I was overdoing it. With some stories just the headline gives me all that I really need to know about that. Other stories I can just skim and get the main ideas and facts. And some I don't bother looking at all. I thoroughly enjoy some of the funnies but some of them I never read. Since I started this approach I've probably cut my newspaper reading time in half, and I still enjoy it. So I have prioritized my newspaper reading.

Priorities

One of the many reasons for my trouble with time is my difficulty in setting priorities. What is truly important and what isn't? What do I really need to get done and what can sit undone forever and not make any difference?

A college student tells me that she studies with a yellow highlighter;   she highlights the important things on each page she reads. When she finishes and looks at the page, it is entirely yellow. She has ADD. We have trouble setting priorities, picking out the more important things from the less important. As I was thinking of her story, I realized that once I learned how to study, I would read each page and be asking myself, "What are the questions here that a reasonable professor would ask on a test?" Not all the professors were reasonable, but I had a pretty high batting average of guessing the actual test questions. Now I recognize that this was a mind game. I was studying but I also was competing, trying to out guess the professor. This is challenge, the kind of thing that will turn our focus center on, and I'm sure that it helped me in the studying itself, not just in guessing for the test. And it was a tool that helped me prioritize the information.

I have a hard time setting the priorities on my to-do lists. Everything looks important or it wouldn't be on there. Unfortunately, the items tend to all look equally important. For the long list, I try to ask, "Which are the most important ones? Which ones need to be done right away?" Then I will put them into categories, 1, 2, 3, depending on how soon I need to get to it. This is difficult for me.

One example of setting priorities is realizing that spending time with my grandson Michael is more important than anything else I could be doing. I can see that this is a good choice. At some point in the future I will look back and be pleased about this; I won't be regretting it. It is unusual for me to have vision this clear.

Summary:

We have trouble understanding or estimating time. Recognizing this, we can use techniques to manage it better. We need to realize that there are limits to what we can expect to do. Therefore we need to prioritize and we need strategies to help us. Keeping our goals in mind can help. We can ask, "What will happen if I don't do this? Or if I don't do it soon?" Prioritizing requires evaluating both how important something is- "What is the payoff or the penalty?"- and how urgent it is – "Is there a deadline after which it's too late?" One guideline in setting priorities is "Do the hard part first." That tells us where to start.

Section IV

Habits

Making habits is a basic part of our principle for coping with ADD: identify a problem, make a strategy, make it a rule, make it a habit. We often have to break bad habits, too. That's harder. But doable.

Chapter 28

Good Habits

A habit is something we routinely automatically do, without needing to think about it. Some habits are good, some not so helpful. I'll discuss how to break a bad habit, but for coping with ADD, how to make a good habit is the more important topic. One good habit of mine is that I brush my teeth every morning. I don't wake up and think, "Gee, should I brush my teeth today or not?" No, I brush my teeth every morning; that's just what I do. I don't have to think about it or make a decision; I just automatically do it. That's a habit. When we can create a good habit, we don't have to remember to do it, decide to do it, or think about it; we just do it.

The state tax department wrote saying that I owed three months of gross receipts tax (another New Mexico aberration?). I was frustrated! I spent an hour digging up records. Each time I make a monthly tax payment I make a record of it - mostly; I haven't really been very diligent about it and sometimes I forget. In general, these payments are also recorded in my checkbook, but sometimes I neglect to record what a check is for (did I mention that I have ADD?). There are substantial penalties for late taxes and I was afraid that this could cost me. I also feared that I'd have to go to the tax office to get it sorted out. Fortunately, I found the records and cancelled checks more or less in appropriate places, a feat somewhat spectacular for an ADDer. I had paid the June tax twice and July not at all. I spent an hour on the phone with a nice lady in Albuquerque. It turns out that they'd misrecorded May, but I'd put the wrong date on one of the two June forms. I hadn't paid July, and it was more than the extra I'd paid for June. Here comes the penalty! However, when she sorted it all out, somehow they owed me $17.98. Wow! So what's the bottom line? I need to make new habits:

1) Double check when I fill out the form to be sure I've done it correctly.

2) Carefully record each payment, not "most payments", not "usually", not "in general", but each.

3) At the same time, check to see that all the payments are up to date.

That should do it. This can save me anxiety, hours and money; I've had to pay penalties before, and I don't like it.

Identify the problem, make a strategy, make a rule, and make it a habit. This tax thing is a big enough issue to be worth the trouble to fix it.

Summary:

Making habits takes time and effort, but can pay off big in the long run. Start by identifying the problem as a problem and decide if it's enough of a problem to justify working on it. Our life is simpler if we're using habits rather than having to make a lot of decisions.

Chapter 29

How To Change A Habit

Some of the problems we identify will be habits, undesirable habits. We can change those:

1. Recognize, identify and become very clear about what you want to change.
2. Make a commitment to change it.
3. Begin "spotting", noticing and remarking to yourself each time you see yourself doing it. You may need to do this for weeks or months before you are ready for the next step. When you have the spotting down and feel ready, then:
4. Change it:

   A) If you are afraid of doing something, do it anyway.

   B) If you are habitually saying an undesirable thing, catch yourself and don't say it. Substitute saying something else.

C) If it's a way of responding to a certain person or situation, decide on a new way to respond and try it. If there's a repetitive script (see glossary), don't follow it.

D) If the habit does something for you (e.g. smoking for relaxation), find a substitute way to do that.

At this point in the process, there are many tools that may help to make the change easier and faster, although none of them may be necessary. Find the ones that fit for you:
1) Think through what are the benefits of the old way vs. the new way. What are the risks involved in changing vs. the costs of not changing?
2) Tell friends what you're working on and that you've made a commitment to change. Ask them to help you spot anytime you are showing the old pattern.
3) Put a large sign on your refrigerator or bathroom mirror reminding you of what you're working on. Change the wording, color and location of the sign every few days.
4) Consciously practice the new way of responding both in your imagination and with someone else. Maybe practice the old way also to increase your awareness.

5) Whenever you are doing the old way or doing the new way, pay careful attention and become aware of the thoughts and the feelings that are occurring during the process.

6) Notice and outline the smaller steps involved in the larger process. Then begin to just do something different at one point. Break one of the links in the chain.

7) Pray for help and strength to change.

8) Substitute something else for the old behavior (e.g. Chewing gum for a cigarette.)

9) Don't try to change too many things at one time. It may work best to start with the most important or with the easiest.

10) Decide ahead of time on a plan for handling a slip, when you revert to the old way. There will probably be some.

11) And, if you're interested in therapy work, you can identify where in your childhood the pattern arose. Recall specific incidents and become aware of the feelings involved; let yourself feel them.

12) You may well be able to think of some other methods to help you change, or you may be able to change without needing any method at all.

Changing old habits is hard work and sometimes progress is slow, sometimes not. Change is quite possible, however, and usually very rewarding. Spotting is the first step, and occasionally that's all that's needed and the habit stops. There will be times when you slip back into the old way; just make sure they are temporary.

You gain strength, courage and confidence by every experience in which you really stop to look fear in the face---
You must do the thing which you think you cannot do.

Eleanor Roosevelt (1884-1962)

Summary:
Habits can be changed with commitment and effort. The first step is to clearly define what you want to change. Then a major tool is 'spotting', simply noticing every time you do the habit; this increases awareness. There are a number of other tools to help make the change. Relying on willpower and trying harder are two of the least effective approaches. We need strategies.

INTERMISSION

So far, two of my editorial reviewers have commented that they found the book "somewhat overwhelming." They both liked it, but they felt flooded with information, suggestions, and things they needed to do. There was too much too fast. So I decided to put an intermission here. Time to pause and reflect, to relax. We can use this spot to review.

First, if you have recognized yourself in this book, and become aware of some of the areas that cause trouble in your life, you are already ahead of the game! Just being aware can be a big help. You don't necessarily need to do anything.

Second, if you decide you want to work on something, remember the principle of small steps. In this instance, this means pick just one or two things that you want to work on. That's enough at one time. You may have noticed more than two or three areas that looked appealing, but you can only do so much. Changing a habit is difficult and so is making a new one, and they both take time. If you just pick one problem and get one strategy working for you, it will make a big difference in your life. Then you can go to the next. I have had ADD for over seventy years, although I've only known it for seven, and I've been working on these things all that time. So I'm not suggesting that you adopt all of these ideas at once and get them all done today.

Now, let's review. Here are the things that I've found most important, most helpful to me:

1. appointment book

Using an appointment book has been natural and essential in my professional life, long before I knew I had ADD, so when I recognized my ADD I already had a book. But some people don't have an appointment book. You'll meet my friend Richard in a bit. Richard keeps his appointments recorded on a big calendar and transfers them to a folded sheet of paper daily. I need to be able to see the whole week, and the whole month, over and over. There's more going on than just being able to keep today's appointments. In order for the appointment book to be most useful to me, I need to review it many times a day. This is one of my most helpful habits.

2. to-do list

This is essential to me, too. If I try to keep all the things I need to do in my head, it will make me feel overwhelmed and give me a headache. I will miss some. Because I'm not good at setting priorities, I'll spend time on some of the less important things while the important ones slip by. But for me, just one big to-do list is not enough. It's very important to make my list of five. That helps get the priorities straight, but even more important, helps me not feel overwhelmed. Then it's easier to actually get started and do something.

3. small steps

I need to break things into small steps so that I won't feel overwhelmed and so that I can actually get started. I need to do this over and over. I will start out with my list of five. Then I may break the first task into small steps. This means that I need to make a new list of five. Usually I will only put some of these small steps on the new list of five. There will still be other tasks that need doing. If I put all of the small steps of the first task on the list, it could make the task seem overwhelming again.

4. the slogan

"Do it now, Do it right, Do the hard part first."

I made this slogan a habit, so it pops into my head anytime I'm trying to decide what to do right now, or how to begin to tackle a task. It gives me a boost, a guideline, and it helps me get started. And it's great to have the hard part out of the way.

5. the principle

Identify a problem, devise a strategy, make it a rule, stick with it and it becomes a habit. Again, it takes time. Maybe you can pick one problem to start with. Once you are on top of it, it will make a difference in your life. Please forgive me; I know that I talk about my personal victory over the lost keys a lot, but I'm so impressed with what a big difference it made in my life! Not having to hunt for those keys three times a week. Just that one simple thing.

So that is a list of the five things that I think are most important in this book. Maybe when you looked at this list of five something grabbed you. You may have thought of a problem you want to work on. Go for it.

Then there are the many tools you can learn to use, like the red flags, or the checking. Just don't try to tackle too much at once.

I hope this intermission has helped you relax and not feel overwhelmed. You may have noticed that the intermission used our principle: we identified the problem of too much at once, and made a strategy. Part of the strategy was to make a short list, the five things most useful to me. Another part of the strategy was small steps, try one or two things at a time. So you may be ready to do it now, do it right, and do the hard part first. Your life will get better.

Now after that short break, let's continue with the rest of the book, which will give you more tools, examples, and understanding, and I hope will also be interesting and enjoyable.

Section V

Unpleasant states of mind

Overwhelmed, overloaded, pressured, rushed, stressed: we spend a lot of time like this. We can really get ourselves tied up in knots, and it can be pretty miserable. There are strategies to avoid these states, and strategies to get out of them if we haven't avoided them.

Chapter 30

Overloaded and overwhelmed

Overloaded is when I feel like I have more than I can possibly get done. Overwhelmed is when I feel so overloaded that I just stop functioning; I can't decide where to start; I can't get started; I just kind of stall and collapse. Feeling overloaded or overwhelmed seems like a basic part of life with ADD. It leads to procrastination, paralysis, and demoralization. If I'd been using my red card correctly I wouldn't have gotten the overwhelmed or overloaded feeling in the first place. But here I am. Feeling overloaded or overwhelmed is a red flag telling me that I need to stop whatever I'm doing and get organized.

To get organized I do this:

I take out a yellow legal pad. I list all the things I really need to get done. This is my big list. I look at this big list and ask if there is anything on there that isn't actually that important; it wouldn't really matter if it doesn't get done or at least not anytime soon. Cross it off. So maybe I can shorten the list a little. Then I pick the most pressing five, the most important and most urgent. Since I have ADD this is difficult, but I pick five anyway and I write the five on a new list. This is my short list. Then I pick the most urgent, and if I can't choose one, then I pick the hardest. I break that one down into smaller steps. Then I pick the step that needs to be done first and if I can't, then yes, I pick the hardest step. I start to work on that one and I forget all the other things on the lists until that one is done. Do one thing; forget the rest. I keep doing small steps until I have completed the first of the five tasks; then I start on the next task from the four that are left. Actually, when I broke the first task into steps, I probably made yet another list, a list of those steps, but I still have my first list of five. Anytime I'm working on one thing, I need to forget about all the other things. They are on the list and will still be there when I finish this one thing.

I repeat this whole process as necessary.

While I'm working, I make sure to take some reasonable breaks. I don't tell myself that this is so urgent that I can't stop for a minute. The break helps me see that I'm not really overwhelmed. Without breaks my efficiency drops and I'll spend more time getting less done. But I also make sure I don't get involved in something else while I am on a break, especially compulsive computer games or starting on some other project. I limit the break to five minutes, ten max, and check the clock. While I'm on my break, it's OK to think about the project I'm working on, but I don't start thinking about the lists. Or when I do, I shift my mind to something else.

When I feel that I just don't have enough time to get everything done, and I'm starting to feel overloaded or overwhelmed, it helps a little to remind myself: "You have as much time as everyone else." I've read a similar slogan: "You have as much time as Edison, or Salk, or Curie, or Mozart had." Another thing that helps a little is to realize that, in fact, I really don't have enough time to do everything. I will never get everything done. There will always be a list, and when I finally die, I will die without having gotten everything done; the list still won't have everything crossed off. I expect that there are no lists in heaven, so it won't matter. So I just do my one thing, and then do the next thing, and keep going. This is like living in the moment.

The strategies in this book will help you not to feel overwhelmed, overloaded or rushed in the first place. That will be nice, won't it? And it also will be different. Your life will be better.

Summary:

Use strategies to avoid getting overloaded or overwhelmed or rushed in the first place. However, when you do feel that way, it's time to stop and organize. List all the things to do, then pick five, then one. Break it down into small steps and focus on one step at a time; forget the list. Take a break when you need it. You have all the time there is; just keep plugging away.

Chapter 31

Rushed and Pressured

If I'm feeling rushed, I need to ask myself what the issue is. If I don't make it to the movie on time, so what? Maybe I won't have the best seat; I can leave and ask for a refund if my seat is too bad. The world will probably keep turning whether I stay or leave. What if I actually miss my flight? Well, there will be another flight, and hopefully it won't cost too much to change my ticket. And what if I don't finish the big project on time and I flunk the course, or lose my job? Well, that's a little more serious, yet again, it's not the end of the world. But if I use the principles here in this book, I won't wind up in a spot like that. And I won't have to get my focus turned on by waiting until the last minute so that I can feel the pressure in order to get myself motivated.

Once I was in a prison ministry weekend in Santa Rosa, and I had agreed to do a workshop at a conference in Albuquerque in the middle of it.

This wasn't too smart, but my practice here was just starting, and I thought the workshop might generate some referrals. From Santa Rosa to Albuquerque is about an hour's drive. I reluctantly left the prison and drove to Albuquerque. I made it on time and I had all my papers with me, which is pretty good, for an ADDer. I found the room where the workshop was. It was empty except for some tables and some trash on the floor, and a janitor cleaning up. He explained to me that the conference ended yesterday. As they say, "A day late and a dollar short." You think this might be related to ADD? The point here is that in the big picture, it didn't really matter. I was kind of mortified and had to make a phone call and apologize, but in the long run, it didn't matter.

I tend to fall into rushing and worry and concern about a lot of things that really don't matter in the long run. Maybe I live with the sense that not only am I going to mess up but that it will be a catastrophe when I do. This seems part compulsive behavior and part ADD. So when I'm feeling rushed, it helps to slow down and ask myself what the importance is. What will it matter if I am late?

Now I'm rarely late to anything anymore because I've found ways to compensate for my ADD, like estimating how long something will take and adding fifty percent, for example. And also because

I tend to be compulsive, which helps with ADD, although compulsiveness isn't always an asset.

When I was teaching at the medical school, there were a lot of meetings. A lot of meetings. I almost always got there on time. And I would be the only one there for a while. Nowadays, as I've said, I have things I can do while I'm waiting and so I don't waste the time. But I hadn't worked that out back then, and I realized that I was wasting a lot of time by arriving at meetings on time. So I quit worrying about it and quit rushing, and I got there when I got there, just like everyone else, and that seemed to work just fine. I'm not recommending making a habit of tardiness, which is typical ADD behavior and can be annoying to others. I am suggesting that we don't have to feel rushed and that usually, being late is not a big deal, especially if it's not a habit.

However, I do recall one administrative meeting at the medical school that I missed entirely. I didn't forget it, just got caught up in other things. At that meeting my friends and colleagues discussed the shortage of manpower that we were all suffering. They brainstormed and problem solved and determined that the obvious solution was to cut the manpower in my area. John Rush, who I previously mentioned as the model of 'No', was in charge of the overall area but wasn't at the meeting. Later he came to my rescue and rescinded that decision. But I never missed another one of those meetings. So, you see, occasionally the answer to the question, "What does it matter?" may be that it could matter a lot. But the question is well worth asking.

I can't refrain from asking a riddle here –
What is the difference between big business and academia?
Well, in big business, it's dog eat dog, but in academia, it's just the opposite.

I don't like to have things hanging over my head. It makes me feel pressured, it makes me feel rushed, and it distracts me. I'm thinking about the things that I need to do instead of focusing on what I'm trying to do right now. And rushed is not a good feeling. I don't function as well when I'm feeling rushed. I rush off and forget to take my cell phone with me, or forget to take the papers that I'm going to need when I get there, or I forget my rule of looking behind me and I back into another car. I try to not let myself get into a situation where I feel rushed.

Strategies:
- Ask: "Will it really matter if I'm late?"
- Organize: put everything I'll need out on the table with my keys the night before.
- Plan: "What do I need to have done before I leave? How long will it take to get there?"
- Add fifty per-cent to any time estimate.

Similar strategies apply to needing to get something done by a deadline. I had set a deadline for myself to get this book to the publisher by the end of April. I began feeling pressured and rushed. Two wise women independently pointed out that this was a self-imposed deadline; there's no reason that I have to get it in by April; it doesn't matter.

Question. Organize. Plan. Add fifty percent.

Pressured

Pressured is not a good feeling either. I've learned (although it's hard to sell the idea to anyone else) that pressured is a state of mind, not a reality. If I can keep my list of things to do down to five, and if I can focus on the thing I'm working on right now, then there is no pressure. When I finish this one thing, I can have the satisfaction of crossing it off, and then I can move on to the next thing. And that's all I need to do. That's really all I can do. There is no pressure.

Also it helps to step back and look at what's going on. Am I feeling pressured because I have taken on things to do that aren't actually necessary? Are all the five things on my list really essential? Can I cross one of them off without actually doing it? Will it make any difference five years from now whether I've done it or not? Or a hundred years from now? Have I picked up something that is a side track or a dead end, not a good use of my time? I do that often, get some idea for some project that sounds interesting, or fun, or even necessary, but actually isn't, and may be a big time waster. It may even be something I'm using to avoid dealing with something else that I really do need to do, something that may be harder, or more unpleasant, or something that I'm not sure I can do or can do well. I've had to ask myself if writing this book might be a time waster. What is the goal? What is the purpose? Will it ever get published?

But I've decided to write it and worry about the publishing later. I've done a little research into the self-publishing concept. I also have one idea of how I might actually find a publisher. Then I've decided that if it doesn't get published, at least I can put it on the internet for free and I can still print it out and give a copy to my ADD patients. So it isn't a side track or a dead end or a waste of time and I've made the decision. So now I can stick to my decision and not be second guessing or doubting, just focus on doing it. But it was important to do some homework first and seriously consider the question of its maybe being a time waster.

Now I need to commit to finishing the book. Because I'm good at starting a project off with great enthusiasm and then just letting it dwindle away when the novelty wears off, or when something else interesting comes along to distract me, or when the going gets hard. So once I've genuinely considered it, then I need to make my decision and just stick to it, and not distract myself by doubting its value. I am going to finish this book.

But you see, I've gone off on a side track, about the book, when the topic of the moment is about feeling pressured. I don't feel pressured to finish the book, but I have chosen to commit to doing so. So, back to the subject: feeling pressured.

You might have noticed that I've been saying, "If I feel overwhelmed, if I feel pressured, if I feel rushed." Because, in fact, those are not facts; those are states of mind.

This is a hard sell. People who are feeling overwhelmed, pressured, overloaded, or rushed really believe that they actually are. But I assure you, it is a state of mind. When you can apply these strategies, and focus on the one thing you're doing, you'll find that the feeling is gone, and you can just proceed with the one thing at a time. Those are pretty unpleasant feelings, and we don't function as well when we have them. It's better to avoid them. These strategies help to do that.

Summary:
1. Use strategies to avoid getting rushed, overwhelmed, or overloaded. Learn to say 'No.' Don't overestimate what you can accomplish. Add fifty percent to your estimated time to do

something. Set realistic goals, and then reset the goal to a little less. Stay on top of things, so they don't pile up. If they do get piled up, go to step 2 below.

2. If you do start feeling overloaded or overwhelmed, stop what you're doing and organize.
3. Use these secondary strategies - the yellow pad, the big list and the little list and the small steps-to deal with the feelings of overwhelmed or overloaded.
4. If you're feeling rushed, stop and ask yourself, "What does it really matter if I am late? What will happen?"
5. If you're feeling pressured, do both: stop and organize, and also ask yourself, "What does it matter?" Look at the big picture. Then focus on one thing.
6. Keeping working on this concept until you truly understand that these are simply states of mind and that you can choose to not feel that way. You will become much more effective and efficient, and life will be much more pleasant.

Chapter 32

Dealing with stress

When things get hard

I've talked about how I deal with feeling over-whelmed and overloaded. But there are other days, when for whatever reason, it's just hard to go. On those days, I pray, "Lord, just help me get through the day." I don't strive to do good therapy. I don't try to accomplish things on my list of five. I just try to get through the day, and sometimes that in itself can be an accomplishment, a moral victory. Actually, I've provided some good therapy on some of those days when I wasn't trying so hard. I did better at staying out of the patient's way and they were able to do the work they needed to do that day. And sometimes, I have to remind myself, "I can only do what I can do. I can't fix everything or everyone. I can't get many, many things done. I can't do things perfectly. I can only do what I can do."

I use self-talk and slogans. I say, "Just put one foot in front of the other." And "Just show up and do your job." I don't have to worry about what everyone else is doing or not doing. Just show up and do my job; the rest of it is not my problem. And sometimes I say, "Just plug away." When the list seems insurmountably long, just plug away, one thing at a time; get one thing finished, cross it off the list, move on to the next thing, just plug away.

These are examples of self-talk, and also of strategies. Show up and do your job. Just plug away. You can only do what you can do. Put one foot in front of the other. Just get through the day; some days that is a triumph.

Works for me, and usually the next day is better. If not, just plug away.

Human nature

All of these feelings - overwhelmed, overloaded, pressured, rushed, even stressed –are states of mind that can be dealt with, eliminated, or avoided in the first place, by these strategies. But I doubt if anyone can avoid them all of the time. There will be times when we feel stress.

I have discovered three rules about human nature:

- When we struggle and struggle with a problem, and we finally come up with an approach that solves it for us, the next thing we do is to stop using that approach.

This happens to me. I come up with a good strategy for something and the next thing I know, I'm forgetting to do it. I have a big foam roll to lay on to help my back. My rule is to use it every day right after lunch. It has helped and my back is much better. So now I realize that I've been forgetting to do it. One of the ways I realize that I've been forgetting is that my back is starting to act up a little.

- When a man feels overloaded and he's too busy and too stressed and realizes he that needs to cut out something, the first thing he will sacrifice is his family. He will cut down not on his work, not on his hobby, but on his family.

I've seen this many times, and I have to struggle against it in myself. This rule is somewhat in contradiction to the next one, but I maintain that they are both true. I don't feel obligated to always make good sense.

- When we get stressed, the first things we quit doing are the things that we do that help us to cope with stress.

I'm really busy this week, so I don't have time to do my exercise, and I will have to skip my prayer time, and the time sitting in the evening with my wife. The problem with this approach, in addition to its being generally unhealthy and not good for a marriage, is that it reduces my efficiency and effectiveness. So I wind up actually getting less accomplished although I'm spending more time working at it. I remember a saying from John Wesley, the founder of Methodism: 'I have a lot to do today, so I'm going to need to pray two hours this morning instead of just one.'

Summary:

Some days it's a moral triumph just to get through the day. Just put one foot in front of the other. Just plug away. One thing at a time. Small steps. You can only do what you can do. Human nature works against us, but we can become aware of this and deal with it. When we are stressed, we need to do the things that help us deal with stress rather than just trying to deal with the stressful situation itself.

Section VI

My friend Richard

This section is about my friend Richard and his ADD and how he copes with it. His set of problems and his strategies are not exactly like mine. Richard's story further illustrates the ways ADD makes our life difficult. It shows that all of us with ADD struggle with similar problems; however, we have them in different patterns, combinations and degrees of severity. Often we deal with them differently. Some of the things that cause me the most trouble are easy for Richard. He has developed strategies for most of his problems, so his story gives us more real life examples of strategies. Richard gives a good illustration of someone not getting help while they are resisting the diagnosis. He also brings up some of the advantages that go with ADD, which was a new concept to me.

Chapter 33

I interview Richard

My good friend Richard has many good qualities; otherwise he wouldn't be my good friend, would he? He's very bright. He's well read, knowledgeable, and has advanced degrees. He's insightful, compassionate and understanding, generous, often wise, and he's been very helpful to me and to many others. From what I've seen, I would guess he has fairly severe ADD. I thought it would be good to hear his viewpoints on things and not just rely on my own.

Richard and I sat on his beautiful patio to begin this interview. I told him that if I couldn't find a publisher I'd maybe put the book on the internet or maybe publish it myself. He said he had a book on self-publishing that he'd lend me, "I'll go get it right now, or else I'll forget it." This is a man who knows he has ADD and who is coping with it. Then he came back and said he couldn't find it (He has ADD). But he made a note on a folded sheet of paper to remember to get it for me.

To-do list

Richard has a different approach than mine, although it's the same principle. He doesn't use cards and he doesn't always have a shirt pocket. Every morning, he takes a clean sheet of paper and folds it twice, into four quarters. He uses each quarter for a specific thing:

1. Things to do today
2. Appointments
3. Calls to make
4. Ideas to remember

When there gets to be too many things in any category, he takes another sheet and folds it and continues. His sheets fit easily in his pants pocket. If he doesn't get all the to-do things done in one day, he puts them on his new sheet the next morning. Richard says that if he has too many things to do, he gets depressed and anxious, especially if he's trying to keep them in his head. Once they're on the sheet, he can relax. He only needs to remember to check the sheet and which thing he is working on now. He doesn't use a rule of five. He particularly likes his paper method because he's creative. When he gets a good idea, he just pulls out the paper and makes a note. Then it's safe and he doesn't need to try to remember anything. This is similar to minimizing decisions in our life; Richard and I try to minimize the number of things we're trying to remember. Trying to remember something is a recipe for disaster; hence either index cards or the folded paper, or some people, younger than me, keep everything on their cell phone and their cell phone is always with them.

Scheduling

Richard says scheduling his time is one of his major tools. He says that he's able to stay on a schedule, but if he doesn't have something scheduled, then he will just do what is most enticing, not necessarily what needs to be done. He will find himself searching the internet for a word for a crossword puzzle, and that will lead him to a chat room. There he gets recognition and pay off for his creative writing, which he thoroughly enjoys, 'While Time Goes By' (song from the 40's which could be a theme song for adult ADD), and the things that need doing don't get done. Richard talks about the strong pull to do what he enjoys, what he's good at, letting what he wants to do crowd out what he needs to do. But he knows that if he follows that pull he will enjoy it and feel good for a little while, but then it will all crash in on him: the things he let slide, the people he let down, the shame, the guilt and feelings of inadequacy. So he chooses getting things done, which then produces its own good feelings when he sees what he's accomplished. Richard says that he's good at staying on a schedule.

Richard recognizes that we can become trapped in TV, or computer games, or solitaire, or running, or anything that we can do well, activities where at least we cannot fail or perform inadequately. But we are escaping from the demands of real life, the demands and the challenges, and we are going to pay for it in the end, aren't we?

Diagnosis

Richard talks about the great relief he felt when he finally received his diagnosis of ADD, even though he had been resisting it.

I recognized that I had ADD at age sixty-four, when I saw that a new patient of mine had it, and then realized that I had the same symptoms. Richard recognized it at age sixty. His wife had been telling him that he had ADD. He, of course, considered this nagging. Finally he gave in and asked his family doctor about it. The doctor asked Richard if he finished tasks on time and he told her that he had only missed one deadline in his life (this is remarkable; Richard does well with scheduling and with deadlines.) The doctor said he did not have ADD. Richard went home and triumphantly reported this to his wife. This shows again that we are all different individuals, although we are also amazingly similar. Most of us have trouble with deadlines. When I tell you my problems with ADD you know what I'm talking about, even though you may not have exactly the same symptoms that I do. And making the diagnosis of ADD is not always simple.

Anyway, Richard was very happy that his doctor said he didn't have ADD. His wife was not so happy. Shortly after that, a close friend told Richard, "You have ADD," and gave him a book to read, <u>Delivered From Distraction</u>, by Hallowell and Ratey. Richard found himself on every page. That's how he received his diagnosis. Almost. He then went to a psychologist who was an expert in ADD, and this time his wife went with him. The psychologist would ask Richard about a symptom. Richard would say he was OK in that area, and his wife would say "Wrong!' and bring up some examples.

The psychologist said, "You have to trust her perspective," and made the diagnosis. People with ADD tend to be poor at self diagnosis.

Here's an e-mail I received from Pete Quily, ADD expert and coach:

"while there are many problems with adhd one reason many adults avoid getting diagnosed or treated is because it's often portrayed as 98% pathology. showing positives and negatives is realistic and helps to soften or reduce denial of adhd esp among men."

Just in case you have any thought that Richard may have been conned or bullied or otherwise pushed into accepting a false diagnosis, I can assure you that I know Richard pretty well and I can further assure you that he indeed does have ADD.

Richard is a good friend and a great guy, and if you have a friend with ADD you learn what to expect and what not to expect. Don't expect being on time, or even always showing up, for example. You work around it. It's not exactly the same as making allowances, but it's close. It's facing reality- you can't count on him for some things. You can count on him to be honest, to be understanding, or to be compassionate, for example, but you can't count on him to show up. You learn to cope with that.

At the time of receiving his diagnosis, Richard had heard that some of the people he worked with thought that he didn't like them, because "When I talk to him, he looks away." This sounds like my wife complaining about my being "inattentive." So Richard told them about his ADD, and "It's not that I don't like you, it's that I'm always distracted, but I will try to do better." And he did do better. Richard trained himself to look at the person he was talking to. He forced himself to concentrate on them and not be distracted, not keep looking at whatever was going on around him or behind them. So things greatly improved. I'm not clear exactly how he does this. Forcing ourselves to do anything, and especially forcing ourselves to concentrate, is not one of our strong points. Ideally, I would like some strategies to help me do this, not just try to force myself to do it. One of the strategies Richard mentioned in another context was to talk to himself about the rewards he would receive if he could concentrate in a situation and the price he would pay if he didn't. This is using self-talk; it's like coaching yourself.

Richard is currently working on his evenings. He tends to do a little of this and a little of that, maybe watch a little TV, maybe read some, maybe work a little on some task. Then he'll notice that it's getting late and he'll wonder where the evening has gone. So now he's scheduling his evenings, like he does the rest of his day. He can even schedule, "8:30 pm -9:30 PM – goofing-off", if he wants. But now, whatever he does, he's doing it on purpose, with intention, and his evening is more likely to turn out satisfying to him. He still has to deal with distractions that would pull him away from his schedule, but usually he can spot that and he says, "Oh, that's a distraction; I don't have to follow it." Naming it helps – "That's a distraction." When he's following his schedule he's doing what he intends to do, not drifting around or following distractions. He's taking fewer breaks in the evening, and they're shorter, and they're intentional,

Acknowledging the problem

It can be hard to acknowledge that we have ADD, probably because of the underlying shame and the fear of being controlled and depreciated. If we can't acknowledge the problem, it's going to be difficult to do anything to make things better. But, if someone is pressuring us to acknowledge it, that probably makes it harder for us to do so.

Richard resisted the diagnosis of ADD and he wasn't coming up with many effective strategies until he could acknowledge the problem. On the other hand, I myself had devised a number of helpful strategies before I had any idea what I was dealing with. Once he acknowledged the ADD, Richard devised more ways to cope with it. The to-do lists, scheduling, and rewards are big tools for him. Rewards not only give us motivation but they are positive reinforcement which helps convert desirable behavior into habit.

Summary:

My friend Richard has severe ADD. He has various problems and various ways to cope, some different from mine. He uses a folded piece of paper instead of index cards. Everyone needs to find the ways that work for them. Scheduling is one of Richard's favorite strategies; it helps him stay on track, getting necessary things done instead of going off on side tracks. We can spot and name distractions – "Oh, this is a distraction," and we don't have to follow them. We can choose. It can be hard to acknowledge having the problem, but if we can't acknowledge the problem, it will be hard to do anything about it and to make our life better.

Chapter 34

Deadlines

Most of us ADDers have trouble meeting deadlines unless they are immediate with severe consequences, the kind that will turn on our focus center. Just knowing that something is important doesn't do it. Richard has the same problems with deadlines that I do, except that he doesn't anymore; he has conquered them. Richard plays a mind game.

Richard says he finds the idea of the deadline exciting, by which I think he means challenging. So first, he makes sure that there is a deadline. When he agrees to do something for someone, he always asks, "When do you need it?" and then he makes that into a deadline. If the task is not for someone else, he just assigns his own deadline. He says that if there is no deadline, the task or obligation will always slide, other things will crowd it out, and it won't get done.

Then Richard thinks about how missing the deadline for the task will disappoint someone else, or himself, and will hurt his self-image and fill him with shame. The particular task may not actually be important, and in reality there may not even be a deadline, but by thinking this way Richard makes a deadline with severe consequences. He focuses on how he will feel if he misses the deadline. Of course, how he will feel is in fact also part of the reality. So Richard uses his mind to create a deadline and severe consequences, and he gets the task done. This is brilliant.

But there is more detail involved. Once Richard has made a task into a deadline situation, he breaks it into steps and he makes a schedule for doing them. By scheduling, he is in effect setting a deadline for each step.

With his deadlines, scheduling, and creating severe consequences, even if only in his own mind, Richard has made completing the task on time a challenge. He knows that when the task is done he may get some recognition and he can certainly give himself credit. Of course, each time he accomplishes something it's positive reinforcement for using this method; he feels good about himself. This is better than feeling that he has failed again and feeling lousy about himself again. That would set him up, so that when the next thing came up, he would be demoralized and be thinking, "Oh, here we go again; I probably won't get this done either." and likely wouldn't. Accomplishments are great reinforcers and boost our self image, which makes it much easier to get started and to do well the next time, and thus to break the vicious cycle of failure and demoralization.

Summary:

'Important' is just not important to our focus center, but we can use mind games to trick our focus center into turning on. Deadlines and schedules can turn on our focus center and help us stay on track and avoid traps. Scheduling provides structure and helps us gain control of our life. We can think about the consequences of not completing a task on time and the rewards of doing it.

Chapter 35

Chaos and clutter

Richard says he can tolerate chaos and that he doesn't see messes. This may be a common male thing. Many women in therapy have said to me, in exasperation, "Doesn't he see the dirty dishes in the sink?!!"

- And I say "No, he doesn't."
- We then learn that if she asks him to do the dishes he probably will do them, but, "Why should I have to ask?"
- "Because he doesn't see them and you want him to help."

But it's a little more complicated than that. Perhaps many of us men do have some laziness when it comes to doing the dishes and we don't mind if our wife goes ahead and does them instead of us. And with ADD we are even less likely to see the dirty dishes. But I also think that if we have good intentions, as I claim that Richard and I do, we can probably be trained. Richard cleans up the house when his wife is returning from a trip out of town and he does a pretty good job (he told me this, not his wife). He says that he thinks about the fact that he loves her and wants the house to be clean for her, and he makes a decision to notice the messes. Then as he cleans up a messy room, he sees things that he ordinarily wouldn't see.

My wife cannot tolerate clutter. That makes me hard to live with. It also makes it harder for me to find things, because she has put them neatly away. If I would learn to put things away myself, it would help me find them later and would make her happier. I'm working on it.

Summary:

We can tolerate mess and clutter; often we just don't see it. But we can learn to pay attention to it, at least at times. We probably do function better if things are neat, clean and organized. We may need to find a way to make it significant to ourselves.

Chapter 36

Organizing

"Where'd I put it?"

My keys always go on the front hall table. That started long before I knew I had ADD. It's a habit; I bat over ninety-nine percent on it now. But that didn't work for Richard. He tried it but he just couldn't do it consistently enough for it to become a habit. Richard's pants have bigger pockets than mine do, so he started always leaving his keys in his pants pocket. Now that's where they always are. First thing in the morning, they're in the pants he took off last night. Works great. For me, I have so many keys on my key ring that it would make me lopsided if I did it that way, and my pants pockets are too small to carry the keys there anyway.

When Richard puts something down somewhere he says out loud where he put it: "OK, the check book is on the kitchen table." And when he parks the car in a parking lot he says out loud where he is:

"OK, the middle of row 13," or "Lined up with the G in the Target sign." This can save much time and frustration but it has to become a habit. I'm getting pretty good at it but it needs more work. I am starting to do the out loud part which I just learned from Richard.

Richard also told me about an electronic gadget, the FOFA, for "Find One Find All." It comes with five little tags. You put one tag in your wallet, so that it's always with you. You can stick a tag on your car keys, and on your check book, or whatever you want. When you've lost a tagged thing, you push the correct button on any of the others and the lost tag will ring. Since the tags all work, even if you've lost your billfold you can find it with any one of the other tags. I'd never heard of this. My immediate thought was, "Only five tags?" Of course, you can buy more.

Illustration 7.   FOFA
Find One Find All

Richard makes copies. If you lend him a document that you'll want back, he will immediately make a copy of it -immediately, before he forgets to and before he loses it, because that's what's going to happen. He also doesn't throw any papers away. He says it's not always easy to find them, but he knows they're there somewhere. He did eventually find the book on self- publishing.

Richard has a green bag that he always takes with him, kind of a big masculine purse or a mini-backpack. At night he puts in all the things that he'll need the next day: a book, papers, his cell phone, appointment book, maybe his laptop, whatever. That way in the morning he doesn't have to run around the house trying to find things, and when he arrives where he's going he usually has what he needs. For me, I put the things I'll need on the same front table where I keep my keys. Since I can't leave without the keys, I can't miss them. That's the theory anyway. When I pick up my keys, if I'm not looking for the other things I may not see them. If they're six inches away from where I'm looking they might as well be invisible. I leave my outdoors cap on the front table, too. I can put the keys in my cap and then put the other things in or on it. Then I have to see them in order to pick up the keys.

My system works pretty well for me, but I'm considering buying a green bag. Or maybe a blue one. Since Richard and I sometimes go to the same places, there's too big a chance of getting our bags mixed up if they're the same color. When we have

ADD we need to think of things like that. And of course, I'm worried that I'll lose the green bag. Maybe I could get the FOFA and put one of the tags on the bag.

Filing

Richard doesn't use a filing system with manila folders like I do. He says that doesn't work for him because he will never look in the files. And, of course, you need to get in the habit of putting the papers into the folders in the first place. So Richard has a very large desk and he puts his papers in piles on the desk. Each pile has a cover sheet with a label of what type of pile it is: work, bills, writing, to read, taxes, etc. When he 'files' a piece of paper he lifts up the top sheet and puts the paper in the right pile. I bet this would work even better if each cover sheet was a different color.

I personally love manila folders, God's gift to people with ADD. I have some piles on my desk, too, but not so well organized as Richard's. Some of my piles are papers waiting to be put in the folders and some of them are envelopes with lists on them. I paper clip them together by topic. Probably many of these papers need to already be in the folders instead of in the piles, but they're all things I'm currently working on and I like to have them handy. As they get out of date I can throw them away or file them. I'm pretty satisfied with my system, although

I need to go through the piles about once a week. Sometimes I find something that has gotten lost in the pile and needs to be taken care of right now. And if the disorganized pile grows too big I will tend to start avoiding it. So as I write this, it becomes clear to me that I need a better strategy.

I've read that one of the habits of highly success-ful people is to touch any piece of paper only once. That means pay the bill when you open it, answer the letter or memo when you read it, try not to file anything, and for goodness sake don't put anything on a pile. This is a good rule and should greatly in-crease efficiency. I try to use it as a guiding principle even though I find it impossible to follow very well. Still, when I'm getting ready to file something, or to put it on the pile on my desk, and I hear myself say-ing, "Oh, I'll need to get to this later," I stop and ask myself, "Could I possibly take care of this now?"

I do have a filing system for things I need to keep. But I try to ask myself, "Do I really need to keep this? Will I really need it or use it later?" The less I have in the files the more effective they will be. The manila folders that I use fairly often are in stands on my desk top, where I can see them. I think they would work even better if I got colored ones. For some reason, colors are particularly helpful in ADD; I guess color catches or holds our attention? I use a big black marker to label my manila folders, and sometimes a red marker. They need to be where I can see them and I need to be able to find the right one easily. Otherwise, it starts to feel like too much trouble and I'll be tempted to just put something on the pile. Things get lost in piles, and eventually I will have to do something else with the paper, and touch it again, unlike the highly successful people. Filing works better.

There's a lot of good information about ADD on the internet, most of it free; I just have never found the time to read much of it. But I have read many of the ADD books and I read the medical articles. I used to keep all kinds of articles from medical and psychiatric journals in a filing system. "You never know when you might need it." But when I would try to use the files, often there was too much in them which made them hard to use. These days, if a question comes up, it's usually easier to go to the internet and find the latest on the topic. I have made a rule: I will only cut out an article and file it if I have read it and I only choose the most valuable and informative ones. So my filing system is again useful to me, even though I usually go to the internet first.

Paying bills

Richard used to have trouble keeping up with the bills, but now he has most of them on an automatic pay system. That works much better. I have an even better system- I used to do the bills, and I did OK, but now my wife does them. I try to delegate what I'm not good at, if I can find someone willing to be delegated to.

Helpers

Richard used to have a secretary and she would gently remind him of things he needed to do, or gently ask, "Have you started on the Bigger's project yet?" I have a hunch that when our secretary does that it is very helpful and supportive but when our wife does it it's nagging. Richard has been able to become grateful for the help his wife gives him in organizing and he has learned to say thank you instead of being annoyed. I'm making progress on that.

It's great to have some one who can help us deal with our ADD. The more they understand ADD the less frustrated they will be with us and the better they can help us. The more they understand and help us the better we   function. The better we function the less reason they will have to be frustrated with us. And the better organizing strategies we have the better we can function.

Summary:

There's no one size fits all approach; we each have to find what works for us. But we all need some kind of 'appointment book'; I use a book, some people use their cell phone, Richard uses a folded paper. And we all need some kind of to-do list. There is more than one way to organize. Strategies, such as gadgets and organizing systems, can reduce our frustration caused by losing things and by not being able to find things. Manila folders and filing systems can be very helpful, but we do need a system and strategies for making them work. Using color makes systems more effective. We are fortunate if we find some one to help us with organizing, so we don't have to try to do it all on our own.

Chapter 37

Sloppiness

Richard gave a good talk this morning on humor in the Bible, which is clearly there if you look for it. Richard has an creative engaging interactive way of presenting. For example, this morning he divided us into two groups, the rich and the poor. As he read the Magnificat we appropriately cheered or booed for our group when the poor were raised up or the rich were brought down. It made the reading come alive. Richard was on time this morning; sometimes he arrives a little late for his talks. His shirttail was tucked into his pants; often it has come out and is flopping loose. However, three buttons on the front of his shirt were unbuttoned and there was a stain on his pants leg. His hair was OK; sometimes it's kind of a mess. But what mattered is that it was a good talk.

When I was a kid, somehow I got dirtier at recess than anybody else, and I frequently tore the knees out of my pants. My shirt tail was usually flopping out. Now I often spill food down the front of my shirt. I frankly don't understand how anyone can eat without doing that. I made a bib holder with little alligator clips and wire. If I can remember to take it, I clip my napkin in front of me when we eat messy food, like at a Mexican food restaurant. My wife gets exasperated when I mess up my shirt again. "Oh, Doug!", she says. She does our laundry and she can't always get the stains out, so it causes her trouble. Occasionally she spills some food on her clothes. I always reassure her, "It could happen to anyone."

Summary:

Sloppiness is a basic part of ADD. We can be aware of that and develop strategies to help. We can try checking ourselves before we go out or we can find someone else to check us. Some wives are happy to do that. We can put napkins on the front of our shirt when we eat. (Richard read this and suggested a tarpaulin). We can organize our desk tops, folders and files. We can put things away when we finish using them. Yes, we can.

Chapter 38

Creativity and follow through

Some of what Richard has told me surprised me. Everyone is different.

Richard says that ADD gives some gifts along with the disadvantages. He says he has a high tolerance for chaos and that he can function well in a chaotic situation. I've read that we tend to do well in a crisis, that we may be the calmest person around. I think that generally applies to me, although not always. It may partly have to do with our ability to hyper-focus.

Richard is very creative, and he says that comes with the ADD. I'm pretty creative; I get a lot of great ideas. I just have trouble implementing them and they often go nowhere. I tend to not follow through. I've had to make a determined commitment and effort to follow through on this book, for example. For a while I was stuck and it was just sitting stagnant. This was because I suddenly realized there are already a lot of ADD books out there and that this one may not get published, or at least it will take a lot of work on my part to get it published. That seemed overwhelming; it's hard enough just to write it. But then I had the happy thought, "At the least I can put it on the internet and people can read it there." So here I am, writing again. Our best move with our creativity is to generate our great ideas and then to find someone else we can delegate them to in order to get them implemented.

In elementary school, I would get wonderful creative ideas. I never did anything about them except to tell them to 'my friend' Nikki. Then he would present them to the teacher as his own. In the fifth grade I got the great idea of doing a weekly newsletter for our class. I shared the idea with Dorothy and Carolyn and we talked about how to do it. The teacher was in favor of it. That was the end of it for me; I never did anything else. The next thing I knew, Dorothy and Carolyn were putting out the newsletter by themselves. This is ADD. We are good at getting creative ideas, but not so good at putting them into action or at following through.

But sometimes, we can go ahead and get started. So then another problem with my creativity is because of my difficulty with priorities. Not all of my great ideas are worth the time and trouble it would take to implement them. They are novel, new ideas, and that turns my focus center on. Then I can find I've wasted hours on something that might be interesting or fun, but actually isn't going to do me much good; it's not heading towards my long term goals. I asked myself about this book: "Is this a dead-end project, a waste of time, a distraction? " But once I really thought about it I needed to just make up my mind to go ahead and write and quit questioning. I needed to commit to follow through. The decision is made, so just go forward and stop rethinking it.

But here I am typing, and what if I suddenly get a great creative idea for another project? I need to hold myself to the task at hand. I can jot down a word or two, and only a word or two, about the other <u>possible</u> project, and then return to my typing. So we can learn to make our creativity work in spite of our ADD problems trying to sabotage us; just being aware of those problems and tendencies gives us a good start.

Summary:

There gifts that go along with ADD, such as being able to function in chaos or in a crisis, and the gift of creativity. Then we need strategies to implement our creative ideas. Delegating is a good strategy. And we need to keep our creativity from leading us astray.

Chapter 39

Hyperactivity and stimulation

There is controversy among the experts about stimulation and ADD.   One group says that we're over stimulated, with too much coming at us for us to handle; our system is overloaded. They say we need to have a quiet simple place to study or work, with no distractions. The other group of experts says not so, that we need stimulation. They say that we actually can focus better if we have more than one thing going on; one isn't enough. So we might study better with the TV on than without it; I play music while I'm writing. My guess is that it depends on the person or on the situation. It would help us to learn how this applies to us; do I do better with quiet or with stimulation, and when? The need for stimulation might explain some aspects of Richard's and my behaviors.

Before he learned how to turn on his super-focus, Richard wasn't looking at people while they conversed. He'd be looking at what was going on behind them or around them, maybe for the extra stimulation. They didn't like it or understand it. I'm uncomfortable in a restaurant if I can't see the room from where I sit. I need to see who's coming in and who's leaving. I don't know why. I'm pretty sure it's ADD though it could be something else, paranoia, for example. My wife says I must think I'm Wyatt Earp. It bugs her; she thinks I'm not paying attention to her. I am, but I guess not one-hundred percent of my attention. Maybe I need that extra stimulation to feel awake or focused, and just one thing is not enough stimulation. One of the ADD theories is that since our brains need a lot of stimulation, we provide it for ourselves through our hyperactivity. Maybe that's why I jiggle my foot or tap the knife on the table in a restaurant until my wife asks me to stop, at which point I start trying to balance the knife on edge.

Hyperactivity and fidgety

I enjoy being with my wife and having a conversation with her. But I get antsy after a while and I need to do something else. This frustrates her and also hurts her feelings. I may get up to go to the bathroom, or to check my phone for messages. I may pull out my cards and write down something that just occurred to me, a creative idea or a to-do that I'd forgotten. I need to check my appointment book or to-do card frequently, to stay oriented. All of this activity bugs my wife, but without it I get increasingly uncomfortable. The antsy feeling is like restless legs syndrome at night; the tension builds up in your leg until you just have to move. You can't not move it. That's the way I feel when I'm sitting too long, antsy. It is strange that I'm less antsy when we are sitting outside, or in a restaurant, or when we're on vacation. Why? When we're sitting in the house, I feel the office calling me, with all of the things I still need to do. Is that it? Or is there less stimulation in our living room than in those other places? This problem is more than simply a short attention span. Some of it feels physical, like it would be there whether I had anything to do or not. When I look at the appointment book or to-do card it helps me locate myself and then I can sit longer. I'm trying to cut down on this hyperactivity, with limited success. Just willpower isn't very effective.

So, I get antsy if I sit too long with out <u>doing something</u>, something beyond conversation. I <u>need</u> to orient myself with my appointment book and to stay up with that and the to-do list. I'm trying to cut down on that behavior because it bugs my wife. That's ADD.

I'm using the term ADD, but the official term is ADHD. ADHD has three subtypes: the inattentive type, which most women with ADD have; the hyperactive type, more common in men, and the mixed type, which is what most men with ADD have, including me. We used to think that ADD wore off around puberty, but now we know that often isn't so. I can personally attest to that. But if we have ADHD, usually as we grow past puberty the hyperactivity becomes milder, or maybe we just learn to control it better. With me, the hyperactivity has always been mild. I just have trouble sitting still without doing something: jiggling my foot, scratching my head, tapping the fork or balancing the knife. Or else I'm stretching something, or exercising. Sometimes people, especially my wife, think I'm not paying attention to them when I'm doing my hyperactivity thing, like Richard with his conversation problem. Or maybe they just find my jiggling or moving distracting and annoying. I've started carrying a wine cork in my pocket. I can pull it out and squeeze it while I am sitting at the table or doing something else that doesn't need my hands. This satisfies the hyperactive need and it's fairly unnoticeable, especially when I do it under the table. The theory says that we need this extra stimulation and that it doesn't distract us but actually helps us focus.

I'm a very fast eater. That may be from ADD but it's also a learned behavior. As a child I enjoyed my mother's cooking, but I learned that it was a good idea to eat and escape from the table quickly before everything turned ugly, which it always did. So I learned to eat fast. Now when I'm at the table with my wife or with friends, and I've finished eating, always before anyone else, I get uncomfortable unless I'm doing something. It's difficult to just sit there and pay attention to the conversation. So I'll get something else to eat, which means overeating and gaining weight. But I love diet popsicles, so at home, I have a diet popsicle while my wife's finishing her meal. Of course I can't do that at a restaurant or at someone else's house. Sometimes drinking a glass of water slowly will help, some. Now, if I can remember, I take out the cork and start squeezing it. Then I can sit comfortably and focus on the conversation and it doesn't appear to bother anyone.

So some of this hyperactive behavior is the need for stimulation and some of it is learned. Some of it is short attention span and some may be just compulsiveness. I have trouble sitting still. I also need to feel like I'm not wasting time, but that I'm accomplishing something. So while I squeeze the cork, I'm exercising, which is a good thing. Yet, if I can sit with my wife at the table while she finishes her dinner, that clearly is not a waste of time.

I'm aware of feeling I have so much to do and so little time to do it in. This is not really healthy, but there it is and I think it's part of ADD. The whole

thing is complicated: ADD, hyperactivity, short attention span, need for stimulation, learned behavior,
compulsiveness, the pressure of things that need to
be done. Anyway, the diet popsicles and the cork
strategies are quite helpful.

Summary:
   Part of our hyperactivity may be that we need
extra stimulation to help us focus. We may not be
able to control our hyperactivity, but we can develop strategies to cope with it.

Section VII
Personality Issues

Our personalities are partly shaped by the effects of our ADD or ADHD, and the way we cope with our problems is partly determined by our personalities. Our genes and our early environment interact to produce our personality. But we do have the capacity to change.

Chapter 40
Discouraged and demoralized

Right now I'm discouraged. I did not organize the writing of this book very well. I had bits and pieces of it scattered around in two computers. Then I pasted all the pieces into one master document. Now I'm editing it and there are multiple repetitions. Some paragraphs are in here four times, the same paragraph. I was feeling great that I had over two hundred pages. I thought I was about ready to go, write the publisher, etc. Then I saw all of these duplications. Lots of them. I'm finally almost finished taking them out. Clearing this up has been a lot of work. It's taken me two days of free time. Now I hear myself saying "That was stupid." and "What a bunch of wasted effort!"

I did something similar when I was working on my autobiography for my family. The disorganization and duplication got me so stalled that I gave up, at least for a while. The task of organizing it and getting going again just seems overwhelming, and I'm stuck.

With this ADD book, I thought I was about finished, and now I have to make myself stick to this tedious boring editing. Furthermore, without the duplications now I'm down to only about one hundred pages and a lot of negative self-talk. But in the editing process I came across one sentence at the end of a paragraph: "I am going to finish this book." That sentence is positive self-talk and I can use it to counter the negative self-talk. I am going to finish the book. This current lament adds a page and I'm about through with the tedious work of taking out the duplications. I'm back on track. So you're lucky; you will be able to read the book after all.

Mr. C: Occupation, self-esteem, discouraged and demoralized

Mr. C, a man in his thirties, came to me in a state of deep despondency. He'd just lost both another girlfriend and another job. I thought he'd want to discuss his problems but in fact he wanted to discuss almost anything else. He was very bright, with an impressive college degree. He told me that the college courses he'd liked were easy for him and he made good grades, but he'd struggled with the courses he wasn't so interested in.

He is a good athlete and an accomplished outdoorsman. He loved to teach me outdoor lore and other things from his impressive store of knowledge. But not much about himself. I gradually learned more whenever I could induce him to talk about himself. Very gradually, because he was slow to reveal much.

I slowly learned that he'd had many jobs, few of which had lasted very long. I learned that his parents helped support him financially much of the time and were pretty fed up with him. They gave him a lot of good advice, a lot of constructive criticisms and a lot of just plain criticisms. His father depended on him for help in a number of areas, but considered him a lazy bum. His sister was the family star; he could never measure up to her. During the time we worked together, Mr. C went through a number of jobs. Somehow he always found jobs in which the boss was impossible, unreasonable, of borderline intelligence at best, and often psychologically impaired (please note the faint sarcasm here.)

I already knew of my own ADD when I started seeing Mr. C and I was able to quickly diagnose his. The job history was the first clue. It made a significant difference in his bottomed out self-esteem to begin to learn what the problem was and to better understand what had been going on, but his self-esteem still remained low. He started Ritalin which significantly helped his functioning, but not enough, and Ritalin couldn't do much for his self-esteem.

Mr. C's way of coping with problems was to ignore and avoid them. He was financially and emotionally dependent on his parents and he couldn't stand up to them when they were criticizing or trying to control him. He was sneaky and he would avoid dealing with them when he could, which was difficult since he was so dependent on them. He had difficulty keeping his appointments with me and with paying his fee regularly, which unfortunately his parents funded, not happily. Eventually we designed a system of penalties and flexibilities so that we could continue working together. In order to have an appointment he had to have paid ahead. That worked pretty well and Mr. C was quite understanding and cooperative about the need for this system for my protection.

I encouraged Mr. C to look into jobs that would play into his strengths, especially his strong outdoors skills, but that never worked out. Gradually it became clear what was happening at work. The field where he had experience wasn't necessarily a good field for him but he could always find a job. He would start off well and make a good impression. Usually he quickly got a promotion, which was disastrous for him as it entailed more responsibilities. He did very well at the things he was good at and he got recognition and approval. The things he was not good at he would ignore and avoid, letting them slide. They would gradually build up to where the boss would notice and bring the problem to his attention. Mr. C would promise to take care of it. And he would try. But by that time things had piled up to enormous proportion. His strategy was to try harder. He would start putting in long days with no breaks. He was trying to keep up with his routine tasks while also trying to catch up on the things he was behind on. He would put in eighteen-hour days seven days a week, working hard at things he was not effective at (his father thought he was lazy). He would eventually have a physical and emotional collapse. At that point he would have a blow up with the boss and either get fired or quit. It would be due to the boss's pathology.

Each time Mr. C lost a job he became depressed and stopped functioning. He would need more help from his parents, who he'd been trying to avoid. This exposed him to more advice and criticism, which was more demoralizing. But eventually he would pick himself up and find another job. The cycle would begin again.

I met with Mr. C's parents twice. He preferred not to attend these meeting, to avoid them. I tried to explain the situation to his parents. I discussed how to be supportive and I encouraged them not to undermine him further with criticisms. I don't think his father bought it, although his mother did, but they seemed unable to change their pattern. It was easy to understand their frustration; at times I'd been pretty frustrated with him myself. I tried to coach Mr. C on appropriate ways to stand up to his parents, but with his dependence on them and long pattern of being sneaky and avoiding them, he couldn't make much progress on that. So his self esteem just kept getting battered and he often was pretty demoralized, which didn't help his performance any.

Mr. C began playing poker on the internet, for play money. Then he wanted to talk about poker instead of about his problems. I was concerned that his poker playing might be taking up time that he needed for other things, like working or looking for work. Of course I was aware of my own previous addiction to computer games. When life is not going well, we find ways to escape. In computer games the consequences of failing are minimal and we can control and master things. We can boost our self-esteem while avoiding real life. The boost is temporary though.

Then Mr. C began playing for real money, which is real life. I worried that he wasn't being realistic about what was going on and that his stories about his poker triumphs might not be entirely accurate. Maybe he wasn't leveling with me, like he didn't with his parents and sometimes even with himself. I feared that he could get into real financial trouble. However, it gradually became clear that he actually was winning. Further, he was using self discipline. He was studying the game. He was handling his money well and not playing impulsively. He could recognize when things weren't going well and take a break. He wasn't getting 'steamed', losing your sense of judgment after you've lost a big hand through bad luck and then impulsively trying to win it back all at once.

Mr. C began to accumulate some money. He handled it carefully, knowing that it was his stake for the next game. His self esteem began to rise. He was finally able to move away from his parents and to another town. I lost contact with him, but I like to imagine him burning up the internet as a poker pro. I don't know what his parents think about this development and it's not the outdoor occupation I had envisioned for him, but it's his life and I think this is going to work for him. Since I like to watch poker on TV I think of him often and imagine that someday I'll see him up on the screen, playing in a big tournament.

I just now called Mr. C. He gladly gave permission to use his story. He's doing fine. He's not a professional poker player and he doesn't have an outdoors job either. He has a job that has structure but is different every day and uses some of his athletic skill. He's not playing much poker but he's coaching others, which he says enhances his learning. He sounds good.

Summary:

We need to find an occupation that works for us, where our weaknesses aren't important and which has both structure and variety. Demoralization can drag us under, but we can capitalize on our strengths and pull ourselves out of the morass. Success enhances our self-esteem, which helps us to function better, which enhances our self-esteem, and so on. This is the reverse of the vicious cycle.

Chapter 41

Shame

You can sense the shame that lay underneath a lot of Mr. C's problems. This shame fed his discouragement and demoralization and they fed the shame, in a vicious cycle. The sense of shame fed his sneakiness and his evasions, and motivated his hiding the truth from himself as well as from others.

Shame is not technically a part of ADD itself, but usually comes along with it. It is an almost inevitable consequence of having ADD, as we build up experience after experience of failing and as we repetitively frustrate those around us who then give us negative reactions.

Here's an ad from the internet, by Bonnie Mincu, an ADD coach. It is about shame, which is a big part of our problem. This ad also is an example of good information available on the internet, and it discusses the shame at least as well as I could:

Shame

Do you feel unworthy and believe that each time you make a mistake, it's one more validation of how worthless you are?

- Do you strive to be perfect in the hopes that perfection will make you seem as good as everyone else?

- Do you live in fear that others will find out how secretly disorganized, late, careless or stupid you really are?

- Has your pattern of avoidance dealing with situations after you've messed up led to lost money, jobs, opportunities and relationships?

If you've answered 'yes' to at least two of these questions, then SHAME is a dominant factor in your life. You may not even be consciously aware of how strongly your feelings of inadequacy influence your behavior.

In fact, shame is such a powerful negative influence on people with ADD/ADHD that it often leads to more difficulties than ADD itself!

Although deep-seated shame is not a simple problem, you can learn to break the hold that shame has over your BEHAVIOR.

ADHD Coaches Bonnie Mincu of "Thrive with ADD," and Nancy Snell, CEC, PCC, have created a telephone class to help you deal with ADD-related shame.

http://www.thrivewithadd.com/shame_tc

I hope you'll join us as we help you break the chains of shame!

warm regards
Bonnie Mincu

I didn't take this course but it doesn't sound woo woo (a Santa Fe term referring to therapies or concepts out of the mainstream and not supported by research. There's a lot of woo woo on the internet. See glossary). This ADD course sounds good and this lady knows what she's talking about. I've never had an ADD coach and neither have my ADD buddies, Richard and Tom, but it's a good idea. I do a lot of coaching for my ADD patients during their therapy, but it's difficult to do both therapy and coaching in the limited time we have. So if you have the time and money, finding both a good therapist and a good ADD coach could be a smart thing to do. The coach can do the teaching about ADD, help you develop your own strategies, and give encouragement and support as you apply them. Meeting regularly with a coach can help you stick with what you're trying to accomplish. The therapist can help you deal with the shame, among other problems.

Mr. D: shame, self image, and self-flagellation

Mr. D, a patient, is competent, accomplished and extremely bright. He might not recognize himself in what I just said, but he will soon. Mr. D talks about always seeing his father thinking of him as a xxxx xx (expletive deleted). He now sees how he began to think of himself as a xxxx xx. He talks about "self loathing." When we started working together he spent much of the time in self criticism; actually, in self berating. I told him that he was damaging himself and wondered if he could begin to let up on himself. He was reluctant to let go of that self-flagellation. He feared that without it he would lapse into laziness and sloppiness and would truly become as his father saw him. This was obviously his self-image, the way he saw his true self. Further, he feared that he might start thinking he was doing OK and then be humiliated when his flaws were exposed, thus repeating a frequent childhood occurrence. Again, shame. Gradually he has been able to let up on beating himself up, and he's been surprised to find that he actually functions better without it. Demoralization is a pretty handicapping condition.

I, too, can remember reading disgust, disappointment and disapproval in my father's eyes. I can't read minds, and my father wasn't saying much, but I believe that he was feeling and thinking what I thought he was feeling and thinking. Like Mr. D, I began to incorporate, take into myself as a part of myself, my father's view of me. Our early identity, our view of ourselves, is formed by what we perceive as our parents' views of us. These identities are not easily changed. And we tend to live up to (or down to) the way we are seen and what is expected of us.

I was fortunate to have grandparents who didn't see me the way my father did and who apparently didn't notice my ADD. One time I was paid to wash my grandmother's car and I scratched up all the paint. Nothing was ever said about it, although I was never asked to wash a car again. But I knew that I wasn't really the kid my grandparents thought I was; I believed that in fact I was the kid my father thought I was. So there was a fear of being exposed and of the truth coming out.

I think my grandparents' positive regard saved my life, but it also had the downside, because I knew that I could never live up to their expectations. So both my father's negative view and my grandparents' positive view fed my sense of shame. We need much work in dealing with shame, self- image, "self-loathing", and self criticism. Many of these problems stem directly from the ADD. The strategies are to find ways to function better, which will stop feeding the shame, and using therapy to help get rid of the old shame and negative self-images.

Summary:

ADD starts building up a sense of shame in us from early childhood on. How bad our shame is depends a lot on how our parents and others reacted toward us around the ADD problems and on what experiences we happened to run into. The shame is an anchor holding us back, a major saboteur of our efforts, and it makes us miserable. Shame can be helped with therapy and with strategies that help us function better.

Chapter 42

How our personality is formed

The beginning

A child with ADD, or especially ADHD, is a challenge and often a frustration for parents and other adults. And those adults' views of us and their reactions to us help shape our personalities and the way we see ourselves.

There is a complicated interaction between our personality development and our ADD. Our basic personality is pretty much formed by the age of six, by the interaction of our genetic makeup with our environment, primarily our parental figures. Our temperament, like shy or adventuresome, quiet or aggressive, is largely inherited. Then our ongoing everyday environment usually has more effect on us than any particular events do, despite what Hollywood says. If we have ADHD, the hyperactive type, we will get lots of reaction from our parents and the rest of our environment very early on. ADD, the non-hyperactive type, may not show up much until we start school, or even until school begins to get hard. Having ADD or ADHD can greatly influence how our parents, and then others, see us and deal with us, and ultimately how we view ourselves. Much depends on our environment: do we get support, help, tolerance and acceptance, or do we get criticism, control and abuse? A negative, disapproving environment lays the foundation for shame. Our parents' views of us become part of us, and this can be helpful or destructive to us.

False self

If we are being strongly affected by our parents' needs rather than their being tuned into our needs, we develop a false self. We try to become what they need us to be. For example, genetically we may have a quiet temperament, but our father, who never did well in sports, might need us to be an athlete to bolster his own self-esteem. If he shows approval when we're active and aggressive and shows disappointment and disapproval when we're not, we may develop a false self. We learn to be active and aggressive and we shut down the side of us that might be quiet, thoughtful, artistic or creative. It shrivels up. Or it could be that we were born with an active aggressive temperament, but our mother needed us to be quiet and sensitive to her feelings. So again, we develop a false self. With our energy and development going into creating our false self, and not into who we really are, we'll grow into adults with a sense of emptiness, with a tendency to depression and to feeling unfulfilled. We may lack confidence in ourselves, although we may cover that up by being aggressive, perhaps overly so. These problems are a result of our diminished true self which was sacrificed to the development of our false self in order to satisfy our parents' needs. It's not so much the false self that's the problem as the lack of development of our real self. ADD or ADHD fosters our sense of shame and just makes it harder to develop our real self.

Outside the family

After age six, we become more involved outside our immediate family and our personalities can be affected somewhat by experiences with others. Teachers, neighbors, coaches, other relatives, and others can have a significant positive or a somewhat negative impact. If we had a good start, probably bad experiences won't affect us much. We're equipped to deal with negative things that come up, and probably the parents who gave us the good start will continue supporting us and help us deal with the rough spots.

If we didn't have a very good start, then we're vulnerable to bad experiences and maybe won't get help from our parents when we need it, so bad experiences will just make our bad situation worse. With ADD or ADHD, it's more difficult for our parents to give us a good start and we almost certainly will have some negative experiences.

In any event, we can still benefit from positive input from the outside world. My wife and I marvel that we both had grandparents who seem to have been life saving. We wonder if that's just coincidence.

Adolescence

If things haven't been too bad, and we aren't too damaged, if we haven't totally lost our true self or been overwhelmed by shame, we get a second chance in adolescence. To some degree our personalities can be dismantled and put back together in new and different ways. We can reduce the power of our parents' influence. We can examine their values and viewpoints, and chose what to keep and what to reject. We can try out different ways of being and find what seems to fit or work for us. We tend to keep most of our temperament and basic personality, but we can come out of adolescence with some significant change, hopefully for the better. On the other hand, some people never progress out of adolescence. This is more likely to happen if we have ADD.

Adulthood

As an adult, therapy offers us still another chance. Again, we don't generally make drastic changes in our basic personality; if we're an introvert we're not likely to become an extrovert. However, we can heal some old wounds. We can reduce the shame. We can drop old ways of coping that are not being effective for us, learn new ways of coping and overcome the emotional barriers that could keep us from using these new ways. We can further develop our real selves. We can gain understanding of how we operate, think, and feel, and how we came to be that way.

"Oh, now I see why I could never make a model airplane!" And how it contributed to my feeling bad about myself.

This understanding can give us some emotional relief and an increased ability to accept ourselves. Often we gain increased understanding and acceptance of our parents with their flaws as well. Nobody ever had perfect parents, and our parents had parents too.

Therapy also helps us develop strategies to operate more effectively. We can make important changes that will have a tremendous positive effect on our lives.

Therapy is not the only way to make changes. Being involved in an intimate relationship can have a positive effect on our personalities, as can spiritual experience and probably a number of other things. Therapy is just the most likely successful and fastest way to go about it.

You can see how some of this information applies to what I've told you about myself. Also some of the stories about my patients reveal the effects of ADD on their personality development and problems. Sorting all of this out is one part of their therapy.

Ms. J - ADD problems

Ms. J, a fifty-seven year old patient, has a stressful job in a very dysfunctional organization. She is bright and has held some good positions, but she is struggling. One of her strongest memories from childhood was of being told, over and over, "You can do better than this!" And she could have done better, if she hadn't had ADD. But whatever she did was never good enough. She has a severe problem finishing things and with organizing. Ms. J has a poor self-image; her inability to finish projects makes it worse. Feeling bad about herself sets her up for trouble with boundaries and taking care of herself and dealing with supervisors

Personality problems

Ms. J is afraid of her feelings, especially anger. She finds it difficult to speak up for herself when she needs to; instead, she becomes strangled on her anger, gets red faced and bursts into tears; she becomes ineffective. She also has trouble setting boundaries and in protecting herself. Her job involves helping people. She gets tangled up in other peoples' problems and swallowed up and used up, and not just on her job. For example, she has difficulty untangling and getting off the phone, so her time gets used up. We've worked on triage, which means sorting out: some problems you can help with a reasonable effort, some you maybe could help but would use up most of your resources, and some you couldn't help no matter how much time, energy and resources you spent. In her particular job, Ms. J needs the ability to triage, and also the ability to take care of herself.

Take care of yourself

An important principle is that you need to take care of yourself first or you won't be able to help anyone else. That's what the flight attendants always tell us: " In the event of an emergency, put the oxygen mask on yourself first, and then on your child." The Red Cross teaches, "If someone is drowning in the pool, don't jump in with them. Use a pole or a life saving ring and stay on the side."

That's one of the reasons I'm taking this week off. I won't be available to help others this week, but when I come back next week, I'll be better able to help. Ms. J gives a lot and doesn't receive much in return; she spends her time taking care of others, but she has trouble taking care of herself.

We don't do well with a boss

Like me, Ms. J doesn't do well with a boss; we function better independently. Although competent, we both carry a sense of inadequacy, connected to our deep shame. So we're hypersensitive to anything that suggests we're not totally adequate, like someone else telling us what to do, for example. Part of Ms. J's problems with her bosses is about not finishing projects, part is her trouble speaking up, and part is not taking direction well. So she is usually mad at the boss. The angrier she gets, the harder it is for her to finish projects, and the more she doesn't finish, the more trouble she has with her bosses, and then that makes her angrier yet. But she's only beginning to be able to be aware that she's mad; she's more likely to feel overwhelmed.

Escape

Ms. J would have a stressful day at work and go home feeling exhausted, worn out and overwhelmed. So she would get on the computer and play solitaire and the things she needed to do at home would pile up. Her to-do list would grow longer and longer; she would feel more and more overwhelmed and exhausted, play more and more solitaire, and fall further and further behind. This looks like an escape from real life, from feelings, especially anger, and from to-do's.

We don't do well with direction

I came up with lots of good strategies to help Ms. J deal with these problems. It took me a while to realize that whatever I suggested, she wasn't going to do, at least not for a long, long time. Sometimes she would eventually incorporate a strategy and her life would improve, but basically, if we planned a project for this Saturday, she was not going to do it. She would just be "too tired". Ms. J does not like being told what to do, because being told what to do suggests to her that her intelligence and competence is not being recognized. Although she is indeed intelligent and competent, her ADD ties her in knots, as does her resistance to being told what to do. She is hypersensitive to that. She feels she's being told what to do even when, for example, I collaboratively work out a plan with her or make gentle suggestions. Of course, sometimes I've forgotten and haven't been all that gentle, which only makes it worse.

Perfectionism

Ms. J grew up feeling that she was never doing well enough and that she always could have done better, and that her intelligence and competence were not being recognized. She developed perfectionism, which is one way to try to deal with a sense of inadequacy and shame. Unfortunately, perfectionism makes it harder to do anything. It feeds into procrastination. Ms. J takes pride in her writing and editing abilities, so she finds it very hard to do what I'm doing right now, which is to just go ahead and write, just to get something down on paper (or into the computer). I can edit later. Ms. J finds it hard to just write; she is trying to make it perfect as she goes. The successful author Anne Lamott makes a big point of this; she says her first drafts are always crap. She just has to get something down on the paper. Ms. J says she can't write without editing at the same time and that's hard and it's never good enough. So she procrastinates, and has trouble finishing, so things pile up on her, and so she feels exhausted.

Ms. J becomes stuck. So life goes for her, in a series of vicious cycles and feedback loops. How much of her trouble is ADD and how much is personality and learned patterns, and how much did the ADD contribute to the personality and learned patterns?

We are pecking away at all this in her therapy. Fortunately, through her hard work in therapy and her learning some ADD strategies, Ms. J is feeling better about herself. She is less self-critical, and is becoming better at handling things, including her anger, her boss, and her to-do list. She is using manila folders at work, and colors, and lists. She is deciding when to end a phone call, and generally paying more attention to self-care. Her life is going better.

Summary:

Our personality is formed by genes, temperament, and our environment and it's reactions to us. Some of our problems stem directly from our ADD, and whatever other problems we may have are made worse by our ADD. Our ADD problems and our personality become intertwined. ADD causes us to mess up and sets us up to feel discouraged, which makes it harder to get things done, which discourages us more. Underlying all of this is a deep abiding sense of shame. If we have developed perfectionism as a strategy to help us cope, we need to find a better one; perfectionism is ultimately demoralizing and disabling.

Therapy can help to sort all this out. Strategies can help with the ADD and therapy can help with the shame. Functioning better also helps with the shame. We can improve our functioning and our lives will be better.

Chapter 43

Self pity

Cognitive therapy

One type of psychotherapy, cognitive therapy, states that there are three fundamental thinking errors, which are said to be the basis of many of our problems:

1. "Unless everybody likes me, I'm no good."
2. "Things should be the way I want them to be."
3. "Life should not be hard."

You can see how each of these errors in thinking could feed self pity.

Sometimes I feel sorry for myself. I think "Oh, my, I have to see a lot of patients today" or "Too much to do" or "Why should I have to work all the time?" I can fall into a "poor me" state even though clearly most of what I'm doing is voluntary and I enjoy seeing my patients. If my practice is 'work', it is the best kind of work for me, except for the part of

dealing with the insurance companies or the government. And sometimes I feel sorry for myself about
that: "Why should I have to put up with all this?" or
"Why should I have to pay these all these taxes?"
A wise accountant once helped me with this. I was
moaning and complaining, "Why should I have to
do all this bookkeeping for the government?" He
looked at me quizzically and said, "Because that's
the law." I was able to let go of that particular self-
pitying complaint. I also got a helpful message from
<u>Zen and the Art of Motorcycle Maintenance</u> by
Pirsig; "It is as it is." The point being: deal with it;
there's no benefit in sitting there complaining.

Sometimes a patient will criticize themself, "I'm
just feeling sorry for myself." I usually jump in and
question this idea. Self-pity is underrated and gets
a bad rap. It is a form of self-compassion, which
many of us are lacking. Learning self-compassion
can be a healing part of therapy. We need to have
compassion and tolerance for others; often we have
to learn to have compassion and tolerance for ourselves before we can feel it for others. So I'm not
opposed to self pity. But we can overdo it, and then
it can become somewhat paralyzing. In the examples
above, I was overdoing it, and doing some distorted
thinking as well. I wonder if Ms. J also overdoes it
sometimes. When she's feeling overwhelmed, tired,
and overloaded, and she just plays solitaire, she

probably needs the break, but she may be overdoing self-pity. She certainly needs to feel compassion for the little girl she was, but not to overdo it for her current adult situation. On the other hand, who's to say that someone else is overdoing it?

Much of Ms. J's feeling overwhelmed and exhausted is due to her procrastination. She's always carrying a long to-do list around with her in her head, things she hasn't finished. She also carries her anger. Her load gets to be heavy and tiring to carry. Self pity may be slowing her down further.

Summary:

We need to have compassion for ourselves. We need to acknowledge the limitations and problems that ADD gives us without blaming ourselves or being judgmental. We may sometimes overdo the self-pity if it helps immobilize us, but we need self-compassion; it's a matter of balance.

Chapter 44

Self-talk and self-fulfilling prophecies

We all are doing self-talk all the time; often we just aren't aware of it. Self-talk can be either negative or positive. I had an epiphany a number of years ago. I don't know what caused it but it was wonderful. It involved self-talk.

I was opening a jar of popcorn kernels, and, of course, I spilled them all over the kitchen floor. And I heard myself saying to myself, in my head, "Oh, I need to pick those up." That's all. Nothing about 'Stupid!', or 'Clumsy!', or 'You should be more careful!' or 'You can't do anything right.' The old tapes did not turn on. It was so amazing and wonderful that I really noticed it. Then I simply and peacefully picked up the popcorn kernels, because they really did need picking up. I didn't make it into a big deal. "It is as it is." Quite an experience. That's my favorite example of self-talk. Many of my other examples are not as pleasant as that one.

Often a new patient will be telling me something, and they'll comment something like "stupid", referring to themself. This is different from saying "That was a stupid thing to do" or "I felt stupid." This is name calling. I immediately interrupt the story and we talk about the name calling. Then I ask them not to do it anymore. That is a quick specific therapy intervention. The "stupid" is an example of self-talk, except they said it out loud. But clearly this is the kind of thing they tend to say to themself. I ask them to begin to pay attention to that self-talk, and to make a note of it anytime they catch it. This process is called 'spotting'. I ask them not to say it anymore in our sessions, because it bothers me to hear them abusing themselves. I don't ask them to stop it in the self-talk, in their head; that is too big a step to ask. The first step to stopping it is to practice the spotting, noticing it every time they call themself a name. This will eventually lead to stopping it. Spotting is part of the way to change a bad habit.

Eventually, I will also try to get them to stop saying, "That was a stupid thing to do." because it's too close to saying "I'm stupid." It would not be a good thing to say to a child, so why say it to yourself? We can say, "Well, I think I've learned not to do that again." or "I wish I had done that differently; I will next time." "Stupid" is just an ugly and unnecessary word.

This negative self-talk is very damaging and we do it a lot. It just keeps eroding our morale, damaging our self-esteem and our self-image. As the patient's therapy progresses, we will be able to identify this kind of self-talk and look at where it came from, when they were a child. We can study the situation now from an adult viewpoint and see how inappropriate that reaction was. Saying things like that is not the way an adult is supposed to treat a child. However, for many of us, especially those of us with ADD, that is the kind of message we got, even if it wasn't always spoken out loud. We just took it in and it became a part of us, as if it was valid. And now we say those things to ourselves.

By the way, ADD has nothing to do with intelligence; we cover the full range from impaired to genius, just like the general population. Thomas Edison and Leonardo da Vinci had ADD. ADD does cause impulsiveness, and our tendency to mess up, and we're often also clumsy, but that's not because we're stupid.

Self-talk is ubiquitous; we're all doing it all the time. But we can learn to use it. As a patient becomes aware of their self-talk we can work with it in therapy. It's hard to stop negative self-talk, although that is the goal. The first step is spotting. The next is countering. I ask the patient to think of a "helpful encourager", a good aunt or uncle or grandmother, or how they would choose to talk to one of their own children. So if the patient is about to take a test and notices the tapes saying, "You're going to fail; you always mess things up. There is no way you can pass this; you've goofed off and you haven't studied enough," they can counter this and give themselves the same kind of talk the encourager would give :

"Wait a minute! You've studied pretty hard. Maybe you don't know it perfectly but you have a good chance of passing. You passed the last test you took and it was as hard as this one. And if you don't pass it, so what? It's not the end of the world. You're still a good person. It just means that you'll need to study some more and then try again. And it will be easier next time because you'll have taken the test once and you'll know what it's like. So just go in and do what you can. Then we'll see how it comes out and what you need to do next."

Thus you can counter negative self-talk with positive self-talk.

I will do some of this countering in the therapy, usually in the form of questions, "So if you don't pass, what would that mean? What would it say about you as a person?" Then we can discuss the answers, but the person needs to learn to use the countering self-talk on their own. They don't have to just let the negative self-talk hog the floor. This is an actual example from work with a patient who was about to take a difficult professional test. She in fact didn't pass it the first time, but she did learn about countering the negative self-talk, and she passed it easily the second time.

There are many ways to counter negative self-talk. You can call on the internal helpful encourager, whoever that may be for you: "It's going to be alright; you're going to be fine." You can bring up facts: "Well, the last two times, I did fine. In fact, I've only really messed up once, and that was a long time ago, and it wasn't the end of the world anyway." You can just argue in your own defense: "I am <u>not</u> stupid! I am a worthwhile person who has accomplished a lot and come through a lot of hard times." You can use hard logic: "Is there any real data to support that idea? Is there any data that refutes it?"

It may be hard to stop the negative self-talk, but there is no requirement that you let it have the floor all to itself or go unchallenged. Therapy can be very helpful with this, but you can learn to handle it on your own even if you're not getting therapy.

Self-fulfilling prophecies

It's clear how the negative self-talk can produce more discouragement and demoralization. It also increases anxiety and helps set up a self-fulfilling prophecy. It's harder to get yourself to study for a test that you know you're going to fail anyway. And the anxiety about failing markedly decreases the effectiveness of your studying. Then the anxiety you have while taking the test interferes with your memory and your ability to think clearly. It can possibly even induce brain freeze, which we'll discuss later. So you fail the test, which is what you always knew was going to happen anyway.

Self-talk tends to lead to self-fulfilling prophecies. "Oh, I'm not going to be able to do this. This isn't going to turn out well. I'll mess this up too." Then we mess it up. It doesn't turn out well. This is what I always used to do with projects before I carefully and successfully built the cabinets I'm going to tell you about. Since I knew that a project wasn't going to turn out well, I didn't want to waste much time on it, so I would rush through it and take short cuts. To save time (and to protect my self-esteem), I wouldn't plan it out or get the right tools for the job. I would just dive in and rush and slop through it. And guess what? It didn't turn out well. I've had to learn to listen to myself, to listen for those negative messages and to counter them. And I remind myself of those cabinets.

Here's a story I sometimes tell my patients:

In the 1930's a guy is way out in the country late at night in his model T car. He gets a flat tire. He starts to change it and discovers that he doesn't have a jack handle. He says to himself, "Here I am in the middle of nowhere without a jack handle and not another living soul for miles!"

But then he looks around and sees a light way off in the distance. He says, "It's probably just an old oil pump or something," but he starts walking towards it.

When he gets closer, he sees that it's a farmhouse with a light in the yard. He says, "There's probably nobody home."

But then he sees there's a couple of lights on in the house. He says, "Well, they won't have a car," but he gets closer and sees that there's a car in the driveway.

He says, "Well, they won't have the right jack handle," but as he gets closer he sees that the car is exactly the same model as his.

Then he says, "Well, they won't let me borrow it."

So he walks up to the farm house and pounds on the front door. The farmer sticks his head out the second story window, and the guy yells, "You can keep your damn jack handle!" and turns around and walks off.

I have worked with some patients like this. Negative self-talk. (This is also an example of "fortune telling" or "prophesizing".)

Self-talk is also an important issue for people with panic attacks. People having an attack are usually saying "Oh my God, this is awful! I can't stand this! This is killing me!" and often, "I'm having a heart attack!" or "I'm losing my mind!" Until they understand panic attacks, most people do think they're dying or losing their mind. What causes a panic attack? Excessive epinephrine released from the adrenal glands into the blood stream. What do these catastrophic thoughts do? They cause the adrenal glands to release more epinephrine, thus strengthening and prolonging the attack. What can someone do about that? Actually a number of things, but here we're focusing on self-talk. A person can't stop those negative thoughts, but they can counter them and not let them take over:

"Oh, I know what this is; this is another one of those darned panic attacks. I don't like them. They're quite unpleasant. But no one ever died from one and I won't either. I've gotten through them before and I'll get through this one, too. They don't last forever. It'll soon be over."

Thus the person coaches themselves through the attack, the epinephrine level drops, and the attack ends sooner. Self-talk is powerful.

Mrs. K.

Mrs. K, a patient and young mother, recently had an exciting session where she talked about using self-talk, most of which she had come up with on her own. Like me, in childhood she had developed perfectionism as one way to deal with her ADD. In this session, she was telling me she was feeling much better, not only not depressed nor anxious anymore, but also much more relaxed. And she wasn't having any more panic attacks. Here is some of the self-talk she told me about which helped explain why she was feeling better:

When she had made a mistake, she said, "I did the best I could. It's not the end of the world."

She also noticed that at four o'clock in the afternoons she had started saying to herself, "My day is over." She meant that she was shifting gears, entering a new phase of the day. She had done what she could during the day and whatever she hadn't gotten done would have to wait until tomorrow. Now she was going to fix dinner and help the kids with their homework, and that's all.

She also noticed that some of her husband's comments which used to bother her, didn't anymore. She had been taking many of the things he said as criticisms. It sounded like probably some of it was. However, since she was expecting criticisms, which she had received a lot of in her childhood, she was hearing some comments as critical when they actually weren't. In any event, now when she heard those comments she was saying to herself, "I've done what I could" or "I've done the best I could" and wasn't taking them to heart. They just didn't bother her anymore.

Mrs. K talked about how with her ADD symptoms she had felt that "I was the only one," until I had told her about my symptoms and about other patients and friends with ADD. We discussed ADD symptoms and how I and others coped with them. This not only gave her strategies to use, but also helped her see that she was not the only one. It reduced the underlying sense of shame from childhood.

She said that now, when she makes a mistake or shows an ADD symptom, she says, "It's OK," like she would say to one of her little girls. This replaces the old critical tapes – "What's wrong with you?! Why can't you be careful?! Stupid!" and so forth.

Sound familiar at all? She says that now she knows herself. She knows that she has ADD and she knows that she will make some of those mistakes sometimes, and "It's OK."

No wonder she's feeling better.

Mrs. K has started an exercise class, which is an excellent idea. She says that there are some of the exercises she just can't do, and she noticed herself starting to say, "You can't do it. Why are you even here? What ever made you think you could be in this class?" but she spotted this self-talk. She caught herself, and said, "It's OK. You can just do what you can do. Those other ladies doing that exercise have been doing this a long time. Maybe I'll get to where I can do some of those. Anyway, I'll do what I can and it will be OK."

If you, dear reader, don't have ADD you might have a hard time understanding why anyone would have the attitude expressed in those negative thoughts. If you do have ADD, I bet you understand the shame and self- image that was built up from childhood and you understand exactly what Mrs. K was going through. I do.

Interestingly, Mrs. K notes that she has also become less critical of other people and she is getting along better with some of them, not just with her husband. Therapy can produce some wonderful results.

Summary:

Self-talk is always going on in our heads and often causes problems. It leads us into self-fulfilling prophecies, usually of failure. The habit of negative self-talk is damaging. If we let ourselves become aware of the self-talk, we can then control its effects to some degree. We can spot it and name it, and we can counter it with positive self-talk.

Chapter 45

Positive reinforcement

Personality formation

One of the principles of modern child rearing and of modern managerial technique in business, is "Catch them doing something good." That means to acknowledge a positive or desired behavior. Such positive reinforcement has been proven more effective in obtaining desired behavior than does criticism or punishment. If we were exposed as a child to the other style, the critical, shaming, punishment approach, it will have a deep and lasting effect on our personality. It feeds underlying shame, damages our self-image and sets us up for demoralization.

A reward, whether it's a compliment, a material reward, or just attention and acknowledgement, is a powerful reinforcer of desired behavior, and we can use it on ourselves. We can practice catching ourselves 'doing something good.'

Rewards

Rewards is a strategy that I use pretty often. After I finish this section, I will take a break and give myself a cup of decaf coffee. I could just leave it like that, but I'm specifically telling myself that the coffee is a <u>reward</u>. That gives me more incentive. Or after I finally get the tax papers to the tax lady's office and go over them with her, my wife and I will go out to dinner as a reward. It's good to have a break after completing something difficult, because there's always the next thing that needs doing. If I just go from one thing to the next, because I feel pressured or rushed, because there seems to be so many things to do, then I don't receive positive reinforcement for what I just got accomplished. This reduces my overall motivation to keep going. And working without breaks becomes pretty demoralizing and tiring after a while. I need to pause and relax and spend a little time feeling good about what I've just finished, give myself a little applause, a pat on the back, some positive self-talk. Those are rewards too. Lots of things can be used as rewards, depending on the size of reward needed and on what's possible:

- Stop and play the guitar, maybe just play without trying to learn anything.

- Playing a computer game would be a neat reward but I know that's addictive for me and I can't let myself get started.
- A dish of ice cream, which is not usually on my diet.
- A diet popsicle.
- An extra massage.
- Whatever.

I need to choose the reward before I start the task in order to increase my motivation, and to help turn on my focus center. Then when the task is done I need to give myself positive reinforcement for having accomplished it. I also need to give myself that break in between things so that I don't burn out or get that "poor me" overwhelmed feeling, which is an impediment to any further functioning.

Acknowledgement

I just read on the internet about using an achievement chart for positive reinforcement to help children make behavioral change, 'gold stars'. I've been doing that for myself for years. On my bedside table is a notebook. Every night I note briefly the positive events of the day, the non-routine things I'm grateful for. This is an anti-depressant technique and I find it useful spiritually. However, that's not what I am talking about here. After I record briefly the grateful things, I then record my achievements:

E Sp G B. Did I do my exercise today? Did I do my twenty minutes of Spanish study, my guitar practice? Did I write the assigned one chapter of this book? Recording these achievements holds me accountable; I'm looking at what I did or failed to do, but mostly it's positive reinforcement. I give myself credit for what I did. Also it motivates me; when I see that I haven't practiced the guitar for two days, I recommit for the next day. The main emphasis here is on the positive. The guilt approach just demoralizes me more and rather than driving me forward it, makes it harder to do anything. We've been dealing with guilt all our lives. This notebook strategy is a way of keeping track, paying attention, being aware, keeping focused, and of rewarding desirable behavior. The good feeling I get as I record the accomplishments is positive reinforcement.

We may be able to teach our significant others to give us positive reinforcement when we do something they like. This turns out to a more powerful motivator than is criticism or nagging. Often we have to do the positive reinforcement for ourselves. Just crossing a completed task off a list feels good, gives us a concrete visible response to our accomplishment, and it's positive reinforcement.

Summary:

We receive a lot of criticism from ourselves and from others, and we see many of our efforts as ending in failure. This feeds our shame, negative self-image, and pessimism, and is very anti-motivating. We need to receive positive reinforcement for accomplishing things, even if we have to give it to ourselves, which is often the case. We're not good at rewarding ourselves and we need to intentionally practice. We can set up rewards as a motivating factor for a specific task. Just the good feeling we get when we do accomplish something is a reward and a positive reinforcement, and it motivates us to do more. When you do accomplish something, take a couple of minutes to admire it and pat yourself on the back before you get distracted and rush off to the next task.

Chapter 46

The perfect is the enemy of the good and all-or-nothing thinking

Perfectionism

We have a history of failing, of not completing things, or of doing a half-way or a sloppy job. We have many experiences of being criticized, often most severely by ourselves. Therefore if we do get up the motivation and courage to actually try to do something, we'd like to do it perfectly. That would be a way to avoid the criticism and the shame, from others and from ourselves. So we develop perfectionism, which is supposed to be a way to prove that the negative image of us held by others and by ourselves is wrong.

Generally we've learned from an early age that whatever we do is not going to turn out well. We will lose the homework or spill ink on it at the last minute or do the wrong assignment. We will knock over the chair and break the vase, drop the fly ball, and step on our dance partner's foot. We will say the wrong thing in the wrong way at the wrong time. We will try to follow the directions, but when we finish putting it together we will have two extra pieces left over and it won't work. We're going to be laughed at and criticized and picked last for the team. So, we learn, "Why try?" That can lead to procrastination, or it can lead to half-hearted careless rushed attempts that are doomed to failure in a self fulfilling prophecy: "Well, I knew it wasn't going to turn out. At least I didn't put much time into it." It can also lead to perfectionism: "If I can just do it perfectly, then I won't get criticized. I'll show them." We may not be aware of this thinking or this self-talk, but it can be there. Perfectionism leads to procrastination; the job looked big enough to start with, but if it has to be perfect, then it's truly overwhelming. And I'm not going to be able to make it perfect anyway, so this will be another failure. So it's a little difficult to get up the get up to get started.

All or nothing thinking

Perfectionism is one example of all or nothing thinking:

"If its not perfect, it's a failure."

"You only made an A, not an A+. Why didn't you try harder?"

Mrs. K, the patient I discussed before, started on medication and therapy and had become very enthused as she started feeling better. She was focusing better and was learning new strategies, and she was exercising over three hours a day. That's ADD - we either don't do it at all or we overdo it. She was especially pleased when she lost twenty-five pounds. Then something happened and she stopped her medicine and she stopped her exercise. She came in and reported that she was "back to square one" and that she had gained ten pounds and so she was "a failure". I acknowledged that she was feeling lousy and was disappointed and discouraged. I persuaded her to do the math and she was able to see that she had still lost fifteen pounds, which is not a small feat. Then I asked her to name some of the ways she was still doing better than when we had started, and she came up with several. This story shows several examples of all-or-nothing thinking: three hours of exercise or none, slipping some is the same as back to square one, regaining some of the lost pounds means failure. Thinking in small steps, I asked her to get in fifteen minutes of exercise that afternoon and she agreed.

When we have this historical record of flops, failures and fiascoes, we tend to become discouraged and demoralized. We get down on ourselves and we develop a deep sense of inadequacy and of shame.

We feel that basically, at the core we are inadequate, a failure, worthless, and that is the true real self. We feel that soon we are going to be exposed and all the world will see it. That is shame. This shame is like a huge anchor that we drag around with us and it really slows us down. It leads to procrastination and it leads to not trying at all. It leads to depression. It leads to perfectionism, which leads to and reinforces all of those negative feelings. But if we can shift out of the all-or-nothing thinking and the perfectionism, we can begin to make a catalog of the things we have accomplished, of the things we are able to do well, and of the good things about us. That is worth doing occasionally. Just writing down our positives is an antidote to the shame. My handwriting is lousy, but I'm an honest person. I can't catch a fly ball but I'm compassionate to others. And so on. It is not all-or-nothing.

All-or-nothing is a not uncommon form of logical error, practiced by many people, not just those of us with ADD. Either I completed the task perfectly or it's a flop. I have to make all A's, or win the blue ribbon, or come in top of my class, or else I'm a failure. She either gives me every thing I want all of the time or she's worthless. You either understand everything I say or you're no good as a therapist, or you don't care about me at all. This is perfectionism, one of the things which feeds procrastination, and these are also examples of-all-or nothing thinking. Perfectionism also leads to my wanting to play the piano well after only one lesson, or without practicing, or without having to learn the scales. So I take one lesson and then I quit, because it's going to take time and effort. Further, since one lesson didn't do it, I must have no skill. So I feel inadequate and ashamed. Well, I knew I was going to fail anyway. Or similarly, I drop out of therapy after a few sessions, because you're saying I need to do homework and it's going to take time to cure my phobia, and I just wanted to come in and have you fix it for me, quickly.

I've given you a lot of examples, because I want you to understand this and to be able spot this behavior when you are doing it. That is the start of the path to changing the pattern: "Hey! I know what that is; that's all-or-nothing thinking again!"

Once we note the distorted thinking, we can use self-talk to correct it. Often, though, just recognizing it can be enough, as it dissolves in the light of reason.

Summary:

We have a tendency to all-or-nothing thinking and perfectionism, which can cause or reinforce a lot of our problems. When we learn to spot this we can cope with it, although maybe with some effort and not perfectly. This is one of the areas where therapy can be very helpful.

Perfectionism, the lies

I grew up hearing, "If it's worth doing, it's worth doing well." That is a lie, especially if by well you mean perfectly. When we lived in Baltimore, we spent lots of time raking up the fall leaves. Was it worth the effort to get every last leaf? Of course not, especially since they were still falling while we were raking. It was just fine to get most of them. How about changing to "Anything worth doing is worth doing well enough."? That way we can avoid both of the pitfalls, perfectionism and halfway-sloppy.

There are other lies that are part of the American tradition, like "You can be anything you want to be." I could never have been an NFL football player even if I had abused steroids. "You can do anything you set your mind to." I was never going to be a good pole vaulter, or a professional singer or a tap dancer. I would never be able to remember where I had put my keys if I didn't have a strategy. It wouldn't have mattered how hard I tried or how much I set my mind or how much I wanted to.

These lies all support a perfectionistic viewpoint, and since we don't measure up to the goal, they feed our sense of inadequacy and failure. They just make life harder.

Another lie, or at least misconception, is that we can do better by just trying harder. Not if we have ADD. That was on the notes home from school, "Johnny needs to try harder." Then we had to deal with the reaction from home. "Why don't you try harder?" (the underlying meaning of Ms. J's "You can do better.") This had a significant effect on us, on our self-image, self-esteem, morale, and eventually on our personality.

Are you beginning to see how all of this ties together?

Summary:

The perfect is the enemy of the good. Perfectionism and all-or-nothing thinking undermine us. We need to learn to love "good enough", if it really is good enough. If we have ADD, trying harder isn't going to work. We need to try smarter. We need to use strategies.

Chapter 47

The cabinets: shame, self-talk, self-fulfilling prophecies, self-image, half-way, sloppy, and a turning point in my life. That about covers it.

I used to know that whatever I tried to do was not going to turn out right, so I would save time and energy by not putting much time or effort into the task. This was especially true with projects, like carpentry projects, for example. I was always thinking that I would be smart and take short cuts and use gimmicks and so I wouldn't need to do it the way other people would do it. I wouldn't take the time, effort or expense to do it right. I would just slop through it and say that it was good enough. In fact, it usually wasn't. And I would get annoyed with my wife when she pointed this out, "I'm not going to have that dog house in my yard!" and "I'm just going to call a plumber; he'll know how to do it right." But I wasn't only saving time and effort and expense;

more importantly, I was saving face and protecting my self-esteem. I wouldn't try to do it the right way, because I couldn't, so I would do it the "clever way," I told myself.

And I wouldn't ask for any help – "You mean you did that all by yourself?"

I have never had a guitar lesson. I've had people show me things on the guitar and recently I found some courses from the internet, but I've never had a lesson. I'm not very good, but "You mean you have never had a lesson!?" I'm actually thinking of taking some lessons. There are some things I want to learn now that I just haven't been able to get on my own. But as soon as I take that first lesson, I will have lost my face saving crutch, "Well, no, I pretty much taught myself."

Shortly after we moved to Santa Fe, in 1994, I started to build some cabinets for our garage. Based on my wife's past experience with my work, she discouraged me from trying, but I went ahead anyway. I was just starting a practice here and things were slow; I had lots of free time. I'd noticed that carpenters tend to work slowly and I'd read that the carpenter's rule was to measure twice and cut once; in other words, be very careful and methodical. So I decided to do the job right. I drew up some plans, which I had never done before. I used to just work out of my head and plan as I went (cute and clever,

"You mean you were able to just build that without any plans!?"). I drew up my plans and I made a supply list. I checked all my arithmetic. I bought good quality supplies instead of the cheapest stuff ("You mean you were able to make that just out of scraps!?"). I also made sure I had the right tools instead of trying to cleverly use a screwdriver when a hammer was needed. Then I built the cabinets carefully. I measured twice and cut once and I took my time; there was no hurry. When some part didn't turn out quite right I took it apart and did it over, instead of finding some 'clever' way to work around it. The cabinets turned out great; even my wife said so. She was proud of me, and so was I. For the first time in my life, I felt like a grown man. I was sixty-four years old.

Summary:

    Even if we have ADD, we don't have to do things sloppy and halfway. We can set our minds to doing it right, slow down, and make things turn out right, if we commit ourselves to that.

Section VIII

Special Topics

There's a lot of varied information in this section, so here's a preview of what we'll cover:

1. Our choice of an occupation can be a major issue for us ADDers. We're certainly better suited for some than for others. Then we need strategies to help us function in our occupation.
2. Learning disabilities are a common accompaniment of ADD.
3. Our significant others suffer with our problems. They can be a major help to us; however, we tend to have trouble dealing with them effectively.
4. ADD causes us trouble in learning situations. There are ways to handle this.
5. The internet can be helpful or harmful, depending on how we use it.
6. ADD actually gives us some special advantages.

We will address these issues here and look, as usual, for helpful strategies.

Chapter 48

Occupations

Strengths and weaknesses

We can identify our strengths and our weaknesses. If we've never actually thought about it, it won't take much time to think about it now. Or we can ask someone who knows us. I bet they can tell us our weaknesses without any hesitation, especially if they live with us. They might even be glad we asked! Just steel yourself for the answer. We need to capitalize on our strengths and make them work for us. This principle is important in choosing our occupation. We need to work on our weaknesses some, but not much, because honestly, they're not going to get much better. My handwriting will never be pretty, or even tolerably good, but I am glad that it's a little more legible than it used to be.

Variety within structure

We need occupations where our strengths work for us and our weaknesses are not too handicapping. We need jobs where there is both structure and variety. We need each day to be the same overall and yet to have details that vary. That's one of the reasons I chose psychiatry over pediatrics. I loved taking care of very sick kids and their families in the hospital, but I realized that isn't what pediatrics is actually like. One red eardrum or runny nose looks pretty much like another. In psychiatry, no two patients are alike, even if they happen to have the same diagnosis. Most patients are different each time I see them, too, especially if therapy is being effective and they're changing. So with my ADD, psychiatry is just right for me. There is structure and yet every day is different. I work on a tight schedule and don't have to be making decisions about what to do next; I simply see the next patient on my schedule. But each session will be different and therefore interesting. That is the perfect job for a person with ADD, variety within structure. And there's opportunity to exercise creativity, which I need to do within each session.

Finding our direction

If we have ADD, we often have trouble finding a direction in life. In high school I had no idea what I wanted to do. The guidance counselor said that since I was good in math and science I should go into engineering. So I started college majoring in engineering and soon saw that it wasn't my thing. The new discoveries about the internal structure of the atom were fascinating, so I changed to physics, but I couldn't do the math. And it was all math. So that wasn't my thing either.

I never imagined that I'd go into medicine. My parents didn't believe in doctors, I got nauseated if anyone talked about their operation and I didn't like blood. But the summer after my sophomore year, I was working as an orderly. I found out that I wanted to be a doctor. No, that I had to be a doctor. This was a shock. I had to take two summer courses in biology to apply to medical school. I feared that my college grades were too bad but I was accepted. This was a shock too.

I planned to go into family practice, but I got fascinated by pediatrics and psychiatry. I never regretted finally choosing psychiatry and have never considered changing. I do see that I've changed jobs and locations about every ten years.

So my occupational path was not a straight one. With ADD, we tend to flounder occupationally, not knowing what we want or what we can do. We also tend to change jobs frequently.

Mr. L

Here I once had Mr. L's story, illustrating the effects of ADD on our lives, the problems with finding a suitable occupation, and the potential benefits of therapy and medication. However, his story is amazingly similar to Mr. C's, the poker player; you were going to read it and say, "Hey, what's this? I just finished reading about this guy!"

These two men are close in age, good athletes, intelligent, and have frustrated parents who are sometimes critical and tired of supporting them. Both men have difficulty with bosses, with holding a job, and with finding a field that works for them. This isn't coincidence, but fairly typical of ADD. I've left Mr. L's story out because it's such a repetition of Mr. C's. But I'd already written it, and it is interesting, so I put it in appendix 10, where you can read it if you wish.

Summary:
Capitalize on your strengths. Don't spend much effort trying to improve your weaknesses: learn to work around them, using strategies. Try to find the right job, one with variety within structure.

Precision and other ADD nightmares
College was a challenge. In chemistry lab, we were given unknown substances to test, either to identify all of the chemicals present or to determine precisely the amount of one specific chemical. Each step required exquisite carefulness, patience, and precision, none of which I possessed. I spent a lot of time scraping my unknown up off the desk top where I'd spilled it, thereby losing half of it and contaminating the rest. I did not make a good grade in chem lab.

I majored in physics, which was mostly math. One of the reasons this wasn't a good choice was the slide rule, an ingenious instrument, now extinct, replaced by calculators. Adding the logarithm of two numbers multiplies them. So the slide rule had logarithms on three rulers, one sliding between the other two.

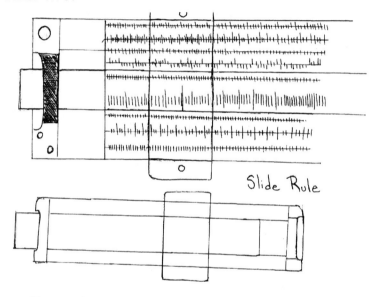

Slide Rule

Illustration 8.   The slide rule
A wonderful tool, if you know how to use it.

By sliding the middle ruler you could work any math problem, if you knew how. I'd never properly learned how. You were supposed to keep track of the decimal point as you slid the ruler back and forth – add one for this and subtract two for that. All in your head. Sound like disaster for someone with ADD? I'd never learned this system, so I was going to be different, smarter, and have a gimmick. Well, I was different anyway. After I worked the problem on the slide rule I would do it again on paper to find the decimal point; this was slow and it worked maybe sixty percent of the time. This wasn't working, so why did I go through four years this way and never stop to learn how to do decimals on the slide rule? Because it never occurred to me to do that. Is that a good answer?

If you didn't understand any of this about the slide rule, then we're in the same boat and you have a sense of how I felt during most of college.

Summary:

We're not good at precision. We need to avoid jobs or situations that require precision. If we can't avoid them, then we need to find help and/or work arounds. If we can just identify that we're having a problem then we can find a solution.

Jobs can be catastrophes

Jobs can be awful for us if they don't fit our patterns of strengths and weaknesses. I've had some embarrassingly catastrophic jobs; more shame. At fourteen I got a summer job with General Motors. They were testing car air conditioners in South Texas, with it's steady reliable temperature of one hundred two degrees and it's straight flat roads. GM sent down two cars and three engineers and hired me to assist them. We would leave the cars out in the sun until the temperature inside reached one hundred twelve degrees. Then we'd turn on the air conditioner and drive at steady speeds back and forth between McAllen and Rio Grande City. From McAllen to RGC at twenty mph, back at thirty, back at forty and so forth, while recording the temperatures inside the car. My job was to record the time and the temperature. All it required was the ability to concentrate and to read this special kind of dial that kept bouncing around. The only problem was, I couldn't do it. I couldn't decide what temperature the bouncing dial was reading. That flustered me and I couldn't keep up. We all got pretty frustrated, as well as hot. The engineers uneasily decided to let me try the driving while one of them did the readings. I did great. I loved the driving, especially at eighty mph, and we were all happy. That job turned out not to be a catastrophe after all. But wait - - !

The summer after freshman year of college I worked for a company that made pipe fittings. In those days blueprints were drawn by hand, requiring precision measuring, precision drawing, precision lettering, and neatness. They hired me as a draftsman since I'd taken mechanical drawing in high school and in college. I didn't tell them that I'd made a C in high school because of sloppiness, or that in the weird college course we didn't actually do drawings, but used the instruments to solve calculus problems. They didn't ask to see a sample of my work. My first drawing startled them. The boss tried to show me the proper way to draw various letters. The problem was, or one of the problems was, that I already knew the proper way to draw the letters. I just couldn't do it. These drawings were to be professional blueprints and, of course, I was sloppy. The boss was dismayed with me, but then he decided that I could work in the print room making copies of everyone else's work for them. This gave the capable draftsmen more time to draw. So everyone was happy, except that the boss had to come ask me to stop whistling in the print room because I was disturbing everyone. Another escape from catastrophe. But wait - - !

After a summer as a hospital orderly, I worked for a company making a special mud used in oil drilling. I was supposed to fill in for the man who ran the lab while he went on vacation. We measured the barium content of ore samples from the field. This required concentration, precision, and routine repetition. You may guess what's coming. Heat the sample to a precise temperature for a precise time, grind it to a precise consistency and then precisely run it through a series of sieves. Mix it into a precise amount of liquid and measure the viscosity by twirling a little metal cup by hand at a precise speed, and precisely reading a fluctuating dial, pretty much like the dial that I was never able to read for the air conditioner tests. My fluctuating dial reading had not improved with time. All of this required precision: precise dial reading, precise temperature, precise weights, precise times, and so forth. Concentration and repetition, every sample exactly the same. Of course, I was no good at it and I hated it. I liked my boss OK, but my boss didn't like me. At any rate, he trained me and then left on vacation.

I ran the samples. One day I got a very high number. I thought they'd found a really rich vein of barium. The big boss asked me to redo the sample. I got a very different answer. I found that I'd run the sample properly the first time but had made a simple error in arithmetic. Sometimes it seems like you can't win. They called my boss back from his vacation (the boss who already disliked me). He was not happy. Besides that, he soon discovered that I'd smoked up his cigarettes while he was gone. It was not a pleasant summer. But I did learn to always check my arithmetic and to never take a job requiring precision.

These kinds of experiences build up our shame and negative self- image: "I can't do anything right."

Shame and the negative self-image are reasons why therapy can be so important and helpful in ADD.

Some jobs are just right.
But the summer before that I had the job as a hospital orderly. I thought I would hate it, but there was a recession and it was the only job I could find. It turned out to be perfect for me. It's the reason I went into medicine. The job was very structured. We started each day with a meeting where we reviewed all the patients and then were assigned our patients for the day. I liked having my own patients to take care of. I checked vital signs - blood pressure, temperature, respiration rate- at certain times each shift. I bathed patients and changed sheets. Everything on schedule. This all required attention but it did not require concentration or precision. The blood pressure gauges and thermometers were easy to read and counting respirations wasn't hard.

The job was structured, but not routine. There were different patients, with different diseases, surgeries, and personalities. I did different things, not only emptying bed pans but catheterizing males, assisting with a tracheotomy and with an ECT. I was helping people. I turned out to be good at this job. I found it very interesting, learned a lot, and realized that I had to go into medicine. Thank God for the recession.

Delegate- an occupational strategy

Strategies are about how to work around our weaknesses rather than about how to improve them. Ideally, we can delegate the things we're weak at. For example, we can be creative, with great ideas, but we tend to be lousy at actually doing the work to implement them. So create, then delegate! If you've been fortunate enough to use your creativity to become CEO of a big company, you've probably already been doing a lot of delegating. Being a CEO is a great position; delegate away. But we can't all be a CEO, even though a fair number of successful CEOs do have ADD. So if you have a partner, and your partner hasn't already given up on you in frustration and disgust, then delegate what you can to them. Negotiate. "If you'll handle the bills, something I'm no good at, then I'll take over washing the dishes; I can do that fairly well." But we can't always delegate, so we need to develop strategies and work arounds for the things we're not good at and can't avoid.

I'm a good psychiatrist. I do good therapy, but I'm lousy at the paper work: keeping notes, billing, and keeping track of who's taking which medication. And especially at dealing with insurance companies. It's hard to find and keep good bookkeepers; some were not so good. One screwed up my whole system and didn't get the bills sent out either. Between paying the bookkeeper and all the taxes, I wasn't keeping much of the money I took in. So I needed to take over the job myself and work in an area of my weakness.

A computer program handles the accounts, but I have to discipline myself to enter the data each night before I leave the office; that's a rule. I stay on top of it so it doesn't pile up, the old dog poop principle. I record the medications in my notebooks in green ink so I can find them, and also in a special folder. These strategies work pretty well. Given a choice, I would enjoy picking up the dog poop more than I enjoy doing all this paper work, but the strategies make it doable.

Ideally, I'd delegate the paper work to my wife. However in this small town she knows a number of the patients, so confidentiality would be a problem. Also it would be potential conflict between us if I were her 'boss'. The current system works OK (I didn't say well) even though I'm working in an area where I'm weak, because I recognize my weaknesses and use strategies to cope with them.

Summary:

Some jobs fit us perfectly and some types of jobs are disasters for people with ADD. They can almost destroy us. We need variety within structure. We need to avoid work requiring precision, concentration, repetition, and neatness. When possible,

we need to delegate the things we are not good at.
Know Thyself.

Chapter 49

The significant other(s)

Let's face it, we ADDers are not the easiest people in the world to live with. Some of us maybe wouldn't be easy to live with even if we didn't have ADD, but the ADD certainly makes it harder. We are unreliable, hyper-sensitive, easily irritated and frustrated, and we tend to take it out on others. We don't listen well. We interrupt and we blurt things out without thinking. All that along with overall poor social skills which cause our partners frustration and embarrassment, and I could go on and on, but why bother? We're just not easy to live with. So in this section I'd like to say something to our significant others to make their lives easier, too. I'd like to, but I really don't know what to say. I asked my wife, and she says tell them to pray for patience. She also says it would help if we could have married a saint. I added, "Since we're fantasizing might as well be a rich saint." (are there any of those?).

My wife didn't think that was funny. Could that be an example of blurting out? So, we're a stress and a burden to those who live with us, care about us, and in any way depend upon us.

It helps if our significant others learn as much about ADD as they can. They could learn what we can do, what we're good at, and try to capitalize on that. They might not keep expecting us to do well on things we're not good at, or to remember things that we aren't going to remember, or to follow through, or to remember any thing at all with out some aids and reminders. Then on those occasions when we do manage to remember or to do something well, positive reinforcement can be very helpful.

"Well, I shouldn't have to praise him for just doing something that he should have just done anyway."

"No, you shouldn't have to; the only reason to do it is if you would like your life to get better."

Our others can be helpful in identifying problems to work on - actually, sometimes they are extremely good at this - and they can help brainstorm and come up with strategies for coping with problems. It was my wife who suggested the keys on the front table rule. Since our memories are not that great, our others can do some reminding - with great tact and finesse, of course, so it doesn't sound or feel like nagging. But probably better than reminding is helping us come up with a strategy that will help us remember.

Our garbage goes out front every Friday morning. On Thursday night, my wife puts a red sticky note up on the microwave where I can't miss it when I make my morning coffee. I see it and remember to take the garbage out, and I don't feel nagged or belittled, just helped to remember.

For years my wife would fuss at me for leaving the toilet seat up when I went to the bathroom at night. I tried to remember to put it down, but I didn't do a very good job of it. I know I was thinking that maybe it was just one of those unfathomable womanly things, or maybe about power or control or maybe just a neurosis. Whatever. But I eventually (belatedly) decided that if it mattered to her, I would really work hard on it and I would do it. So I started making progress, slowly, and she was still fussing. I asked her for patience; I'd explain that I was trying and that it took time for me to form new habits. But I was trying and I was making progress. Then one night she told me that when I left it up - I'm not sure that 'told' truly captures the way she conveyed this information to me - that sometimes when I left the seat up she got up in the middle of the night sleepy and groggy and she fell in. That was powerful information and it created a powerful mental image. I never left the seat up again. Well, almost never. But it was like a miracle, for me to be able to abruptly change like that. After that, just to reinforce it, I came up with a two part rule:

1. I always put the seat down.
2. I always check to make sure that I have put the seat down.

Somehow I'm better at remembering to check than I am at remembering to put it down in the first place. If I go back to bed and can't remember that I checked, I get up and go back and check. So now it's strategy, rule, and habit, and I do pretty well. But it started with that sudden shock - she was falling in- and that powerful image.

We do have trouble remembering, and learning a new habit is hard and slow, but sometimes apparently a shock or a vivid image can speed things up.

We need to be careful that we're not using ADD as an excuse, maybe for something we just don't want to do, or don't care about, or are just lazy about. That just puts more unfair burden on our already overloaded significant other. We are responsible for trying to do something about our ADD problems; it's a lifetime's work. This is like someone with alcoholism. They are not responsible for being alcoholic, no one ever chooses to be, but they are responsible for doing something about it. Same thing.

I'm talking about life partners or spouses, but these things can apply to our bosses, friends, colleagues, teachers, or any others in our lives. Our ADD behavior has effects all around us. A new book, The ADHD Effect in Marriage, by Melissa Orlov, has many good ideas for a couple handling the ADD problems in one partner. Her tips include letting the ADD person take responsibility for their life and problems and treatment. That way the non-ADD spouse doesn't become a parental figure, or a nag or critic. Then the couple needs to sit down together and do problem solving, come up with strategies for improving the things that impact the non-ADD partner. They can work as allies.

Mrs. M

Some years ago, before I realized I had ADD, Mrs. M came to me for help. She is a very nice lady; as it turns out, she was maybe too nice. She was very unhappy, had some depression and some anxiety, and was feeling overwhelmed. She had many complaints about her husband. In fact that was most of what she talked about. As a good therapist, I tried to help her look at herself more, but she kept talking about her husband. She couldn't get him to do things around the house without nagging. Then if he did them, he wouldn't do them right. He would let important responsibilities slide and spend a lot of time on things that didn't actually matter much. He would take on a responsibility, like paying the bills, and then he wouldn't do it. Eventually their phone service was cut off. He left his clothes lying around all over the house. Without consulting her, he would commit them to doing something and then if there was any work involved, it would fall on her. But if they were ever going to do anything as a couple – go to a movie or out to dinner or on a trip - it was up to her to initiate it and then she had to make all the arrangements. He spent a lot of money on things that she considered unnecessary. They would agree on some budgeting but then he would just go on spending like before as though they had never talked about it. Many of their arguments revolved around money, but also around the things that he wasn't doing and promises that weren't being kept.

Mrs. M did have some personal problems that we eventually worked on. She had trouble saying "No". She was always feeling overloaded, doing a lot of things for other people that she really didn't want to do, going places she didn't want to go, spending money on people when she didn't want to. It was hard for her to do anything for herself, to spend money or to carve out time for herself to do what she wanted. She was too caught up in doing things for other people, mostly things she had agreed to do when she really didn't want to. And she was very responsible. If she said she would do something, she did it. This just made her more angry at her husband because he often wouldn't do what he had promised and she just could not understand that.

Mrs. M had learned early in her life that it wasn't nice to be angry. She rarely felt anger. If a patient like that is Christian, as she was, I usually refer to some passages in the Bible that show Jesus, who we were taught as children was "little Jesus, meek and mild," was madder than hell much of the time. He went around calling people names ("whited sepulchers," a huge insult to the Jewish people, as sepulchers were ritually unclean), and kicking over tables, and beating people with whips; so I'm not sure that we're supposed to try to be 'better' than Jesus. This approach sometimes helps some people somewhat. Mrs. M and I were finally able to realize that when she came in shaking her head and wringing her hands, and saying over and over, "I just don't understand him!" that she was really pissed off. And it wasn't always just about her husband. Many people are not as responsible as Mrs. M.

We tried some strategies to help Mrs. M deal with her husband; some helped and some didn't. I suggested they separate their finances and have only individual credit cards, not joint ones. She didn't go for that. I suggested that if he was supposed to do something she could set a certain number of days to have it finished. If he hadn't done it in time she could hire someone to do it. This would be better than nagging, or just staying angry, or doing it herself, which would only make her more angry. When she got totally fed up with finding his clothes on the floor all over the house, I suggested that she put a brown paper bag in each room. Then if there were clothes on the floor she could put them in the bags, and she could tell her husband that she would only launder clothes she found in the dirty clothes hamper. He was a good dresser who cared about his appearance so this strategy worked. He started putting his clothes in the hamper and eventually she didn't need the grocery bags.

I suggested she only ask him to do things that wouldn't have great consequence and not important things like paying the bills. She needed to be very clear about which things were going to directly affect her and which things would only affect him. If a problem was going to cause her harm, then she would need to continue to step in and be sure that it was done and done properly. This usually meant she was going to have to do it herself. However, if its not being done properly was only going to affect him, then she could let it go. For example, she no longer had to keep track of his golf dates and remind him when it was time for him to go. This approach helped some. She was able to let go of a lot of things and no longer felt "I have to do everything!" and she wasn't so overloaded. Although she still resented having to do things that she felt he should have done, the important things did get done.

But as I described, Ms. M's problems weren't only with her husband. So she learned a new habit, starting with a rule. Whenever she was asked to do something or to give time or money, instead of automatically saying "Yes" she learned to always say "I'll have to think about it." Then she often was able to say "No" later. That's not entirely accurate; she never did become very good at saying "No". But she learned to say, "That won't work for me." She and I practiced that. I would ask her to do something and she would say, "That won't work for me." I would say "Why not?" and she would say, "That won't work for me." I would say, "Well, come on, it's not really that much to ask, and blah blah blah." Then she would repeat, "That won't work for me." She became good at that and her life improved quite a bit.

My wife and I just went to a wonderful presentation by Anne Lamott, a gifted very spiritual author. One of her one liners was " 'No' is a complete sentence." But I didn't have that line yet while I was working with Mrs. M.

It turned out that Mrs. M's husband is also a nice guy, which seems surprising in view of what I've written about him so far. I gradually learned about many good things he had done for other people. Then I learned that he had accomplished a number of things, including completing a triathlon and writing a book and getting it published, which I can tell you is no easy job. So it became clear that he wasn't just lazy or a goof off.

I finally realized that Ms. M's husband had ADD! Then it was important for her to learn about ADD. This did not reduce her frustration very much but it did help her not to be so angry at him so much of the time. It also helped her realize why she needed to use some of the strategies we had worked on and also to develop others on her own. So her husband's diagnosis was a very useful part of her therapy.

I touch base with Mrs. M occasionally, and she says she's doing very well. I ask her what's causing that, and she says, "I learned to take care of myself." She sounds good. I just called her to obtain her permission to use this material in the book and she mentioned that she and her husband were reading, The ADHD Effect in Marriage, by Melissa Orlov, and finding it very helpful.

Another source of help in an ADD relationship might be AlAnon, or at least AlAnon literature. Some of the AlAnon principles are related to ADD: "You are not the cause of nor responsible for his problems. You can't fix them and if you keep protecting him from the consequences of his behavior, i.e. "enabling", he won't have any motivation to try to improve. Nagging only makes things worse. You need to protect yourself from damage to yourself caused by his behavior but it is not your job to protect him; so only deal with the things that will harm you personally." This attitude may sound harsh, but actually it's loving. It maximizes the chances that he will try to do something about his problem, which will make his life much better, as well as yours.

I read somewhere that when we really and truly love someone, we also love their faults. That sounds good to me, but it also sounds like a bit of a stretch. It may be a huge stretch some days, and maybe even more so if the person you love has ADD. But we can work together on strategies.

Summary:

If one partner has ADD, both partners need to address it. It will help greatly if the non-ADD partner understands ADD, and if they don't become a critic or a nag. The responsibility for dealing with ADD is up to the person who has it, but hopefully with help from the other. All of this applies to anyone we are involved with. One of the ways we ADDers can help our significant others to deal with us is to teach them the best way to help us. This will be clearer after the next section, describing how I don't do well with a boss.

I don't do well with a boss

You may have noticed that several of the people I've mentioned, Ms. J, Mr. C and Mr. L, either have had terribly bad luck in the numerous bosses they've had or else they might have had some difficulty getting along with a boss. I fit in that latter category.

Most of us don't like to be told what to do. I don't know how much that's part of the ADD. We tend to have a demoralized negative picture of ourselves. When someone tells us what to do and how to do it, or critiques or criticizes our efforts, or makes helpful suggestions, or generally supervises us, it just taps into those ideas that we're incompetent and can't do anything right. Since I tend to mess up, I also tend to attract a lot of those suggestions and critiques and other helpful interventions. I tend to not react well to them.

I have had bosses in my professional life, but I've been blessed, perhaps not by coincidence, that my bosses left me alone for the most part, and let me do my job the way I wanted to do it, as long as I didn't mess up. Beyond that, I could go to them for help if I needed it. I didn't do that often, probably for the same reasons we're addressing here. For most of my work, I've been my own boss. This disliking supervision occasionally causes problems with my wife. She sometimes expresses her love for me by giving helpful advice, like how to repair the faucet, for example. She might feel that I need instruction on how to wash the dishes properly. She may offer constructive criticism on something else I might not be doing quite the way she would. These helpful comments make me feel that she sees me as incompetent. They tap into my sense that I really don't know how to do things and that what I try to do can't possibly turn out well. In other words, all I hear is that I'm incompetent. My wife feels hurt when she's sincerely trying to be lovingly helpful and it's quite clear that I'm not appreciating it. She tends to be lovingly helpful a lot. I don't know how much this is just part of her personality, or how much it comes from her previous experience with me; she may indeed believe that I can't be relied on to do something right. Either way, it doesn't always go well.

Advice

Yesterday my wife had a recipe for hummus out on the kitchen counter. Our friend Charlie had just given us some of his homemade hummus and it was fantastic. It had a real bite to it - picante! I asked if she was going to make some and I said she might think about putting some chile in it. She retorted that if I wanted to make it myself I was welcome to go ahead. It almost seemed to me that perhaps she possibly was a little tiny bit slightly miffed. Many people don't welcome unrequested advice. I surely don't, and that is a weakness of mine. I might do better sometimes if I listened more to other people's ideas. Having ADD has exposed me to more than my share of unrequested advice. Those who know me and especially those who live with me may have gotten used to my messing up, forgetting things, misplacing things, doing things halfway or "good enough". They may feel they need to head off trouble in advance by giving me helpful suggestions. But when those suggestions remind me of my own sense of inadequacy they're a little hard to take.

This dislike of unrequested advice may be a trait pretty common among men. In our culture we men are raised to believe that we're always supposed to be competent at everything, at least at everything that is considered masculine. I've also read that for women, giving advice is seen more as a form of caring than as intruding or controlling or depreciating.

Still, I have noticed that sometimes a woman may not be too appreciative of unrequested advice either. Like about hummus, for example.

I'm working on not being so reactive to advice; then I can consider it and perhaps benefit from it. I also am trying to limit the amount of advice I give in therapy. Often I don't know enough of the details and nuances of the situation to be in a position to give good advice. Therapy is not really about advice anyway, although occasionally it can be helpful. It is a masculine trait to want to problem solve and come up with helpful solutions, even though often what is really needed is just listening.

Finally, another of my favorite sayings :
"One of the best things about good advice is that it does so little harm, because no one ever follows it."

Summary:
We tend not to do well with advice, supervision or bossing, which may revive our feeling that we are basically incompetent. If we can somehow improve on this reaction, some of the advice or suggestions could be helpful to us. That's a hard improvement to make, though.

Teach our significant others how to help
I have let my wife know that I don't respond well to supervision. She doesn't always respond well to my letting her know that; after all, she is only being loving and helpful. I do think that she is getting better about this. She sometimes manages to phrase her suggestions in a way that helps me not react so negatively.

Last month we dealt with a habit my wife had recently developed which was bugging me. At night she putters arounds in the kitchen at the last minute while I retire to the bedroom. Once I turned off the lights on her by accident. So she got into the habit of saying in a desperate voice, "Don't turn out the lights!" as I went into the back. Every night. Finally I asked her to try an experiment for one week. I asked her to not say, "Don't turn out the lights" and to see what happened. She tried it and hasn't said that since and I don't turn out the lights.

I got my wife's help with the lost keys problem because I was bugging her to help me find them. Frequently. If I had recognized the key losing as a problem, I could've asked for her ideas, and we could have solved it sooner. She's gotten used to the idea that I can't find anything and usually will offer to find something for me when I start looking. And she doesn't seem to mind it when I ask for her help after I've given up on looking for something myself. Which is pretty often. This is working together on the problem.

I often put things out where I'll be sure to see them because if I can't see it, it doesn't exist. I might need to remember to take something with me, or there's a bill I need to pay, or a book I want to be sure to start reading. My wife doesn't like clutter. She neatly puts it away. Then I not only don't know where to find it, I forget that it exists at all. So I request of her that if something I've put down somewhere bothers her, to ask me to move it, rather than moving it herself. If I put it somewhere else myself, at least I have some chance of finding it, if I can remember. And I can use my cards for that.

It's harder if we don't have a partner, although in some ways it's easier. But we can get some help with these things from friends, colleagues, or even bosses. And if we are closely involved with them, it's helpful if they know about and understand our ADD problems, although we need to use some care in who and what we tell.

Summary:

We can let others know what kinds of things are helpful to us and what kinds of things don't work so well with us. Our ADD problems can have a huge effect on our partner and our relationship. Both partners need to work on it. Our partner can be a huge help with the things we have trouble with. We can get some help from others too.

Chapter 50

Learning disabilities and coordination problems

Learning disabilities are not a basic part of ADD, but many of us with ADD also have learning disabilities. We have trouble remembering things, which is part of the ADD, but learning problems go beyond that. We may have letter or number reversal when we write or type or dial a phone. I have that a lot, so I've made a habit: whenever I write down a phone number I check to see that I have it right. I also check it to see that it's legible, that when I come back to use it I will be able to read what I just wrote. Actually, that's true for any kind of notes I make. I need to make myself slow down and write them legibly and then check them again to be sure they are legible. Otherwise when I return to my note I'll have:

"call m#$$c&*# at 50#-XX3 ##*4!", which is generally pretty useless.

I used to use lots of scraps of paper: "Here, let me just jot that down." Now I keep a steno pad by each of my phones, and I have cards in my pocket. When I get a phone number, or some other important thing to note, I don't put it on some scrap of paper somewhere. And I make sure it's legible. And now I have a long term record of the call or the information. Works a lot better.

Some of us have trouble with math. I don't, although in college when I would manage to get the complicated formulas worked out and solve the equation correctly and be just about to get the right answer, I would mess up the simple arithmetic and miss the answer anyway. But that was inattention and rushing and carelessness, pure ADD, not a math disability. Many of us had trouble learning to read. I didn't have that either. But my handwriting has always been terrible. I'd always thought that was due to the way I learned to write. Only after I realized I have ADD did I also realize that my terrible handwriting is mostly due to poor fine motor coordination, made worse by my always being in a hurry. My teachers always told me, "Doug, you have terrible handwriting," and I would say, "I know." They would often mark me off for it. They would tell me I had to improve. Only two of them ever made any attempt to help me improve; unfortunately, their attempts weren't very successful. I have recently improved it a little, which amazes me, after over sixty years of illegibility. I discovered that if I slanted the first part of a script " *ℓ* " (small L) way over to the right, then the second part would cross it and it would wind up looking like an " *ℓ* " is supposed to look. Wow! Now I say to myself, "*ℓ* alert", when I see one coming up in a word and I get myself ready to do it right. After that improvement I realized that if I drew the first part of an "e" extending way over to the right, then the "e" would look like an "e". So I started also doing 'e alerts'. And my handwriting improved. Then I realized that I didn't have to rush. Just by using these alerts I had slowed down. I also saw that I didn't have to crowd everything in to save paper. Actually, these changes saved time in the long run, since now I or perhaps even somebody else can read what I've written. Right now I'm working on my "r"s, but I don't have those down yet. I'm not yet using the speech recognition computer programs, but those could turn out to be one of the technological blessings for ADD.

In high school football I played in the line. I was too small for the line but I had no fine motor coordination. I was small but slow. I couldn't pass nor catch, and so I played in the line. Not being able to see didn't help either. The vision problem has nothing to do with ADD, unless there's some brain damage affecting both, which I doubt. With no fine motor coordination nor ability to see, I couldn't play baseball or basketball, but I could play in the line, somewhat.

So it's not enough that we have ADD, we also tend to have problems with reading, math, writing, and coordination. These can be addressed, too, but generally I wouldn't expect great results and it may not be worth the trouble. It's better to find ways to work around these problems rather than trying to improve them. I am pleased and surprised though that my handwriting definitely is better.

Geographically challenged

I'm geographically challenged, too, another learning disability, not a key part of ADD itself. My wife can be in a foreign city, go to a place once, come back to the city five years later and know how to return to that place. I've seen her do it. I, on the other hand, can go somewhere in Santa Fe fifty times and the fifty first time is like the first time all over again. I have to ask my wife for directions or use the GPS (which I'm no good at because I'm also both technologically and patience challenged) or use a map. If I'm going to use a map, I need to do it before I start and to write down the directions; it's harder to use once I'm moving, lost, and frustrated. My wife has a hard time giving directions because she often doesn't know the names of the streets, she just knows when to turn. She can't say how she knows; she just knows. On the other hand, I'm pretty good with maps and she isn't; if you hand her a map, her mind goes blank. So this has something to do with learning disabilities, right brain and left brain, and visuo-spatial capability. I can get lost in my own house. I recognize this geographical handicap and use strategies, like looking at a map ahead of time and carrying my cell phone so I can call my wife, "So do I turn left or right on Rufina Street?" This reduces the level of frustration in my life.

Summary:

Learning disabilities are not a basic part of ADD, but many of us with ADD have one or more learning disabilities and often poor coordination also, probably all due to some mis-wired brain circuits. Both ADD and learning disabilities contribute to our underlying sense of shame and demoralization, as does our clumsiness. We need to be aware of our disabilities and come up with strategies to deal with them. Then things can get better.

Chapter 51

Educating ourselves

There's a lot of good information on the internet about ADD, most of it about how to try to manage your ADD kid - read it and have some compassion for what your parents went through with you. There's also a lot of information about adult ADD. Some of it's free; for some of it you have pay. Some of it is good. Some of it is garbage. And some of it is woo woo. There is some woo woo also in some of the ADD books. Some of the woo woo may turn out to be good. A current fad is multi- modal therapy; I've read a little about it but I don't understand what it is. I've read some discussion of Yogic unilateral breathing. I haven't tried that.

Some studies suggest that the cerebellum is not functioning properly in ADD. The cerebellum is the back end of our brain that has to do with coordination and balance and probably other things.

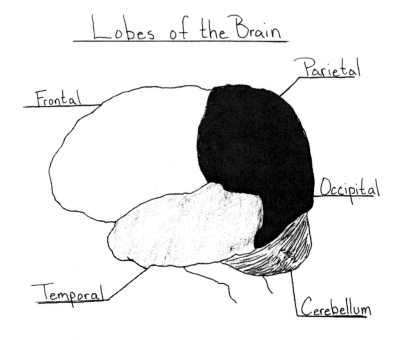

Illustration 9. The cerebellum
Controls balance and coordination

There's a program for treating ADD by strengthening the cerebellum through things like balancing
exercises and juggling. My friend Richard, who is
very smart and has advanced degrees and a severe
case of ADD, is also a juggler. It might appear that
the juggling hasn't helped his ADD much, but then
I didn't know him before. Still, I like the idea, even
though it's woo woo, and I've been practicing bal-

ancing on one foot. That's easy enough to do, or rather, easy enough to find the time to do. I do it while I'm brushing my teeth. The book says it may take six to twelve months to see results. I've been doing it for about six months and can't say I've seen any improvement in my ADD, but my balancing is definitely better. That can't be a bad thing.

I haven't looked at much of the ADD material on the internet. The part I include in this book is good. I'm still a book person; I like to hold the book in my hand and turn the pages. I don't use a Kindle or those other machines yet either, but I suspect I will. If I had more time I would look at the things available on the internet too. At the end of the book are some recommended books and some web sites.

I do suggest that you learn all you can about ADD; use your common sense to weed out the garbage. See what seems to be commonly accepted and not just unique to one place, for example, or what seems to be just too good to be true. If it seems weird and it's expensive too, I personally would stay away from it. In general, the more you know the better off you are.

I do believe that what is really going to help you are the strategies, the principles and the tools I'm telling you about, and maybe the medication, which can help you focus and help you use the strategies.

Life can be hard sometimes and having ADD definitely makes it harder, all of the time. So, if you bought this book, or checked it out from the library, or borrowed it elsewhere, or even if you shoplifted it, I hope you will feel committed to actually read it and not just put it on your shelf or in your things-to-do pile. And not because you 'should' read it, but because it will help you and your life can be better and you might like that.

Summary:

We can help ourselves by becoming educated about ADD. There are other good books besides this one. The internet has a lot of helpful material about ADD, much of it for free, but keep your garbage sensor active.

Chapter 52

Studying and learning

I didn't learn how to study until medical school. School had always been easy for me; I'd never had any concern about a test until college. I got into Rice, a prestigious school, and suddenly I was in with the top students from the top high schools in Texas. And I was in way over my head.

Back then, I thought that you studied by reading the book and underlining. I didn't catch on until medical school that, No, you read a page in the book, then close the book and see if you can recite or write down the important parts. When you have that page, then you go on to the next page. It's work. It works. (See a more detailed explanation in Appendix 1.) I never asked anyone about studying; I didn't know that I didn't know how to study. I hear that nowadays in some places, they actually teach kids how to study. No one ever taught me. It was assumed that you knew how to study. I assumed that I knew how. Wrong!

Finally learning how to study was wonderful, like a whole new world opening up. It got even better when I discovered the forgetting curve. I developed a system which gave structure to my studying. I started really learning things, not just passing the test. That was great!

Studying with ADD means dealing with focus and concentration issues and avoiding distractions. We also need to know how to study. Even after I learned how to study though, the ADD still caused me trouble. Once in medical school, I was studying for the last exam of the year. I was tired, it wasn't a subject that interested me, and I couldn't concentrate. So I sat in the library writing poetry and bugging the other students who were trying to study. I didn't do well on that test. This is one of the things that came back to me and finally made some sense, once I realized that I have ADD.

Reading

I love to read. I read fast; I can't wait to see what's coming next. I don't remember anything I've read. If I'm reading solely for pleasure this is OK. But if I want to retain something - to be able to discuss, or because I want to learn something- then I need to slow down. Every page or so I need to stop and ask myself, "Now what did I just read?" This a much less intense form of the study method. But it makes a big difference in how much I get out of the reading. You might want to try it with this book and see.

Focus

It's hard for me to focus. It's hard for me to prioritize. It's hard for me to acknowledge that I can't do it all, and that I will just have to let some things go. It's easy for me to let myself become distracted and try to ride off in eight directions at once. I've been learning to play the guitar for many many years. I've vastly improved, but I'm still not good at it. The books and the print outs from the internet course are just sitting on the coffee table and the course is waiting on the internet for me to find the time to get back to it. Naturally, I can't do all of this. I also bought a wonderful Spanish program, Yabla, on the internet. I enjoy it, whenever I find the time to go to it. That's not often. So, what am I actually doing? Well, at the moment I'm trying to learn "Brother Can You Spare A Dime" on the guitar. I just about have it and am ready to start on "I Remember You" next, which I previously half-learned. I'm also trying to learn the irregular predicate verbs in Spanish. What I'm also trying to remember, and to learn, are the rules - focus on one thing at a time; really learn, not half learn; just because you bought a book (or a course) doesn't mean you know the material in it. But I tend to scatter myself out, and go in many different directions at once. And thus I often don't get anywhere at all.

So, I will learn those two songs, one at a time, and overlearn them, Overlearn means really learn the heck out of it; keep studying it even after you have it. And don't stop at "I've got it pretty well." Then I plan to go to the internet guitar course and work my way through it. Often when I start something like that, I go along until I hit something difficult and then I drop it. This time I plan to stick with it; I'm making that commitment, just like I had to commit that I <u>am</u> going to finish this book. I have to acknowledge that I can only learn one thing at a time and that I have to focus on that one thing and overlearn it. I do have a plan B: if I hit something hard in the guitar course, unless it's a necessary foundation for what comes next, I can skip it and go on, not skip it and drop the course. There's no rule that says I have to learn everything in that course; I'm not working for a grade. If it were a college course, it still might be smart to skip the hard part and come back later, rather than just becoming discouraged and starting to find distractions and eventually just letting the whole thing go. Another approach for when I hit a hard spot, whether in college or in my home guitar course, might be to find some help. There also is no rule that says I have to do it all on my own.

That's one of the strategies for ADD, which I didn't have (the strategy, that is), to recognize where I'm having a problem and to ask for help. This is similar to trying to delegate tasks that we aren't good at; first we have to recognize that we aren't good at it and then we have to find someone who is good at it and is available. Unfortunately, I didn't know that I didn't know how to study. So I never tried to get any help.

Summary:

Our ADD problems will make studying and learning more difficult for us, but there are strategies that help. We can get our focus center turned on. We can learn how to study so that we're learning, not just studying. We need to make ourselves focus on one thing at a time and not just learn it but to overlearn it. We need to recognize that we can only do so much; there are only so many hours in the day. (See appendix 1 for more on studying, learning and the forgetting curve system.)

Chapter 53

Advantages of ADD

I was surprised when Richard mentioned creativity as a gift that comes with the ADD. I do think I'm a little creative; this is my second book. But I had never thought of my creativity as related to ADD. And I do tend to problem-solve a lot, sometimes when I would do better just listening. Then I found this on the internet, courtesy of Pete Quily, an ADD coach in British Columbia:

Top Ten ADD Advantages in a Hi Tech Career.

1. The Ability to Hyperfocus.
Hours of full engagement and concentration in a task, IF you find it interesting. You can get into the zone and be totally immersed in what you're doing while the outside world disappears. When I went on the internet for the first time in 1993 at an Internet

cafe I got on the machine at 8 pm and around 4 am decided it was time to go home.

2. Rapid Fire Mind.

Your brain processes information at hyperspeed. You can do things in 30 minutes on a computer that might take other people hours. Downside if you're stuck with an old machine and not enough RAM you'll be frustrated cause it can't keep up with the speed of your brain.

3. Multitasking at Will.

Able to run 14 apps at a time and effortlessly switch between each without breaking a sweat. Able to do several projects at a time with ease.

4. High Energy Level.

You're able to keep going on a project (if it's interesting, ADDers are more into creative and en-trepreneurial activities than clerical and repetitive ones). 14-hour days? No problem. Adrenaline is my fuel source:)

5. Highly Creative.

Able to think beyond the idea of a box. This comes naturally for ADDers, while others pay thousands of dollars to try and learn this. Since you take in more information than the average person, and you're easily distractible, you're more likely to view a problem from many different angles than vanilla people (non ADDers), and therefore come up with more possible solutions to a problem. Need an idea generator? Find an ADDer.

6. Quick Learner.

IF it's something you're interested in. ADD is mainly a condition of boredom; you have no trouble paying attention to something if it's interesting. Most people find it difficult to do boring or repetitive things but these can often totally shut an ADDer down. Your rapid fire brain + highly creative mind + the ability to hyperfocus equals fast absorption of new information quickly. Dr Ed Hallowell, who has ADD and has written Delivered from Distraction : Getting the Most out of Life with Attention Deficit Disorder, said he stopped teaching Psychiatry at Harvard University because the non-ADDer's brains were just too slow and they took so long to get it. He got tired of being continually frustrated waiting for them to catch up to the ADD students.

7. Stimulus Seeking Brain.

A perfect match for the wired world, an under stimulated brain and an over stimulated virtual environment. Being an info junkie can be a good thing. Well, not always:)

8. Constantly Scanning your Environment.

Allows you to notice more and find information and resource that others miss. Also allows you to see possible problems before they arise, and opportunities that others may not see because they have tunnel vision vs. multiplex vision. An ADDer invented the electronic ticket.

9. Great in a Crisis.

High energy intense situation? Lots of chaos and change? Sign me up; I thrive on stimulation, change and chaos. We can create order from chaos effortlessly. We can also create such an environment as well if needed.

10. Risk Taker.

Impulsivity means you're more willing to take risks and have a bias for action, act now while the opportunity is hot instead of getting into analysis paralysis. Many entrepreneurs have ADD i.e. Paul Orfalea who founded Kinko's, JetBlue Founder and CEO David Neeleman who attributes his creativity to ADD. Both are Billionaires. **Imagine how successful a high tech CEO would be if they didn't take many risks.**

These are just a start of the advantages of ADD, for more go to the list of 151 positive characteristics of people with ADD at my ADD Resource website.

http://adultaddstrengths.com/2006/02/09/top-10-advantages-of-add-in-a-high-tech-career/

Pete Quily is an ADD coach and has lots of good information on his web site. http://www.addcoach4u.com.

So when we feel discouraged, we can remember our advantages. One of the benefits is the ability to multi-task. I had never particularly noticed that but apparently I can do it. I ordered some wonderful courses on CDs from The Teaching Company and I enjoy learning things while I'm driving. My wife says she can't do that; she can't even listen to them while she's a passenger. Score one for ADD?

Summary:

I notice that I do have some of the other positive traits that Pete Quily lists. I'm not sure that ADD is something I would choose to have, but it's good to recognize our strengths and assets. It helps against feeling discouraged and demoralized and it helps us choose our occupations.

Section IX

More of the typical problems

Most of the problems here are pretty familiar: disorganization, losing things, procrastination, stuck and paralyzed, impatient, impulsive. Brain freeze may be new to you, but it's a significant problem if you have it. Let's go through these problems and, of course, some strategies for coping with them.

Chapter 54

Disorganization

Inefficient, ineffective, and disorganized
You may think it's been easy writing this book. You would be wrong. I have ADD. I've already told you about the duplications when I put the different parts of the book into one file; here's some of the painful details.

It wasn't easy to find those duplications. First I tried opening two pages to compare side by side.

That was slow and laborious. Then I realized I could use the "find and replace" tool in Microsoft Word. I would put in a phrase from page sixty-seven that sounded vaguely familiar and see where else that phrase occurred in the manuscript. But I was very afraid of losing something that wasn't actually a duplicate, so before cutting I would go back and recheck the first page. I did a lot of cutting and copying and a lot of rechecking to make sure I didn't lose anything. Whew!

One of the things I'm learning is to plan ahead when starting a project or before applying a solution to a problem. Sometimes the attempt to solve one problem can create new problems.

I type without a lot of niceties. For example, I don't type "ADD"; I type "add". Also I type "tho" and "thru" and "santa fe". So I used the "find and replace" tool. I put in *"find add and replace it with ADD."* That worked pretty well, except then I found things like, "ADDed" or "ADDiction" and had to correct those. I tried *"find tho and replace it with though."* So where I had typed "thought' it came out "thoughught".

I put in *"find santa and replace it with Santa."* That worked fine. Then *"find fe and replace it with Fe."* Not so fine. I found a lot of things like "I am Feeling --" and "It takes Fewer--". So I had to go through and change those. Just now I realize that if

I had put in *"find santa fe ---"* instead of each word separately, it would have saved some trouble.

I have ADD. I am not well organized. I take shortcuts, like not capitalizing when I type, because I'm impatient and I'm trying to type as fast as I can because my thoughts run a lot faster than I can type. If I had slowed down to think it through before I started using the "find and replace" tool, I'd have saved a lot of time and trouble. But then, slowing down to think and planning things out ahead are not my strong points, nor is patience for that matter.

All this shows what tangled messes ADD can get us into, making things so much harder than they need to be. Slowing down, thinking ahead, and careful planning can save lots of trouble. Short cuts are not always time savers. When I worked on the cabinets, I was able to think ahead, plan and slow down. But it's clear that I still need to improve on this.

Summary:

We tend to plow into things; we tend to be impulsive and impatient. We need to train ourselves to slow down and plan ahead, not easy for us.

Chapter 55

I can't Find Anything

I was just looking for the bottle of Presidente, a good Mexican brandy. We've finished dinner and I enjoy a little brandy after dinner, especially while I'm writing. There's a picture in my head of the hard working author with sleeves rolled up, cigarette dangling from his lips, eyes squinted from the smoke and with the glass of something at his right hand, pecking away on the typewriter. Maybe Hemingway or something from the movies. Well, I don't smoke, and I'm not Hemingway, and I couldn't find the Presidente. I looked in the liquor cabinet and didn't see it. I moved some bottles around, because sometimes I forget to look behind things, but it wasn't there. Then I found it. It was right there, on the front row, out in the open, in my face as a matter of fact. But it was turned around, so I was seeing the back of the bottle, where it had a very clear label, with Presidente in large red letters. I must have been looking for the front of the bottle, so I had looked right at it and never saw it. At least I didn't have to call my wife for help. It's always a moral victory and a personal triumph when I can find something without needing my wife's help.

I can't find anything if it's not where I expected or if it looks different than I expected. If I'm looking in the refrigerator for the pickles, and they're on a higher shelf than I thought, I'll look there but I won't find them. If the jar is different than I expected, I can look right at it and not see it. Oliver Sacks, a noted neurologist, just had an article in the New Yorker about his cognitive impairment, prosopagnosia, not being able to recognize faces, surprisingly a not uncommon problem. I'm good at recognizing faces, but poor at remembering the name that goes with the face. The not seeing things I think is a similar problem to the prosopagnosia, but I don't know a fancy name for it. Both are probably based on a brain mis-wiring.

There are strategies for this not finding problem. My best one is to call my wife. It also helps if I follow the old fashioned principle, "I have a place for everything and everything is in it's place." I don't like the prissy way that sounds and I don't follow it too well. However, I do try to put something away when I'm done with it, rather than just laying it down wherever I am and "Oh, I'll get to it later." If it's in the right place, I'm more likely to find it, if it looks like I expected. I can try to remember to look more carefully, and use strategies like remembering to look behind things, and to look up and down. But the fact is, even if I'm looking right at it, I still may not see it.

Summary:

We ADDers are not good at finding things. It helps some to put things away as we use them rather than waiting until later. We can train ourselves to remember to look behind things and to look up and down.

Chapter 56

Procrastinating and avoiding

I was going to write this earlier, but I kept putting it off. I couldn't get around to it.

Actually, some years ago my wife gave me a round tuit. It's a metal disc that says "This is a round tuit. Now you have one. You can't say "When I get around to it." anymore." I think she was trying to tell me something.

Illustration 10. The Round Tuit

Now you can't say that you don't have one anymore!

I procrastinate a lot. Often it's because something seems unpleasant. Maybe I haven't cleaned up the dog poop for a week and the prospect of a whole yard full of poop is not appealing. Of course, if I keep putting it off, it's not going to get any more pleasant. More often I procrastinate when I'm not quite sure I can actually do something.

I'd been putting off and putting off cleaning the dust out of my computer, and the fan was getting louder and louder. Finally, yesterday I did it, and l felt greatly relieved to have it done at last and pleased with myself for having been able to do it. It went fine and the computer works fine after I finished and the fan is quieter. But I was very unsure of myself. If you open a computer you can destroy it with static electricity if you're not careful. And when I had the side off the cabinet I was worried that I might not be able to get it back on, but it went on easily. And I didn't mess up any of the components or knock them loose. When I finished and put the side back on and plugged all the wires in and turned it on and it actually worked I heaved the traditional sigh of relief. But before I actually did it I'd been unsure and uncomfortable about it and I kept avoiding it.

So something will seem uninteresting or difficult or unpleasant, or I'm not sure that I can do it. Maybe I'll think "I don't really have time today, I'll do it tomorrow," which is self-talk; or I'll just think of it as something that I need to do, sometime in the vague future. That's procrastination, isn't it? If it's because I'm not sure I can do it, that's from a long history of messing things up, or if I'm not sure I can do it well, that's perfectionism. If there's a deadline, at the last minute the deadline may turn on my focus center and I get to it; if there's not a real deadline, I may never get it done. If it's something that affects my wife, she may get on my case and become unpleasant enough that I go ahead and start, but that's not a good way to run a marriage. Anyway, once I get started, a task usually isn't as difficult or unpleasant as I'd imagined and I can usually go ahead and finish it. That's good, because we're talking about not getting started, but not being able to finish things is also a common ADD problem.

For getting started, once again the strategy is to break a task into small steps and do one step at a time, and to not think of it as one large chore. I tell myself that in reality I probably can do it, or at least I won't know until I try (self-talk). And sometimes it helps to set a deadline, a specific time and date that I will get started.

Of course, it's better if I just go ahead and start a task now, if possible. Sometimes I just bite the bullet, put it at the top of my to-do list, underline it in red, put a big 1 in a circle beside it, and just make the decision to do it. And it helps to realize "I'm procrastinating on this." because I don't like to procrastinate; I don't like this aspect of myself and I know that I'll be happier once I go ahead and get it done and don't have it hanging over my head anymore (I can use all of this as self-talk). Also, sometimes I just don't know where to start; maybe there's a bunch of tasks in no particular order. If I can't pick one, I can decide which one is the hardest and start there, or I just make myself start at the top of the list and work down. But there's a lot of inertia and I may have to use all of these strategies to overcome it.

Avoiding

What is the difference between avoiding and procrastinating? Not much, but I think procrastinating implies it's uncomfortably hanging over my head, is unavoidable, and that I will get it done sooner or later. Avoiding means the task is a little less pressing and a little less certain.

I have a white card in my pocket titled 'Avoiding'. That's another strategy. If I'm consciously aware that I'm avoiding something, then I'm more likely to figure out a strategy and go ahead and do it. I ask myself every day or so, "What is it I'm avoiding?" Then either I can stop avoiding and start to do it, or at worst I can write it on the card. At least I'm aware that I'm avoiding it, and when I check the card occasionally I'm more likely to go ahead and start the task. Maybe it's an uncomfortable phone call, or some record keeping that isn't fun, or some part of Spanish that seems particularly difficult. I wish I could just do those things, but since I don't, it helps to have them on the avoiding card and stay aware of what's going on. And occasionally, when I'm about to write something on the avoiding card, I say "Oh, what the heck." and just go ahead and do the task and can avoid needing to write it down.

Summary:

We tend to avoid things; paying attention to what we're avoiding will at least give us the chance to use strategies to get going, and the small steps is useful again.

Chapter 57

Stuck and getting unstuck

Inertia: an object in motion tends to remain in motion; an object at rest tends to remain at rest.
Newton's First Law of Motion

As an extreme example of procrastinating and avoiding, and often as a direct consequence of it, we can sometimes become totally stuck. We can be stuck, demoralized and paralyzed.

Many things in life work in feedback loops, like vicious cycles or whatever the opposite is - beneficial cycles?

When our ADD wins out and we drift away from our track, get distracted, can't get started, can't finish, and so on, then we get down on ourselves; we feel frustrated and demoralized. We say bad things about ourselves, to ourselves and often to others. That makes us get further down and further demoralized. And that makes it harder to start anything or to make progress on anything, which makes us more demoralized. That's how a feedback loop works. We can spiral down into the pit and become overwhelmed with inertia.

Sounds awful doesn't it? But it doesn't have to be that way. We can use strategies to break a link in this chain of events. Although it is hard to use a strategy when we are demoralized – which of course is pretty demoralizing.

If you're trapped in the negative feedback loop, the vicious cycle, the downward spiral into the ADD demoralized paralyzed pit -

You Can Get Out!! Trust me. Use strategies:

1. Check yourself for negative self-talk. Identify it and counter it.
2. Pick the smallest easiest task that you could do. Let go of the 'hardest part first' principle for a moment.
3. Break that task into even smaller steps and pick the smallest and easiest one.
4. (optional) If needed, call an understanding friend and tell them what's going on and what you plan to do. You are looking for encouragement and you're also making a commitment.
5. Do the small step. If you can't, you haven't broken it into small enough steps.
6. Give yourself applause and a pat on the back. Counter the negative critical self-talk: "Of

course it shouldn't have been hard, but it was, and I did it!"

7. Repeat the process. You have broken the ADD cycle and you're on a roll! You're coping.

OK, you can't clean the kitchen. It's too much. You're stuck.

But maybe you can do the dishes. Or maybe not.

But you could wash one fork. Yes, you could.

But if not, get the soap out and set it on the counter. You can wash the fork tomorrow.

OK, you have a lot of big important things to do and washing one fork isn't going to take care of them. Right! But washing the fork is doing some-thing; you were stuck and you weren't doing anything and that wasn't helping anything either. Now you're interrupting the vicious cycle paralyzing negative feed back loop.

You are unstuck.

Good for you !

Often we have some task that seems overwhelm-ing and we procrastinate. But we won't let ourselves do some other task, because it isn't as important; the big task is important and we 'should' be doing that. Well, maybe it would be good if you were do-ing that, but you aren't. So if breaking the big task down into small steps is not enough to get you moving, and you're still stuck, find some other small task to do. Get yourself moving and break the log jam, the stuck, the inertia. Then go to the small step of the large task.

Summary:

We get stuck in negative feed back loops and become paralyzed. We can get out of them by breaking the cycle. The trick is to do <u>something</u>! Find something small enough and easy enough that you can get yourself to do it. You will need to counter the negative self-talk with a lot of positive self-talk. Defend yourself, argue against it, use facts. Be a good defense attorney in your own cause. Then do something, anything, to break the inertia. And if necessary, break the small steps of the important task down into even smaller steps.

Chapter 58

Short attention span and inattention

If we have ADD, we generally have a shortened attention span, although if something has really turned on our focus center we may be able to stick with it for a long time. We're on a roll. We're in hyper-focus. Sometimes while I'm writing this book I'm really into it and I'm not ready to stop writing, but I do notice that my typing errors become more and more frequent with time. Most people, even without ADD, cannot effectively concentrate for more than an hour. I can enjoy a movie or a concert that lasts two hours, but with something that requires my intellectual concentration, like a lecture or studying, my limit is about an hour. I've been at workshops where the presentation goes two hours at a time - the second hour is wasted. And if we're studying, or doing other intellectual work, after about an hour our efficiency markedly drops, and it drops more and more as we go on. We will accomplish more in a two hour session if we take a ten minute break in the middle then if we work the whole two hours.

The first strategy for dealing with our short attention span is to be aware of it. We need to know our own personal attention span and plan our work around it. We need strategies to turn on our focus center and we may need extra stimulation while we work. (I'm playing music while I write this.) Plan the work so that the small steps fit into our attention span. Plan breaks to fit with our attention span, and strategies for getting ourselves back from the break and refocusing.

Summary:

We generally have a short attention span, unless something really turns on our focus center. Then we can become hyper-focused and time can go by without our noticing it. We need to plan around our own attention span.

Inattentive

My wife has been doing me a great favor by wading through the first draft of this book. That's a chore because it is still pretty disorganized (I have ADD) and there are still a lot of repetitions in it, and she does have other things to do. I asked her feedback and she told me I had left out my major problem!! - inattentiveness. She sounded a little annoyed. I thought I had put it in, when I talked about getting antsy at the cocktail hour or the need for stimulation in the restaurant, for example. Anyway, I know what she's talking about. Having the cocktail hour every night is very important to us and to our marriage. It's our scheduled time for conversation. She feels like she doesn't have my full attention. I'm fidgeting, jiggling or scratching my head, checking the appointment book or the cards. I'm jumping up to check on something and then coming back in. Anyway, I can only sit there for a certain amount of time before I get antsy and the cocktail hour doesn't usually last a full hour. In a restaurant, I'm seeing what's going on and not always looking at her. I can see why she feels that I'm inattentive. Richard seemed to solve his similar problem by willpower. I'm impressed. I've been working on this problem and I think that I'm improving but I haven't asked her opinion about that. It's still a problem. So far I'm just trying harder and instead I need to come up with some strategies.

Summary:

Our inattentiveness can be misinterpreted and can distress or annoy others. We need to be aware of the problem and takes steps to deal with it; we need strategies.

Chapter 59

Impulsive, impatient, and irritable

Once in high school, I was feeling pretty high after we won an away football game. Coach let us walk around town a little before we took the bus home. Mistake. I walked into a store. No one was there. I put my quarter into a shuffle board game and it didn't work. Filled with righteous indignation, I put the shuffle board disc in my pocket and left. I napped on the ride home. The next day Coach showed us the disc that someone had left on the bus. I was in some trouble.

So did I outgrow impulsiveness as I matured? I did not. While I was on faculty at the medical school, I received a complimentary letter about my book on crisis intervention, asking for information. I was very pleased; maybe I got a little high again. I was quite busy, but I responded. I sent a long rambling letter which I didn't bother to edit; I just explained that I was very busy. There was no response. When later I read what I had sent, it was terrible. I was very embarrassed. Impulsive.

That high feeling may be a red flag.

Impatient

From an early age I wanted to work. When I was eleven years old my parents got me a job at Mr. Bird's grocery store where they shopped. I made twenty cents an hour. I swept, washed windows, took care of the shipping boxes, burned the trash, and cleaned up the cans on the shelf. More or less. There was a fiasco the day Mr. Bird told me to dust the food cans. I took them off the shelf and dusted them but I just couldn't get them stacked properly back in the shelves. I finally just dumped them in and then made a neat stack on the front edge to hide them. Mr. Bird was pretty mad.

One day I was ready to burn the trash, but Mr. Bird told me to wait. I enjoyed burning the trash. I was impatient, so I started bugging him, "Can I burn it now?" Finally he got exasperated and told me to go ahead. I did. Soon a very angry lady stormed into the store. The smoke had blown into the clean laundry she had just hung on the line. She was not happy. Neither was Mr. Bird.

From an early age, I did not have patience.

I have a GPS for my car. It should be very helpful, because I'm geographically challenged, frequently lost, and have no sense of direction. One day I was totally lost way out in the boonies. The GPS was wonderfully helpful. I hardly ever use it. You have to know the exact address of where you want to go, so I would have to look it up in the phone book and then enter it into the GPS, before I leave. Nothing can be entered while the car is moving. Entering it takes some time and it's not easy to get it right. So I would have to carefully enter the exact address before I start out, when I'm ready to go. When I'm ready to go, I'm ready to go, now. If I had any patience, the GPS would be very helpful.

My wife helps me with the book, as an editor and a representative of the general reading public. Plus of course she has the experience of living with someone with ADD. She just now came in to give me feedback. I took notes. She suggested I take a part out because it might be offensive and could turn some people off of the whole book. I saw her point at once. She kept trying to convince me to take that part out, after I was already convinced. I was eager to hear her other ideas.

I interrupted her, "OK, OK, I got it already. What else?" I may have sounded a little abrupt.

I could see that I'd hurt her feelings and she was a little miffed. After all, she was doing me a favor and trying to help me like I'd asked. But she was able to go on and give me some more good ideas, which I appreciated.

A little later we talked about this exchange. I explained why I had interrupted when she was trying to convince me of something I had already agreed to. She said that she wasn't trying to convince me; she was just trying to have a conversation. She said that this was an example of my impatience, that I can't stay with a conversation.

So here's my ADD again, impatience, with a little touch of blurting out. On the other hand, it's partly a man-woman thing. In her book, <u>You Just Don't Understand</u>, Deborah Tanner explains a fundamental difference:

Men use talking mainly to convey information, and sometimes for problem solving or for exerting power. Women use talking mainly for connecting. This difference can lead to a lot of problems.

So I was trying for information and was impatient; my wife was trying for connection. Sometimes my wife gets quite impatient with my lack of patience, but she was great this time.

Irritable

I'm very irritable, easily annoyed, often over small things. I thought it was just me, one of my character flaws. Then I looked up 'ADD irritable' on the internet and got 648,000 hits! How come I didn't know this??? The internet says that the medicines don't particularly help with this symptom.

But I'm working on strategies:

1. Mindfulness - just note to myself, without judgment or trying to change it — "Oh, I'm feeling irritated right now."
2. I ask myself – "Why?"
3. Logic – "Is this really something to be irritated about?"
4. Empathy –"I wonder what this looks like from the other person's point of view?"
5. Laugh. Just laugh. Try it.
6. A short prayer.
7. Step back – try to see the situation in the larger context; "What difference does this make in the big picture?"

Some combination of these works pretty well, much of the time. The irritation usually evaporates, especially if there is no good reason for it. The irritation itself is the red flag to remind me to use the strategies. I'd never connected this before with ADD; I thought it was just the way I am.

At times, irritation is a normal and healthy response to a situation. Harriet Lerner, PhD, says in her book The Dance of Anger (highly recommended), that there is nothing wrong with anger; it is neither good nor bad. It's a signal that something is wrong in the situation and that we need to do something about it. But with ADD, we can easily be overly-reactive, so we need to be careful about our anger.

So irritable is a symptom of ADD. It can also be a consequence; anyone feeling overloaded and frustrated might be somewhat irritable even without ADD. Other than being aware that we are irritable, there's not much we can do about it, other than trying to avoid getting overloaded or tired or those other states which make us more vulnerable to our ADD and to irritable behavior. Awareness is a first step in dealing with being irritated: "Oh, I'm irritated right now." The feeling itself is the flag, which signals us to start using strategies.

Summary:

Impatience, impulsive and irritable all have to do with our relative lack of self-control. These three cause us a lot of problems in relationships. They are unpleasant in their own right. We need to have awareness and to have strategies on hand to deal with these.

Chapter 60
Socially inappropriate behaviors

Blurting out

I used to blurt things out in school. Early, it was mostly funny comments. Later, in junior high and high school, it was jokes harassing the teacher. Someone raised his hand and asked our elderly (fifty?) Texas History teacher, "Miss Jones, how do we really know what happened at the Alamo?" So I called out, "She was there!" That got a laugh from the class; I'm not sure about from Miss Jones. I don't know how I got away with it. This kind of behavior was only with certain teachers; there were some I knew not to mess with. So I did have some self control and social judgment, but, like patience, they weren't my strong points.

Many of us were the class clown in school.

At the end of junior high, there was an assembly to present the award for good citizenship. Everyone knew that Nikki would win it. So when my name was called, I was astonished. I loudly blurted out an obscenity (junior high, remember?) and then went up to accept my good citizenship award.

My son, Duane, also had ADD. He was always in trouble for blurting out in class. What he would blurt out was the answers; he wouldn't raise his hand, just blurt them out. He was also in trouble because he couldn't stay in his seat. He was up wandering around the class room or going over to talk to some other kid. Ritalin helped him some. ADD runs in families, especially through the male side.

Inappropriate behavior

I used to like playing "the bad boy", wild, daring, free spirit, not constricted by the staid conventions of society. I have a tendency to push the envelope. This is similar to blurting out. I will say or do something questionable after a moment's hesitation. For a split second I wonder if I'm going too far, if it's going to be too offensive, but then I say or do it anyway. Now that I'm aware of this, I do it less often. I've learned to notice when I'm getting that "bad boy" state of mind, which is a red flag telling me to stop and think.

My friend Richard loves to tell jokes, often inappropriately. It might be the wrong time or the wrong place or the wrong joke. For example, there are some jokes you just don't tell to the widow at a funeral. He learned to stop himself and to consider before he told a joke. He just trained himself to do this, and it has become a habit. I, too, have learned to pay more attention to that little question, "Is this really appropriate?" Then I made a decision to start erring on the side of caution.

Richard's training himself to stop and think before he tells a joke shows that this is doable, whereas trying to train yourself to stop and think before you speak at all is probably too big and beyond our capacity. The urge to tell a joke is the red flag for him.

I mentioned that my wife asked me to take out an offensive story. This is a good example of how our significant other can be helpful to us. She was right, but I wouldn't have seen it myself. She also asked me to take out another story that was a great example of my blurting out and the harm it can cause. The reason for omitting this one was because it's still painful to her, even after a long time. So we'll have to get by without it. Our blurting out can cause real and lasting harm.

Summary:

We tend to be impulsive, to blurt out, and to lack patience. We can be inappropriate. By recognizing these problems, we can do something about them. We can identify in what circumstances they tend to happen; sometimes we can catch it on the tip of our tongue before we say it or catch ourselves before we do something inappropriate. We can learn to be on watch for it. Sometimes there is that little warning voice, if we train ourselves to listen to it. We can notice ourselves being irritable, and use strategies to control it.

Chapter 61

Brain freeze

Brain freeze

My first experience with brain freeze was on my first test in college. It was a chemistry test, the first test in my life that I had any doubt about. I wrote my name on the answer sheet, looked at the questions, didn't have a clue, and froze. My brain would not work, and there was nothing I could do. This was the first of many college tests on which I did not do well. I don't recall any more brain freezes in college, so the next one, in medical school, caught me by surprise. The junior medicine exam was the most important exam of the four years. I was doing well in medical school. I had learned how to study. It wasn't over my head and I was enjoying it. So I don't know why I had this problem. I got the exam, wrote my name on the answer sheet, looked over the questions, and did not know a single thing about any of them. I went into brain freeze. Fortunately

I was able to get up and go drink a Coke. When I came back, my brain had cleared and the test wasn't actually so hard. I made the second highest grade in the class. Brain freeze is, of course, simply caused by anxiety.

Mr. B, my patient, has some learning disabilities. He also has an advanced degree. He gets brain freeze anytime you say the word "computer". I don't think he has ADD but I'm not sure; we have some other things to deal with for the time being. He has tried to learn how to use a computer, but he freezes at the thought. He has tried to get help, but people try to teach him several things at once, which is too much. They also try to explain to him how it works and why, when all he needs to know is how to do it. He freezes. He has tried to take notes, but his brain is frozen and I doubt if he takes very good notes. Then he doesn't find the notes very useful and guess what? When he tries to use them, his brain freezes. Nonetheless, he has persisted and has gradually caught on. He can now use e-mail and Google. He can navigate web sites. And yet, if you say "computer" to him, his brain still freezes.

My wife clearly does not have ADD, but like Mr. B, she used to freeze if you said "computer". Now she loves it. But she also hates it. She sends and receives lots of e-mails. She can Google and navigate web sites. She can use Word. But she seems to think that computers should work well. So when anything doesn't work well, which is often, she calls me in frustration. Since it's her computer that's not working, she thinks the problem is the computer and that she needs to get a new one. That's kind of like if your car doesn't move when you step on the gas, then there must be something wrong with the gas pedal. She understands that better now. So now she thinks the problem is Comcast. She may be correct. She no longer freezes with the word "computer," only if there is a problem. Like Mr. B, she has made a lot of progress.

My wife's real issue is with math. She's quite bright, but she's convinced that she can't do anything that has to do with math. Her brain freezes. This is partly a learning disability, but it is partly just her belief that she can't do it, as it is with Mr. B with computers. If you could convince her that it was a puzzle, or grammar, or maybe even arithmetic, probably she could do it, as long as she didn't realize that it was math.

It isn't clear how much brain freeze is related to ADD; some people without ADD can get it. In those cases it seems to be because of self- perception- " I can't do math"- and thus anxiety and thus self fulfilling prophecy. But it is probably more common with ADD, and then those same factors- perception, anxiety and prophecy- make it worse.

Summary:

Brain freeze is related to anxiety, which is certainly increased by ADD. If you're caught in brain freeze, the best thing to do is to take a break, because if you don't, you're not going anywhere. You may be able to become aware of your perception about the situation and to question the validity of it or to counter the negative self-talk.

SECTION X

Interview with my friend Tom

When I interviewed Richard I was surprised by some of the ways that he and his ADD were different from me and mine. So I thought it would be a good idea to get yet another view point. I made an appointment to go interview my friend Tom at his house. Once again I became impressed by how unique we each are, with our own special set of ADD problems and our own stories, and yet we have such strong similarities too.

Tom's story further illustrates the difficulties that ADD can cause in our lives, especially educationally and occupationally. Tom particularly has difficulty with finishing things. He also struggles with using strategies. This shows that they're not always easy to use and certainly not the magic answer, and how our ADD, and maybe our personalities, can make it difficult for us to do the things that would help us. It also shows that the strategies are not one-size-fits-all; we each have to find the ones that will work for us and apply them in our own way.

Chapter 62

Tom's story

As I drove into Tom's driveway I saw him walking back into the house from his garage. I rang the front door bell, and in a while he welcomed me inside. He explained that he'd been on his way to my house for the interview, but he'd forgotten something and had gone back inside for it. (You may recall that the appointment was for his house.) He said that he thought he'd seen a car in his driveway; I guess it didn't register though because he hadn't checked to see who it was. If he hadn't been late we might have passed each other on the road as he made his way to my house. Did I mention that Tom has ADD?

We walked into his dining room. The table was covered with papers and folders, as was the floor on one end. Tom cleared off a space on the table for us. I joked that I wanted to take a photo of this to use as an illustration in the book. Tom explained that he'd been organizing and cleaning out some files. "For quite some time now," he added.

Tom has ADD; that's why I was interviewing him.

Tom didn't realize he had ADD until he was fifty years old. He likes to learn things and he reads wide-

ly. One day he chanced to read an article on ADD
and he said, "Boy! Oh, that's why!" He suddenly
understood why his life had been "so screwy". Then
he went to see a psychiatrist and had his diagnosis
confirmed.

From childhood, Tom's big trouble has been not
finishing things. "If something is boring or uninteresting, I just can't do it. If it's something I enjoy,
I can really get into it, until I get it conquered, but
then somebody else needs to finish it."

Tom says he also has trouble staying on track.
"If I'm not really zoned in on it, something will distract me, and if it doesn't, I will make up something
to distract me."

Tom is obviously smart, and as a child he was
always being told that he wasn't living up to his
potential (i.e." You can do better."). I thought that
must have been pretty demoralizing, but Tom said
that it didn't bother him. He liked learning and he
knew that he was learning a lot, just not the right
things at the right time. He never thought he was
dumb, he just thought that he was "a goof-off". But
the criticism did have an effect. He decided that if
he was going to be seen as a goof-off, he might as
well be a really good goof-off, and so he goofed-off
even more. He never liked "the rote stuff", like getting homework done or handing things in on time.

In college, Tom did very well in the courses he was interested in, mainly accounting. He liked accounting because it was logical and it involved math, which he was good at, and because he had set a goal to become an accountant. In the other courses he just scraped by, without doing much work. He particularly did not do well with languages. But he went to graduation and received his diploma and got a job. For a few years no one found out that he hadn't actually graduated; he had 'incomplete' in three courses. He had just skipped one final and hadn't turned in a paper in another course, and something else about the third. The problem was that he needed that degree to get his CPA, which his firm expected of him. They kept asking him when he was going to get it and he kept telling them "soon" until he ran out of "soons". He went back to the college and talked to his professors. With hardly any effort on his part they all gave him a passing grade and he finally actually graduated. And he got his CPA right away. Which of course would have been easy enough to do from the beginning. Tom has trouble finishing things.

Later, Tom went to graduate school. There was one required course he couldn't fit into his schedule, so he had a friend tape the lectures for him. Then he sat down and listened to the tapes so he would be prepared for the test.

Sure he did.

So when he had completed all the courses except that one, he talked with the professor, who offered to just let him take the test. Then Tom would pass the course and receive his graduate degree. But Tom said "No", that he wanted to do it right, so he was going to listen to the tapes and then come back and take the test.

So Tom always says, "I did a master's degree," not, "I got a master's degree." Because of course he didn't and Tom is honest. But Tom says he got a good education even if he didn't get the graduate degree.

Summary:

We are talking about Tom's problems, especially with finishing, pretty typical of ADD. Now we will get to strategies. Like me, Tom developed some strategies before he ever knew he had ADD.

Chapter 63

Tom's strategies

When I asked Tom if I could interview him about strategies for dealing with ADD, he said that he had no strategies. I was doubtful. It's hard to imagine someone living with ADD for over fifty years without developing some strategies. It turns out that Tom has a few more strategies than he told me. I guess he didn't think of them or didn't regard them as strategies.

Tom got his first job while he was a still a senior in college and, of course, some years before he actually graduated. He enjoyed the job. It was new to him; it was challenging; he was learning lots of new things. And he was good at it. However, after a few years, he had it pretty well down. Then it was no longer new or challenging; he wasn't learning new things and he began to get bored. And he was no longer good at it. Things began to slide. Some things were getting done kind of halfway; he began to miss details and deadlines. His focus center was no longer turned on.

So Tom found a new job. And, of course, with time the same thing happened. At that point, Tom took a look at himself. He didn't realize that he had ADD, but he realized that there were things he was very good at and things he was not. He was very creative, good at research and at solving problems. He was not good at details, deadlines, finishing things, or at doing anything that was repetitive, routine, or not challenging. So he found a job where he could be creative and do problem solving. He was the company problem solver. People came to him when they were stuck and he'd come up with some novel creative solution for them. Tom says, "I did the fun stuff, things that were challenging, that they didn't want to deal with." I wondered how he dealt with deadlines, but he said there actually weren't any deadlines. Most of the problems weren't urgent and just needing solving in the next month or so. I also wondered how he got a job like that. He was able to go to the company and explain to them what he could do for them and to sell himself. He basically created the perfect job for himself inside this company.

So if you're in the position of wondering what would be the right job for you, I hope you will remember Tom.

Then Tom had an even better idea; he started his own company. Now he could be creative and come up with projects and then have other people do the detail work and finish them for him. And he could do the problem solving. There would be no one over him asking him why he hadn't met a deadline. I said this sounded perfect, and that it must have gone very well. Tom said that it only went pretty well. When there was work he was 'supposed to do', he might get it done or he might not. When he was supposed to review some of his employees' work, sometimes he had trouble getting around to it. Although he didn't have a boss, some of his customers did have deadlines for their projects. But he came up with a strategy that helped with this, somewhat. We'll get to that in a minute.

Tom said that with his own company he got by, didn't do great, but he did what he liked, and he didn't actually work very much.

Tom has retired, but he stays busy doing consulting work. He gets work that is problem solving, novel and challenging, where he can be creative. Tom also does a lot of volunteer work. And he uses his strategy: if he's doing something for someone and he thinks he can finish it by the fifteenth of June, he tells them that it should be ready by the tenth of July. So Tom recognizes that he isn't good with time, and he uses a variation of the strategy I use when I estimate how much time something will take and add fifty percent. It's a good strategy.

Tom says he tries to keep expectations from other people low. That's a strategy. For example, he visits his family in the Midwest every summer, but he never tells them when to expect him. He tells them he'll be there "around mid June." This is because he often doesn't get away on the day that he planned to leave, and he can't really tell when he'll arrive.

The strategy is to avoid making commitments you might not keep. I've had a rule for years: I never make a promise. I tell people "I will try to " instead of "I will."

So see, Tom does have some strategies after all.

Organizing

Tom has another strategy: he uses a computer program called a PIM, a personal information manager. It has a calendar, a to-do list, a very fancy address book, and lots of bells and whistles. It will pop-up reminders onto the computer screen: reminders of things to do, appointments, people's birthdays, and anything else he wants. He can set it to ring an alarm whenever something pops up and anytime he wants to be reminded of something, like when to take his pills. So the alarm can give him immediate reminders, like needing to leave for an appointment right now, or for long term things - that he has to pay his quarterly taxes; the tax pop-up will come up every three months. He also has a spread sheet that tells him when his bills are due.

It sounds wonderful to me. The only problem (well, in fact it isn't the only problem), the only problem for the moment is that it doesn't work very well for him. Why not? Because he tends to ignore the pop-ups and the alarms. Another problem is that the program is old and will not work with Windows 07. He needs to buy a new program, and transferring everything to the new program is going to be a hassle. I think it's going to feel overwhelming and maybe he's not sure that he can do it right. So he hasn't gotten around to it yet. Maybe he's procrastinating on it.

This PIM is a great program and Tom says it is helpful, just not too helpful, since he ignores the pop-ups and alarms a lot of the time (generally, when we find something that helps us, we quit doing it.) Tom was being helpful to me by giving me this interview; he wasn't asking me for any help. But here's the way it seems to me:

Tom would need strategies to make this PIM work for him and he doesn't seem to have any. He just tries harder, which is not a strategy. If we leave a reminder on the door for an ongoing thing-"Be sure to lock the door."- then after a few days we won't see it. Our brain accommodates and it becomes invisible. The note on the door only works for a today thing-"Carry out the garbage today"-so that it's novel, and it's not supposed to be there, and we notice it. Of course, then we still need to make ourselves carry out the garbage, but it's a good start. But Tom has had this PIM program for years; these pop-ups and alarms are not new to him. Probably when he first got this program he was enthusiastic and spent a lot of time setting it up the way he wanted it. I bet that it worked well, for a while.

But now the PIM is repetitive and familiar and not new. Also, it's both too much and it's not enough. Maybe this program is the only strategy for daily living that Tom has, except for one calendar. And it's all there on that computer. He doesn't put notes on his phone, or use cards, or have an appointment book. So the computer becomes routine and familiar, maybe oppressive, and maybe overwhelming. Maybe it feels 'bossy'. He has the pop-up notices, but he didn't talk about reviewing his schedule for the day, and doing it five times a day, or about reviewing his to-do list.

Calendar

Aside from the computer, Tom keeps a paper weekly calendar and puts his appointments on it. This is another strategy. He keeps it in his briefcase, so he doesn't always have it with him. And he doesn't look at it very often. Still, he says he's fairly good at keeping those appointments, because they involve other people and he doesn't want to let them down.

	SUN	MON	TUES	WED	THURS	FRI	SAT
8							
9				brkfast @ Johns			Bridge tournament
10							
11					committee		
12							
1							
2							
3				call Jar			
4							
5		group					
6							
7							
8					date!!		
9							

Illustration 11. Tom's weekly calendar
He doesn't look at it very often.

Tom says he's fair at getting things done for other people; it's his own personal life that seems out of control. For example, the pop-up tells him when it's time to pay the electric bill, but he ignores it, and then winds up paying a penalty. I'm not sure he has a strategy for actually paying the bills. His paper calendar works fairly well for novel, one-time appointments, but he has trouble keeping routine appointments. Tom is only fair about keeping our appointment for Monday prayer group. He intends to, but it's routine; he gets distracted, other things come up, he schedules something else in that slot, or he forgets. I don't know if he has a pop-up for the meeting.

Possible approaches
So, Tom didn't ask for my help, but here are some things I might try if I were in his situation:
1. Rely on the computer system for fewer things, so it wouldn't give me so many messages. Program it for variety; make the pop-ups a different color and the alarm a different sound each time.
2. Have backups to the computer system, using my phone or my cards also.
3. Make a habit of checking whatever tools I was using several times a day. Use anchors: maybe every meal time, or every bathroom visit, or every telephone call. Maybe have the to-do list of five pop up on the screen every hour on the hour and the bigger list at the end of every day, in a different color every time; have the pop-up play a different song each time instead of just an alarm.
4. Make a strategy for paying the bills; maybe pay each bill as soon as it comes in, or maybe every Saturday. They wouldn't pile up and become a chore. Put a sticky note on the wall and record each penalty I paid and the total penalties for the

year so far, to increase my motivation. Richard has most of his bills paid by automatic withdrawal, which is another strategy – if you trust it.

5. Keep a notepad by my bed, and every night mark down whether I had made all my Appointments, kept up with the Bills and followed through on the Pop-ups. So on a good day, I would mark down: 'A, B, P' (today, appointments were made, bills were paid, pop-ups honored)

6. I would only make one or two of these changes at a time. Make rules and then make them habits.

I don't know which of these strategies would actually work for me. If they didn't, I'd try other strategies. We're all different; I don't know which of them might work for Tom. He apparently doesn't think in terms of strategies. Maybe he still thinks of himself as a goof-off and that's just the way life is. Or maybe he thinks of the whole thing as one big problem, which should be solved by one big computer program, and he hasn't broken it down into separate smaller problems. Or maybe he just doesn't think the problems bother him enough to be worth the effort to do anything about them. The idea that it's not worth the effort could come from some of the demoralization and defeatism we get from our

ADD experiences. And Tom says he's an easy going guy; probably things don't bother him as much as they would me, but I would hate having to pay a penalty on the electric bill. Maybe Tom just keeps applying the strategy of trying harder, which doesn't work very well. But Tom is a bright creative problem-solver. Maybe if he approached each of these problems, one at a time, to figure out a strategy that would work for him, it would turn out to be worth the effort. Maybe his life could be better.

Long after all of this was written, Tom told me he'd that realized he does have another strategy, but he says it's not a very good one. He deliberately lets things with a deadline sit until the last minute. He says his internal clock tells him when the last possible minute is and then he waits a little longer. Then he can start because the deadline, the sense of pressure and the challenge turn on his focus center. He may stay up all night, but he gets it done and usually does a good job, because he's smart and his focus center is turned on. That is a strategy and it works for him. It's not one I would choose for myself.

Summary:

We ADDers each have our own pattern of ADD symptoms and problems, and our own ways of coping with them. Tom has some strategies for major problems but he seems to let the smaller things go by. Maybe that's a strategy too. Would his life be better if he used strategies for those smaller things?

Chapter 64

Finishing

Many of us with ADD have trouble finishing things: the term paper, the cabinets we're building, the house cleaning, even the book we're writing. Tom says it's his biggest problem. Richard says it's not much of a problem for him. For me, it's in-between. I do sometimes start a project and then get stalled, but I usually get it done eventually. But not always. I got stalled on the guitar courses. There were some projects I started and then realized they were dead-end time wasters and stopped. That's different though; it's good that I didn't finish those.

Why would I have trouble finishing something? I start something, usually with great enthusiasm. I get into it and then the new is gone. I've got it down and it's not a challenge anymore and there's a bunch of new challenges calling for my attention. Maybe there's not a heavy deadline built in and setting my own deadline for myself is not very powerful.

Maybe I run into a hard part and it just seems too difficult or too much effort. Maybe I'm not sure I can actually do it. Some of the problem is perfectionism; I may fear that it's not going to turn out well, so I'm afraid of finishing and finding out that I was right.

I'm currently stalled on my autobiography, for my grandchildren, which is nearly completed. It's pretty disorganized and I don't know how to go about organizing it; it seems overwhelming. Plus, I ran into a part that's hard to write and I've been avoiding it. Also, I've written the most interesting part, but there are some odds and ends that need putting in and I'm just not that interested in them. Then the idea for this ADD book came up, and here I am. And there the neglected autobiography sits.

So I need strategies for finishing things. Richard sets a deadline for himself and that works for him. Tom delegates things to others to finish for him, which is a great strategy if you can do it. He also notes that if it's a personal commitment to another person, he's more likely to finish, but that's not actually a strategy. It sounds like a fair number of things he just doesn't finish.

I don't like not finishing something. It feeds the shame feeling. And if I haven't given up on the thing entirely, then it's hanging over my head. I don't like things hanging over my head. And if I don't finish,

I feel bad about wasting the time and energy I've already invested in it. I try to use strategies to help me avoid the not-finishing trap. First, I question myself before I start a project: "Is this really useful? Is this a good use of my time?" If I decide to do it, then I make a commitment. I've told you about the struggles I had about writing this book before I finally made a genuine commitment.

Then I take a moment to think about the project: "What will it be like to finish it? What are the payoffs and rewards? What will be the consequences if I don't finish? How will I feel if I just let it go?" This is similar to what Richard does.

Not finishing is actually a form of procrastinating, isn't it? So I use some of the same strategies: Break it into small steps. Pick the hardest one. See if I can break that into even smaller steps. Pick the hardest step and do it. Then it seems downhill from there.

I think I will be able to finish the autobiography once this book is finally done. And it will get done.

Summary:

Finishing, or rather, not finishing, is a major ADD problem. The strategies include planning ahead, being sure that the project is worth doing and why, and that it's not biting off more than we can chew. Then if we're stuck, we can break it into small steps and get unstuck. We can also discuss with ourselves the benefits of finishing and the consequences of not finishing, hoping to make the benefits and consequences heavy enough to motivate us.

Chapter 65

Irresponsible, unreliable, and lazy

Irresponsible

Tom says he's not responsible. I assume he means that he can't be relied on. He feels bad when he lets someone down. He probably is responsible; he takes responsibilities seriously; he just doesn't manage to get responsibilities done. Tom's negative comment is an example of how ADD damages us. We create negative images and labels for ourselves and that feeds the demoralization. The demoralization then makes the problems worse, not only because it makes it harder to try, but the negative ideas becomes a self fulfilling prophecy if we do try:

- "I knew I would screw it up."
- "I'm not a responsible person."

So Tom says he's not responsible. He tries to keep other peoples' expectations of him low. If he thinks he can get something finished in June he

348

tells them July. He doesn't tell his family exactly when to expect him. Yet, he is devoted to his two granddaughters, and when they had graduations this year, he made both ceremonies. He left a day later than he'd planned, so that he had to drive eighteen hours straight, and he left things undone here that he needed to do before he left, but he made those graduations.

Tom explains this by saying, "Because it really matters to me. I made it top priority." He says he can establish priorities, which is a problem for most of us, but that he doesn't do well on things that "should be a priority." In other words, if it doesn't personally matter to him so much, he will have trouble. It makes a big difference whether it's what he 'should do' or what he wants to do. I believe that 'should's are poison to us. I have worked on eliminating them from my vocabulary, especially my internal vocabulary, and I say something like "I would prefer not to pay a penalty on this bill" instead of " I should pay this bill."

We ADDers are often called irresponsible, unreliable, and lazy. I don't think I'm lazy. I like to work. I'm very good at manual labor. I have chopped cotton in the fields, hauled hay, and rolled cotton bales around. I'm a hard worker, at manual labor, but intellectual labor is hard for me. I tend to put it off. I don't look forward to it. I procrastinate. I tire easily. Once I finally get started I tend to take breaks and often don't get back from the break as soon as I meant to. I can have trouble meeting a deadline. All of this can make me look irresponsible, unreliable, and lazy. I don't think I'm lazy.

In fact, I don't think Tom nor Richard nor I are irresponsible either. We all take responsibilities seriously. We get upset, mad at ourselves, and ashamed when we miss something that we were supposed to be responsible for. We may try to laugh it off, "Well, that's ADD for you." for public consumption, but we're not laughing inside. But the truth is, you can't rely on us - unless we've come up with a strategy that works for the situation.

Getting help

Once Tom realized he has ADD, he tried Ritalin, Straterra, and Adderal, the three different types of medications for ADD. (see appendix 4) Obviously the ADD was bothering him enough for him to try the medications. He doesn't take any of them now. He says they had no effect whatsoever on him. Nada. That suggests that he never tried a high enough dose. Otherwise, he would've either noticed them helping or he would've noticed side effects. For me, the Ritalin just didn't help enough to justify the side effects, but I had both benefit and side effects so I know I was on a high enough dose. From that experience, I decided it wasn't worth the trouble to try the other two medications, because my symptoms are pretty well handled by the strategies. However, I'm not sure that's an entirely rational viewpoint.

I asked Tom if he'd done much research on ADD, because it helps to learn all we can. Tom likes to read and to do research and he's bright and interested in many things –but, "No, I haven't learned much about ADD." He has bought a number of books on ADD though; I saw them on his book shelf. He said he's actually looked at a few of them. You probably know the principle: if we buy a book, we not only own it, we now own the knowledge in it. We don't actually have to read it. So Tom hasn't read the books, but he says that when he runs across an article on ADD he does read it.

I wonder if Tom might be thinking that strategies, like the medications, don't work for him. He might be thinking that they don't work because he believes he lacks the willpower to follow them. But maybe if he broke them down into small steps and tried one or two at a time he could do it. It does take time, effort, and a decision. It helps to recognize the importance of using strategies and how much they will make your life better. Maybe he's doing OK and it doesn't seem worth the effort; he did make it to his granddaughters' graduations.

After I finished writing this, I had even more surprises in store from Tom. For more of the unfolding saga of Tom, see appendix 9, "Follow up".

Summary:

We ADDers can look lazy and irresponsible. That's a bad rap, although the outcome often looks the same as if were true. We are indeed unreliable, at least sometimes. This can be helped with strategies.

Section XI

People with ADD

Some people with ADD don't know they have it, some won't acknowledge it, and some won't or can't get help with it. Some are very successful in spite of it; think of Benjamin Franklin, Thomas Edison, Leonardo da Vinci, and Paul Orfalea, the founder of Kinko's, who labels himself "a hyperactive dyslexic".

Chapter 66

ADD unrecognized, unacknowledged, unhelped

Kids

Daydreaming about "what if?" is a fruitless exercise. Some of us with ADD spend a fair amount of time daydreaming. I started school early and matured late. I often wonder how I would have done athletically if I'd been with kids my own age. I was in my own age group once at summer camp and did well. But if I'd been in the appropriate grade - the grade behind me - I never would have married my wife and those grandkids would not exist. So I'm lucky it was as it was.

Sometimes I wonder what it would have been like if I'd had received some help with the ADD. No one knew about ADD back then, so that wasn't going to happen. But could someone just have noticed I was having trouble, without having to make a diagnosis? Two teachers tried to help with my handwriting, but that was it. So sometimes I wonder, but that's a waste of time. Still, I'm sensitive now to people who need help and don't get it.

For some years I worked part time for the Juvenile Court of Baltimore County. I would evaluate kids for the judge. The kids were in court for anything from chronic truancy to bank robbery and even murder. I would send for whatever records I could to help in the evaluation. Over and over the school records included evaluations these kids had already had:

- 3<u>rd</u> grade - reading at first grade level.
- 5th grade - testing: learning disabilities, visual processing impairment. Poor attention span. Discipline problem. Reading at second grade level.

- <u>7th grade</u> - four suspensions. Reading at third grade level.
- <u>8th grade</u> - Permanent suspension. In juvenile custody. Records sent to juvenile court as requested.

If the kid ever got any help, it wasn't indicated in the records; just evaluations, which had been made and just filed. The kid had been evaluated, promoted and ignored, except for when he caused disciplinary problems.

We know a lot more about ADD now. There are very effective ways to help kids with ADD and there are good approaches for adults too. I hope things are better in the schools now. But I keep reading about budget cuts: no nurses, no counselors, no art, no physical education, and maybe no help for the children? Maybe not even evaluations any more? I hope I'm wrong. ADD/ADHD are childhood problems. They do not begin in adults, they just sometimes carry over into adulthood. The kids need help.

Summary: (you may picture me ranting)

School systems sometimes seem to just be going through the motions. Today schools "teach to the tests" to protect the teachers and the systems, rather than trying to give the children an education. I'm not a fan of "No Child Left Behind", which really means "No Rich Child Left Behind". It makes things worse rather than better. (Sorry for the political insert.) We now have the knowledge to diagnose and help kids who have ADD/ADHD, if we have the will. That would, in many ways, make things better when these kids become adults.

(I wasn't really sorry.)

Adults

O wad some Pow'r the giftie gie us
To see oursels as others see us!
It wad frae mony a blunder free us,
An' foolish notion!
Robert Burns - To a Louse (On seeing one on a lady's bonnet, at church.)

I hurt for people who have ADD and don't know it, or for some reason are not getting help for it. Once I recognized that I have it, I began to find additional strategies that have greatly helped me. And I began to notice lots of other people who seemed likely candidates for the diagnosis. Each one of us is different, but those of us with ADD tend to have a lot of characteristics in common.

Some people who have ADD are not willing to acknowledge it. This has to do with shame, and with pride, especially with us males, who are not supposed to have any 'weaknesses'. Regrets could be part of it too, regrets about things we've done or not done, and even about how things might've been different if we'd had some help. If you have ADD, it sure helps to know you have it, to acknowledge it and to get help.

Harry, another friend of mine, makes lots of mistakes. He's a very nice man, very compassionate. He forgets things, things he's supposed to do. He forgets to do them. A lot. He's very agreeable. He agrees to do a lot of things. But often he doesn't do them. The things he does do, he tends to mess up on. Harry has a good sense of humor. When he has forgotten to do something, or when he messes up, he openly acknowledges it. He gives a little laugh, and says, with a nice smile, "Whoops! Messed up again." He says this a lot.

One day I offered Harry something to read on ADD. He was cordial as he declined, but he appeared slightly miffed. He pointed out his substantial academic achievements, implying that they made the possibility of ADD obviously ridiculous. That was several years ago. He is still saying, "Whoops! Messed up again." A lot.

A nephew of mine just graduated from high school. Late. Barely. He's a gifted athlete, great at every sport he tries: football, baseball, basketball, golf, bowling. He's a personable kid, though shy. But he had difficulty getting up in the mornings, and difficulty getting to school, and difficulty getting to class once he was there. And difficulty doing homework. And difficulty getting the homework to school even if he had done it. He could've done very well in athletics if he'd ever been able to keep his grades up long enough to stay eligible for a team. As I understand it, he did get an evaluation and a diagnosis, but no organized help. He tried some medication, but it gave him side effects and that was the end of it. This is third hand information; it may not be accurate. He did manage to graduate from high school, late, after a great deal of struggle. Now he's trying to find a direction.

Sometimes with a new patient I begin to consider a diagnosis of ADD right off the bat. Someone calls and makes an appointment. Then they call to ask the time of the appointment again; they either didn't write it down or they lost the slip of paper. Then they show up late –"got lost" or "couldn't get away". They forget to bring the questionnaire they had "mostly" filled out. And they can't find their check book to pay me for today. Finally, when they leave the office, their car keys or their cell phone are still sitting on the sofa in my office. By that time, I'm more than a little suspicious.

ADD tends to run in families, especially on the male side. My daughter-in-law, Queenie, read a draft of this book and said she thought her two sons, my grandsons, have ADD. I don't know. The older grandson is extremely bright. He's personable and in many ways mature for his age. He doesn't do homework. The teachers generally don't appreciate this. Yet he does well on tests. He's done well in some advanced placement courses but sometimes they drop him from the class because he doesn't do homework. He explains that he understands the material so he sees no reason to do the homework; he is a teenager, after all. His mother explains that he's so bright that he's just bored. I thought he might be just a wee bit lazy; however, he's on the wrestling team and I've seen him work his butt off in practice, so I can't say that he's lazy. I'm not clear why their mother thinks the two boys might have ADD, but from the book she thought she recognized some patterns.

Queenie also thought that my son, the boys' father, might have ADD. He and I have somewhat different views about things medical, so I wasn't too surprised when his response suggested that he doesn't believe in ADD. I personally haven't seen anything that made me think that he has it. He did have some trouble with school as a child, but when he had a good teacher he did very well.

It never occurred to me that my father or grandfather might have had ADD. Now that I think about it, I never saw my father just watching TV. He was always doing some paperwork from the store at

the same time. And he always double-checked the
door lock at the store. But I never saw him rushing around frantically looking for his keys, or being
late, or forgetting to show up. I don't think he had
ADD. His father, my grandfather, was messy, a terrible driver, had zero patience and a horrible temper.
But he didn't show any other symptoms. Maybe?

Queenie made some helpful comments about the
book. She said that these strategies could be useful
to anyone, not just people with ADD. That makes
sense: while they could be helpful to anyone, they
are essential to anyone with ADD. Certainly to me
anyway. After she read about me driving off with the
gas hose twice, and backing into guest's cars twice,
she asked whether people with ADD can learn from
experience. I believe so, although I could see where
her question came from. But after all, I only did those
things twice, so I did learn, just a little slowly. Still,
I do repeat many of my mistakes over and over, and
with some mistakes, even twice is a lot. So I made
strategies and rules for those situations. I appreciate
her help with the book and will certainly send her a
copy when it's published. And I am determined that
it will be published.

Diagnosis

Sometimes it just seems obvious that someone
has ADD; the pattern screams out the diagnosis. But
sometimes in less severe or less typical cases it's

more subtle. And some things, like anxiety or depression, can mimic ADD. Diagnosis is best done by a professional, who will look at childhood history, family history, current difficulties, and often at results of testing. They might also interview family members or others who have been close to the person, preferably for a long time. The pencil and paper tests for ADD are very helpful, but they alone cannot definitely say someone does or does not have ADD.

Some of the typical problems of ADD are not limited to people with ADD. Many people sometimes procrastinate, or sometimes lose things, and so on. But we ADDers do almost all of these things, and we do them almost all of the time; that's the difference. In those ways, our ADD lives look very similar to each other and different from non-ADDers.

Summary:

ADD/ADHD are problems of childhood. Sometimes people outgrow them, often not. If diagnosed and treated in childhood, this can make a great difference in the life of the child, and later for the adult. Adults can be diagnosed and helped also, and their life can be better. Sometimes the adult ADD diagnosis is pretty obvious; sometimes it is more subtle. Unfortunately, some people aren't getting

the help they could benefit from, because of lack of
knowledge or because of shame or other factors.

Section XII

Doing better

The good news, of course, is that if we do have ADD, there are lots of things we can do to make our life better.

Chapter 67

Four S's: Structure and scheduling, sleep, and some physical activity

These four things are important for anyone's basic healthy living, but they're especially important for those of us trying to cope with ADD.

Structure

I do best with structure in my life. What does that mean? It's not just a schedule, although a schedule is certainly structure. Structure means that my days have a shape. I don't get up in the morning at some indefinite time and wonder " What should I do now?" or "What will I do today?" I don't wander aimlessly through the day, wondering, "OK, what do I do now?" Structure gives me anchor points that help me stay oriented in time. I follow my basic routine nearly every day unless on a trip, and even then I try to keep some vestige of it.

I do best if I get up at roughly the same time every morning.

Then I:
- bring in the newspaper
- have prayer time
- eat breakfast and read the paper
- brush my teeth, take my pills, shave
- exercise, shower and dress
- work until lunch
- lunch
- work until cocktail time
- dinner
- relaxation/free time until bedtime.

Some evenings we watch a movie and some evenings I do paper work. I try to study Spanish and play the guitar every day. At bedtime I read my daily devotional and write down the things I'm thankful for from that day. I get ready for bed and then read until I'm sleepy. Then I say my prayers and go to sleep. Pretty much the same each day unless there is something else specific planned. That's the structure of the day. It's flexible; some days I go fishing or to the prison, and those days have a different structure, but they still have structure. For example, the days that I go fishing pretty much look like each other, same routines.

I believe it's healthy to eat three meals a day, though some people do well with more. With ADD, the meals are anchor points, time markers which help me know where I am in time, what's coming next, how much time I have left in the day.

There is also a structure to the week. Mondays and Thursdays are days off, and on most of those days I either go fishing (weather permitting) or volunteer at the penitentiary. Sundays I go to church and take a nap in the afternoon. Tuesday, Wednesday and Friday I see patients.

That is structure, the general shape of my life, most of the time. Following this routine helps me stay organized and to function better.

Some jobs have structure; you mostly know what you're going to do and when you're going to do it. For most of us, a job where you set your own hours and schedule your own appointments, like a traveling representative for a company, for example, won't work out well. I learned in college that I could not study at home. The new trend of working from home sounds almost impossible. There will be nothing but distractions all around. It would be hard for me to make a schedule and stick to it. So the point is to have structure, a more or less routine general shape to your days, and then have specific schedules within that as needed. Life will go better.

Schedules

Within the general structure of my life I also have some schedules. Life goes better if I stick to a schedule. This schedule isn't written in concrete and it is not a straight jacket. Things happen or opportunities arise and they need to be responded to. On days when I see patients, it's a strict schedule: I see patients at 10:30, 11:40, then lunch, then patients at 2:00, 3:10, and 4:20. So I know what's happening, and when, and I don't have to make decisions about what to do. On days when I'm not seeing patients I usually make a loose schedule for the day, what I plan to do. Schedule can be very helpful; it's one of Richard's main strategies.

Sleep

We do best if we get up at about the same time every morning and go to bed at about the same time every night, again with flexibility depending on what's happening. This keeps our internal clock on track, which is often difficult for us, and it helps us to get good sleep. Good sleep helps us with our ADD. We can focus better, organize better, and function better if we've had a good night's sleep. The amount of sleep we need varies from person to person. People with ADD don't need more sleep, it's just more important. So I do what it takes to get a good night sleep; I practice, mostly, good sleep hygiene. For me, that especially includes no caffeine after 5 PM, not even decaf coffee. When I used to drink regular coffee, I needed to have none any later than 2 PM; it stays around about eight hours. Also I have no alcohol or chocolate after 8 PM. The rest of sleep hygiene I'm putting in appendix 3; however, it is truly important.

Some physical activity

I used "some" to make it four S's, and "physical activity" sounds so much nicer than "exercise", doesn't it? But there it is, the E word. Regular exercise benefits general health, but with ADD, it also improves our functioning. It helps with focus, and with stress, irritability, impulsiveness, and mood. Coincidentally, it helps prevent Alzheimer's. We need to find exercise we enjoy, or at least that isn't a chore. We won't stick with a chore. We need to take it easy, and if we're out of shape, to start slow and gradually increase. The activity needs to be specifically for the purpose of exercising; cleaning houses all day or hauling bricks around is healthy work, but for some reason work doesn't provide all the benefits of exercise.

I record the exercise I've done each day along with my weight, which I struggle to keep down. This gives positive reinforcement, motivation and awareness. I don't watch much TV, but I record poker and football games and watch them while I treadmill. With fast forward, I can skip all the commercials and timeouts. So I actually look forward to my exercise periods, partly because it feels good and I like the treadmill, but also because I can watch the poker or football.

Why is exercise particularly good for ADD? Maybe it strengthens both the cerebellum and also the basal ganglia, a group of cells near the middle of the brain which is what goes bad in Parkinson's disease, and like the cerebellum, is related to movement and has been implicated in ADD.

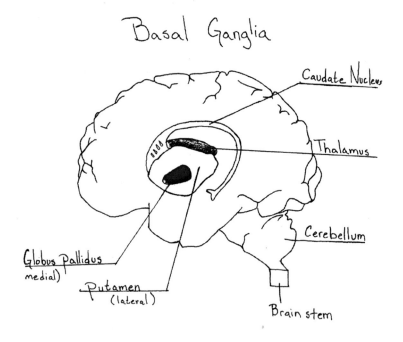

Basal Ganglia

Caudate Nucleus

Thalamus

Cerebellum

Globus Pallidus
medial)

Putamen
(lateral)

Brain stem

Illustration 12. The basal ganglia. Mid line section of the brain.

Maybe exercise improves the basal ganglia.

Meditation (see appendix 6) and probably Yoga are helpful for ADD, as may be massage, acupuncture and Tai Chi, but I haven't read any good evidence for those.

Summary:

Exercise is one part of treatment for ADD. There are strategies to make it easier to keep up with the physical activity. So, we have the four S's: structure and schedule, sleep, and some physical activity. These foster healthy living but specifically they help us ADDers to focus and to function better. Using these four S's provides a foundation on which to build the strategies, rules and habits. Meditation and yoga can also help.

Chapter 68

Mindfulness and awareness

The concepts of mindfulness and awareness are currently fad topics. I think they are centuries old Buddhist concepts. A mentor recently tried to explain them to me; it's a little confusing though.

Mindfulness

Mindfulness is the act of focusing attention on what's going on: "What am I feeling right now? What am I thinking right now? What am I doing right now? What is happening around me right now?" Awareness is the result of mindfulness; we become aware of what's going on, in and around us. We have the answers to those mindfulness questions: "Right now I'm aware that I'm feeling uncertain that I have explained these concepts correctly."

Mindfulness includes a nonjudgmental attitude; you don't judge what you become aware of. You don't label it good or bad. You don't try to change it. You just be aware of it and let it be. It is as it is.

Mindfulness is quite different from being preoccupied with one thing and oblivious to everything else, which of course is what we do when we hyperfocus. De Mello, the Buddhist Jesuit, says that most of us are sleepwalking most of the time; we're not paying attention to what is really going on, we are not aware.

Mindfulness and awareness can help with ADD:

"What am I doing right now? How does this foster my long term goals? Am I doing what I intended to be doing or need to be doing right now? Is this the best use of my time right now?"

Awareness

So it's good to be aware of what we're doing. Sometimes what we're doing is taking a break, or it might be goofing-off. There's a difference: a break is something I'm intentionally doing, maybe goofing off on purpose, and it may be the best use of my time right now, because I need a break. That's different from goofing-off goofing-off. That's when what I'm doing is a distraction that led me astray, or is helping me avoid doing something else. I'm doing something that's not in my schedule and that I didn't intend to do. The goofing-off took over, instead of my being in charge and taking a break because I decided to. So I want to be aware of this.

There are programs for awareness. One is to pause at every hour on the hour and practice awareness. That just means stopping what we're doing and asking the mindfulness questions. Notice what is going on right now. This can take about thirty seconds, maybe less. It's a very useful practice. Personally, I do it once or twice a day; I could improve on that. One book, <u>10 Simple Solutions to Adult ADD</u> by Sarkis has a good section on using timers, like kitchen timers or a wrist watch or cell phone with an alarm. Set it to sound every hour and practice awareness.

The timer can also be used for other things: "I'm going to watch TV for half an hour and then get back to work." Good intentions, but maybe we need a timer. The timer can help whenever we need to be sure that we don't get lost in the TV, or on the computer, or whatever. We can set it to ring every hour so we can pause and practice awareness. Or we can use other things to remind us; after every telephone call, or every bathroom break, or any recurrent thing. This is using anchors, which is discussed in the next chapter. I find practicing awareness twice a day is enough to be useful, although more often would be better

Summary:
Mindfulness, paying attention to what's going on and to the situation, is not our strongpoint.

Awareness can be practiced and helps us stay on track and not get lost, diverted, or distracted. We can get better at it. We can use alarms or other cues or anchors to help us practice awareness.

Chapter 69

Memory aids

I have many different kinds of memory aids. That suggests that memory is a real problem for me. It sure would be if I didn't have the aids.

Anchors

Anchors are cues in our daily life that remind us to do something that we want to do routinely, so that we're not relying on our memory to get it done. They could be called triggers, as they trigger us to do the thing. They could be called signals or reminders, but I like 'anchors'. They anchor the thing to do to the spot or situation that's the reminder.

There are some strange exercises that I need to remember to do. They involve moving my pelvis and my jaw. Don't ask me to explain. Fortunately, they can be done in the car, even while driving. One of the main streets in Santa Fe is St Michael's, which I'm on at least five times a week. So I've made that street the anchor for my pelvis-jaw exercises. Every time I'm on St Michaels I remember, "Oh, yeah, I need to do my exercises." So they get done.

Anchors support my spiritual life: I made stirring my coffee the anchor for remembering Jesus; every time I go to the bathroom, that's my anchor for saying the prayer of St. Francis.

Some of my patients have trouble remembering to take their pills. But they all brush their teeth at least once a day, or so they say. Most of us don't have to remember to brush our teeth or decide whether we will or won't; we just do it automatically. So I suggest that they put their pills next to their toothbrush, and use tooth brushing as an anchor.

There's a window at the end of the long hall from my office to the rest of the house, so every time I leave my office and walk down the hall I'm looking outside. In the original house plans, that would've been a blank wall but my wife came up with the idea of putting a window there. I call it the Martha Memorial Window. Every time I walk down the hall I look out that window and remember how much I appreciate my wife. The window is a good anchor for me.

So what things do you need to do repeatedly that you could use an anchor for? If you need to check your blood sugar, you might use eating as an anchor. If you need to review your appointment book, you might use the bathroom anchor. Other possible anchors could be talking on the phone, getting in the car, putting your shoes on or taking them off, stopping at a red light. You just tie the thing you want to remember to do to the anchor. It becomes a habit.

Other memory aids

I have many different memory aids.

I use mnemonics. I use cards for to-do lists, and the blue cards for information that I might need but don't need to remember. I use the envelopes to make working to-do lists and I also use them to make notes about things I want to remember, or learn, or keep handy: Spanish vocabulary or grammar, stocks to check on, or information that I've just gotten off the internet. I also have two white boards and five calendars in my office. And remember my rhinoceros doll?

Sticky Notes is a free computer program that makes little yellow notes that I can bring up on my computer desktop. All kinds of information and reminders on the notes: which keys print Spanish letters on my computer and other keyboard shortcuts, principles to remember, frequently used phone numbers. I can bring up all the 'stickys' at once or any one that I want.

I wear a black wrist band, to remind me to pray before everything I do. I carry a card in the back of my appointment book, with principles to remember:

- "With God, all things are possible"
- "Is this the best use of my time?"
- "Beware of assumptions and expectations."
- "Focus on one thing/over learn."
- "What am I avoiding?"

Right now there are nineteen principles on the card. I'm working on learning to review that card daily, like when I'm waiting in line, or waiting for the computer to boot, or whatever. So far I only review it about once a week. It's always helpful. In a way, it's like having a good grandmother or good uncle who's coaching me about important things I need to know and remember. Another memory aid.

I have trouble remembering names, although I'm good at remembering faces. So when I meet someone:

"Hello, Sally. Nice to meet you, Sally. And Sally, where are you from?" I try to be sure to say their name at least three times right off the bat. This helps, some.

There's lots of other tricks that people use to help with memory. The internet is full of them. Remember to use your memory aids, because you can't rely on your memory. Remember?

Mnemonics

Mnemonics are a powerful memory aid that I like a lot. It helps if the mnemonic has something catchy or clever in it to make it easier to remember. I use YALPA and LEQBLF, which happen to also be acronyms. Somehow I find them easy to remember, although they're not catchy or clever. I want to remind myself daily that I'm young, aware, loving, prioritizing and assertive, YALPA. When a situation comes up, this mnemonic helps me to remember that I need to be and can be assertive, because I tend to avoid conflict. I want to remember, especially while doing therapy, that I listen, have empathy, and ask questions. I want to notice beauty, be loving, and be fearless (like assertive), LEQBLF. Sometimes when I'm momentarily down I can remember the B and notice something beautiful around me instead of focusing on the grim or the negative.

I may need to explain the "young" part.

A few years ago, I was feeling old. I thought of myself as old. I noticed that I was walking kind of hunched over and that I would groan whenever I stood up or sat down. When I became aware of all this, I asked myself, "Why? What benefit am I getting from this?"

I couldn't think of any benefit, so I decided to stop it. I straightened up, stopped groaning, and decided to think of myself as young. I noted that many of our presidents have been in their seventies and many CEO's are too. I am actually in the prime of life, at the top of my form. This change has made me feel better and gives me more energy. It's easier to get things done.

This used to be called, "The Power of Positive Thinking." Now we call it the importance of perception and of attitude. The new age folks say that we create our own reality.

So, YALPA, "Young!" Works for me.

My favorite mnemonic I learned in medical school, where mnemonics are very popular because there's so much to memorize. The bones of the wrist:

"Never lower Tillie's pants, Grandma might come home."

Navicular, lunate, triangulate, pisiform, greater and lesser multangular, capitate, and hamate.

Who could remember that?

Then there's the twelve cranial nerves, coming from inside the skull:

"On old Olympus' towering tops, a fat assed German vended some hops."

Olfactory, optic, oculomotor, trochlear, trigeminal, abducens, facial, auditory, glossopharyngeal, vagus, spinal accessory, hypoglossal.

How old do you think that is? It must've been passed down by generations of medical students.

Another mnemonic I like uses a different concept and is very clever and creative:

"How I want a drink, alcoholic of course, after the heavy lectures involving quantum mechanics."

That gives you the value of pi to fifteen places, if you count the number of letters in each word. 3.14158265357969. Neat!

What do you need to remember? Even if you're not a student, if you need to memorize something, you can make a mnemonic, something catchy and memorable. If there are principles that you want to apply in your life, or if you're working on making a new habit, then a mnemonic can really help.

In other words-

Memory never evokes misery, only new interesting connections.

Get it?

It's a mnemonic, for remembering "mnemonic".
Memory Never Evokes Misery, Only New Interesting Connotations.
i.e. MNEMONIC.
Oh, well; never mind.

Reminders

Every Thursday night my wife writes "garbage" on a red sticky and puts it on the microwave, so I'll take the garbage out on Friday morning. Richard puts his reminder notes like that on the coffee pot or his computer. A reminder note will only work if it's new, out of place, and preferably brightly colored. Otherwise, in a few days you won't see it anymore. Since the red sticky is clearly out of place on the microwave door, and is only there once a week, I don't become used to it. So I can see it and the method works. My wife, who doesn't have ADD, has no trouble remembering to put up the sticky.

When Richard had a secretary, she had a folder for each month. If something came up that would need attention in the future, she would file it in the appropriate month. Then at the beginning of each month they would review that file together. Richard doesn't do this anymore; if something's important he just puts it on his calendar. But he says he's thinking of using a file like that again.

Summary:

We need more than to-do lists; with ADD, we can use all the help with memory we can get. There are many types of memory aids and tricks. I use anchors, cards, mnemonics, and stickys. And my wife helps me.

Chapter 70

Moderation

"All things in moderation."
----- *including moderation?*

Sometimes it's hard for me to get myself to do something. I forget. I procrastinate. Sometimes I suddenly realize that I've stopped doing something that was being helpful; I'm just forgetting to do it. For example, I read a paragraph in my little blue inspirational book almost every time I go in or out of my office, which is the anchor for that. This helps me keep focused and to stay in a positive attitude and in the spiritual mode I want to be in. But I notice that lately I've been forgetting to do it. Also, I forget to check my avoiding card to see what I'm avoiding. Well, you get the idea. That's enough, I'm starting to get in a down mood just writing this. But the point here isn't just about not doing, it's also about overdoing. Once I do get doing, I also have an overdoing problem.

Moderation is not a word that's really in our vocabulary. We procrastinate and avoid, so we tend to not do anything. However, once we're into something, we tend to overdo it.

I like to exercise. I was very proud of myself when I got up to two-hundred reps with twenty pound dumbbells. Then I moved up to twenty-five pounds. I try to exercise every day; if I set that as my goal, I'll generally manage to get in five days in a week. I'm afraid that if I don't aim at every day I'll wind up not doing it at all. Each day it'll be too easy to say, "Oh, well, not today." So now every day (almost) I'm doing the twenty-five pound dumbbells and pushing myself to get back up to two hundred reps. The result is that I tear up my shoulder and have to give up the weights altogether for a while.

But I'm very pleased with how I'm doing on the treadmill. I'm doing over two miles in around thirty minutes, every day (almost); my goal is three miles in forty-five minutes. Of course, this overdoing it gives me plantar fasciitis (very painful irritation in the instep of the foot) and I have to give up the treadmill for a while too.

After time out for healing I've been able to start exercising again. Right now I'm using the smaller twenty pound weights and only twenty minutes on the treadmill and now I alternate days between them. I have reset my goals, lower. Moderation.

When we find something new that interests us, or that's a challenge, then our focus center is turned on, really turned on. A friend takes me out biking and loans me his spare bike. Then I'm really into biking, for maybe a month and a half, or maybe even two. Buy all the equipment. Two year subscription to American Biker. $500 racing bike, special shoes, outfit, gloves, helmet. Then my interest is grabbed by something else and the biking stuff goes in the closet, where it joins the bowling stuff I put in there a couple of months ago. (This is just an example, and the only thing in the book that isn't factual. I never got into biking.)

When we do something, we don't do it half way - well, that isn't true. We often do it half way, because we know it isn't going to turn out anyway and because we have trouble finishing. So we do a lot of things half way. What I meant to say is that we don't get into things half way. When we get into them, and our focus center is turned on, we really get into them – full- bore, nothing but the best - for a while. Not, I repeat, not, in moderation. Not let's try it for a while at a lower level and see how we like it. Not let's rent or borrow some equipment and check this out. Not in moderation.

My daughter in law asks, "Can you learn from experience?" Yes, it's possible. By now I recognize this pattern of great enthusiasm at the beginning and overdoing. My wife recognizes it too, and will say a word of caution, which I sometimes am wise enough to pay attention to. On the other hand, I recently bought a set of CD's from The Teaching Company. They have great college lecture courses on a variety of interesting topics. I listen to the CDs in my car. The first course was fantastic. I bought some more. Now I've bought six of these courses in the past two months, which is over a year's worth. I will not buy anymore until I finish these. I will not!

A few years ago, my neck was hurting. A massage therapist showed me some stretches. I started doing them and they helped. So I did them more often and more intensely. If I'd been stretching my neck to the right a little, I started stretching it <u>way</u> to the right. And so on. Gradually my neck got worse again. It took me months to realize that the stretching was making my neck worse - not actually the stretching, but the overstretching. But if I'm doing something, I usually don't do it in moderation.

Balance

I need to work some and to relax some. I need to be careful about what I eat but not go on some extreme diet. I need to keep working on this book, but also to keep up with the other things in my life. Balance is one of the basic concepts of mental health; not too much nor too little, not all work nor all play. Not all one thing and none of the other. Stay in balance.

Summary:
> *Too much is not enough.*
> *Old Texas saying.*

With ADD, we tend either to not do at all or to overdo, another trap. Too much or too many. We can be aware of that pattern, and learn to put the brakes on. Moderation and balance.

Chapter 71

The paradox

All of this is very good information, but so far I have been avoiding a difficult topic: The Paradox.

The paradox is this: most of these strategies involve some willpower. Set a rule, stick to it. When you mess up just keep trying; don't give up. Willpower. And willpower is something we have in short supply. That's not entirely accurate though. Part of my prison ministry involves bringing in home-made cookies for a multi-day program. This is a very powerful tool in the ministry. The inmates realize that there are people who still care about them, plus, they really like the cookies, especially chocolate chip. So for days I'm surrounded by homemade cookies, and by people eating homemade cookies. Mostly chocolate chip. Lots of them.

I know that I can't eat just one cookie. This has been well-proven. I can't keep a balance, can't eat them in moderation. So I don't let myself eat any.

No cookies. I don't get started. So I lack the will-power to eat just one cookie, but on the other hand I do have the willpower to keep myself from starting with the first one.

I'm not sure whether lack of willpower is a basic part of ADD or not. If my friend Tom can't finish a project, is that lack of willpower, or is it because once we master something it loses novelty and chal-lenge and we can't keep our focus center on and we can't finish it? When I made the rule of keys always on the front table, at first I had lots of slips. Sometimes I'd just forget, but other times I'd find it inconvenient. I'd say, "Oh, just this one time won't matter." Is that lack of willpower, or laziness, or just ADD? I did have the willpower to stick with the rule and not give up, even when I messed up. So eventually the rule did become habit. Realizing how much my life improved from just this one strategy is a powerful reinforcer. Knowing that if I don't try to follow the rule every time it won't become a habit motivates me, too. And once it's habit, then it doesn't involve much willpower anymore.

I still have trouble keeping the red card list down to five. It's always easy to pull out the red card and jot something down that properly would have gone on the orange card. But the orange card has so many things on it that I don't trust it. I'm afraid that I'll never get to it. Maybe I need to make a rule that there can only be ten things on the orange card list? Anyway, I have trouble keeping the red card list to five. Is that lack of willpower?

And what if these things do turn out to be due to lack of willpower? That sounds like a moral weakness, a character flaw:

- "Doug, you have terrible handwriting!"
- "Yes, M'am, I know."
- "Doug, you lack willpower!"
- "Yes, M'am, I know."

I didn't ask to have terrible handwriting or lack of willpower, so is it my fault? No one ever told me how to get more willpower. If I started every day with an icy cold shower, would that somehow help develop willpower? Maybe if I fasted one day a week that would somehow help with willpower? Those approaches don't sound very promising to me. I'm not willing to try them unless I have some reason to believe they'd actually work. Recent research has shown that we each have a certain amount of willpower, and if we use a lot of it on one thing, we will have less available for the next thing. That sounds discouraging. As I write this though, I realize that while I pray for a lot of things, I haven't been praying for more willpower. That might be worth trying. Like asking for a miracle?

On the internet I have read opinions that we ADDers do have willpower, we just need to learn how to turn it on, like turning on our focus center. So guess what, we need strategies. The tricks for making something interesting to ourselves, using rewards, and positive self- talk are all ways to help us turn on the focus center and the willpower.

Summary:

I'm left with the paradox and the question: Is part of the problem a lack of willpower? If so, how much of the problem is due to that? Clearly, some willpower is required to make and follow the rules. I hope that we have some or can find it somewhere. Making habits requires some willpower, but once we have the habit, little willpower is needed. Strategies can partly make up for the willpower deficit. I do best with strategies that require minimal willpower.

Conclusion

Well, you've gotten the message by now and it's true:

Your Life Can Be Better!

I hope you've found some things that click for you and that you want to try. I'm not trying to tell you what to do with your socks at night, nor your blueberries in the morning, or even with your keys. I want you to have the concept that if something is a problem for you, is causing you frustration, you can do something about it. The heart of the approach is the principle: identify a problem, make a strategy, make a rule, make a habit.

Then there are tools that will help you deal with ADD : appointment books and to do lists, red flags, slogans, memory aids, structure.

I hope you're not feeling overwhelmed with all the information and concepts. Just take one or two things that sound good to you and work on those.

Just one will make a difference. Later you can do others. Small steps.

I hope you're not feeling discouraged, because these things do work. And remember also that there are some positives to having ADD.

Finally, let's give a tribute to our significant others, the ones that put up with us and try to help us. We thank them for being our allies, who understand the ADD and are willing to work with us to help us cope with it. As you work and make your life better, it's going to make theirs better too.

Good luck.

THE END

APPENDICES

There's a lot of appendices here; you might take a look at them and see which ones would interest you. If you have managed to finish the book you get a gold medal just for that.

Appendix 1. Studying

Part 1 goes into more detail about some great strategies for making your studying more effective. Part 2 discusses the heart of studying, the technique for learning. Appendix 2 is fascinating, whether you're a student or not, because it discusses the forgetting curve. Then it gives the forgetting curve system, which is the power system for studying and learning, learning anything!

How to study- Part 1: manage ADD

How can you manage ADD so that you can study effectively? If you're truly interested in the topic you're studying, great. You probably won't have much trouble, if you know how to study. Here are some standard study helps, whether you have ADD or not:

1. Find a "kindergarten" book on the subject. Go through a very simple version before the course starts. Then it will be easier to learn the more complicated material. I learned to do this for any course, whether I was interested in it or not. The "For Dummies" books, Cliff notes, a junior high text, can be useful for this, or the internet.
2. Make sure you have the right setting to study. Do you do best with quiet or with stimulation? Maybe you need music or even the TV.
3. Take reasonable breaks. Few people can study effectively for more than an hour at a time without a break.
4. You will get more out of lectures if you skim the relevant textbook chapter and/or read the kindergarten book section before each lecture.

Depending on the subject, you may need some of these strategies:
1. Use mind games to turn on your focus center. For example:
    *   Try to outguess the professor. What are the test questions going to be?

- Pick someone in the class to compete with. Make up your mind that you're going to get a better grade than Joe.
- Imagine that you're trying out to become an astronaut. You've passed every trial except this final test.
- Make a point of being sure that you really thoroughly totally know the material, have over-learned it, even if it's not interesting. You can make it a challenge.

2. If you're really short of time, pick some sections to just skip. Maybe you kind of know the material, or maybe it just doesn't look important enough to be on the test, or maybe it looks so complicated that it would take too much time to learn it. You don't have to make an A.

3. You can study with someone else. Ask them to call you back when you're wandering off track.

4. Pick the least uninteresting small aspect of the subject. Become an expert on that. Do extra reading and know more about that than anyone else in the class.

These are some ways to work with ADD to get the learning done. Most of them are good study techniques whether you have ADD or not. You might already know some others. You need to find the things that work for you.

How to study - part 2   Own the information

If you're taking notes, glance through them later the same day, to make sure that everything is legible and clear to you. This also orients you to what you're going to learn. You see, it's about learning, not about studying. We study in order to learn. I didn't know that. I thought I just had to study and pass the test and that was enough.

If you're studying a book, first turn to the end of the chapter. Read any summary or questions. Then go through the chapter and look at the headings and subheadings. If there are none then just skim the chapter quickly. You want to get a picture in your mind of what you're going to be learning and of the structure of the chapter.

If you're studying from the computer, the same principles will apply. You can highlight and save. You will need some scratch paper, but maybe you could open another file to use as "scratch paper."

Now you're ready to learn. From here on it's the same whether it's a book or your notes. Read the material and as you read, underline one to three points on the page that seem the most important. In most books, each paragraph contains a theme or summary sentence and the rest is expansion or explanation. Look for those sentences. Also, try to guess what on that page a reasonable professor might ask on a test.

Do the first page. Close the book and from memory write down the three most important points from that page on scratch paper. You don't need to be neat or use complete sentences; just scribble the points in a couple of words. Write just enough to show you that you have the idea. When you can do this for the first page, go on to the second page and repeat the process. When you have finished a few pages, close the book and scribble down the main ideas or points so far. If you can't, start over. If you can, then go on and work your way through the chapter. At the end of the chapter, close the book and scribble down the most important points of the entire chapter. This will be much more than two or three points and it might take you a whole page of scratch paper. If you can't remember all the points, go back and review and try again. Do this until you can reproduce the whole chapter from your memory. Then you have studied the chapter and you have learned it, for the moment. This same technique applies to notes, lists or illustrations that you need to memorize. You need to be able to reproduce them from your memory.

Next, when you find yourself with some empty time, review the chapter in your head; you need to be able to reproduce the chapter from your memory. You can do this while you're in the car or waiting for something. Depending on where you are, you can scribble it down or just do it in your head. If you can't get it all, then review whatever you need to.

The summer before medical school, I was taking two biology courses. The drive to college took a half-hour. I'd leave a little early before a test and review everything in my head on the way. Then if there was anything I couldn't remember, I had a few minutes to review it before the test. I remember reproducing in my head the picture of the brachial plexus, a very complicated network of nerves in the shoulder. I did very well on those tests. So at that point I did know something about studying properly, although I didn't understand what I was doing. It just happened because of the situation, that half-hour drive.

Studying and learning means that you need to be able to reproduce the material from your memory. You start with small chunks of information at a time until you have it all. This is the same way to learn to play a song on the guitar.

If there is a lecture, most teachers will somehow emphasize what they think is important. Many of the test questions will come from that. While reading a book, you can see what would be good test questions; you can probably guess some of the actual test questions. Then you'll be set on those, but somehow this kind of guessing helps even for the questions that you hadn't anticipated. Trying to outguess the teacher provides a challenge, and that turns our focus center on. So does the challenge of reproducing the ideas on paper or in our head.

With this method of study, and especially if you use the forgetting curve system, you aren't just studying for the test. You're learning, which is different.

Appendix 2.
The forgetting curve system

The forgetting curve was a wonderful discovery for me and the system I developed to use it was very effective. When I worked in the student counseling center at the medical school, I taught this system to a number of medical students. The feedback I received was mixed. About a third of the students said that this system is hard but they found it helpful. About a third said, "This is fantastic! It is so great! I wish I had known about it years ago." The last third was like, "Well, thank you, Dr. Puryear, but obviously you don't know anything about what it's like to be in medical school." They were referring to how much time this approach takes. It does take time in the short run, but it saves time in the long run. That's because you're actually learning the material as you go. You've put it into your long term memory banks. Otherwise, you're cramming at the last minute and regurgitating it on the test from your short term memory. Then it's gone. But once you truly learn it, you don't have to do much studying for the midterm or the final. You just brush over the material and see if you have any weak spots to bone up on. You own the knowledge. Even after the course is over you still have the information. We assume that some of it will be useful information in the future striving towards your goals. At the least you will pass the tests.

So---

The forgetting curve.

This comes from an experiment performed in 1885! Let's reproduce the experiment with you as one of the subjects. You memorize a list of nonsense syllables. Let's say it takes half an hour to learn them to the point where you can recall them perfectly. Then you start forgetting. The scientist plots a curve of your percent recall vs. time. The curve slopes up as you're learning and it reaches a peak at 100% recall. Then the curve slopes down as you start forgetting with time.

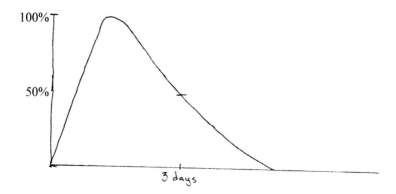

Illustration 13. The forgetting curve
At day 3 you still know 50 percent.

Everybody is different, but for most people the point where you only remember 50 percent of the syllables is at about three days. At that point you learn the syllables again. Two things happen: first, it will take you much less time to relearn them to 100 percent. Let's say ten minutes. Second, the forgetting curve begins to level off; you remember more syllables much longer.

This time, after learning them the second time, you'll still remember about 50 percent seven days later, ten days after the first learning. At that point you learn them a third time. The results are similar. You relearn the syllables much faster, say five minutes, and the curve flattens out even more. At six months you still know 80 percent of the syllables! Then you will lose any more only very slowly. If

you haven't actually been using the material, you
might still know 70 percent at a year.

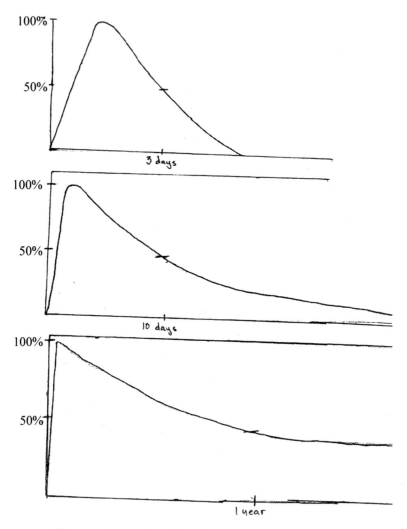

Illustration 14. The forgetting curve
Learn it completely at 0, 3, and 10 days]

The fabulous forgetting curve system

So here's the system:

Today, learn your new material. Then relearn the material from three days ago and from ten days ago. For each day's material make sure you can scribble down the points on scratch paper without referring to the book or notes. In our experiment, that took you half an hour for the new material plus ten minutes plus five minutes; total, forty-five minutes. When you are actually applying this system it can take longer, because you need to do the reading, but you are not just reading and underlining, as I used to do, you are learning each page as you go.

Again, each day you learn today's material, the material from three days ago, and the material from ten days ago. You really learn it. Seeing that you really know it is part of the positive reinforcement that helps make this system work. The challenge of actually learning it and of trying to outguess the professor helps keep the focus center turned on. That is important, because this system does require time and concentration and self-discipline and we with ADD are in short supply of all three of those, unless we have strategies.

Appendix 3. Sleep

Sleep hygiene

Getting good sleep makes a real difference in ADD. The paradox is that it's best if you don't worry about sleep, since in fact being concerned about not sleeping is a major cause of poor sleeping. If you miss a night's sleep, it's not such a big deal. You'll still be able to function that day and the next night you'll probably sleep fine because your body will try to catch up. Still, it's better to get a good night's sleep every night.

The rules for good sleep hygiene will help you sleep well. Most people, though, don't want rules for sleep hygiene; they want to just take a pill and not worry about it. The problems with sleeping pills are tolerance, habituation, and side effects, as well as possible addiction and abuse.

Most of the sleeping pills lose their effectiveness over time as tolerance builds up. This is tolerance. But then you're stuck still needing them even though they're not helping anymore, because if you stop them abruptly your sleep will get even worse. This is habituation, which is like addiction although not nearly as bad. Many of the sleeping medications pile up in your body over time and gradually cause you side effects, such as poor memory (we sure don't need that), poor coordination with a risk of car accidents or falling, poor concentration, and sometimes grogginess. These are especially significant problems in the "elderly", meaning anyone older than me. If the only side effect is grogginess or morning hangover, that usually can be taken care of by taking a lower dose and taking the pill earlier in the evening. If you use good sleep hygiene, you probably won't need medications. If you still need them then you won't need to use as much.

Rules for good sleep hygiene:

1. If you aren't asleep in twenty minutes, get up. Do something relaxing or boring. Watch TV, use the computer, read, or listen to music; just don't get into anything stimulating. Stay up until you feel drowsy and then go back to bed. If you don't go to sleep in about twenty minutes, get up again. There's nothing more tortuous and more guaranteed to keep you awake than lying in bed, tossing and turning, and TRYING TO GO TO SLEEP. That's not only guaranteed to keep you awake, but it also trains your brain that the bed is a place of tortured awakeness rather than a place of sleep. As your brain becomes trained to that, it gets increasingly difficult to sleep. Get up, do something quiet and relaxing until you're drowsy, and then go back to bed.

2. Use the bed only for sleeping or sex: not for reading, TV, playing games on the computer or for anything else. Again, your brain is becoming con-

ditioned and you want it to associate the bed with sleep.

3. Your sleep will be better, as will your life in general, if you have the structure of a pretty regular bedtime and a pretty regular getting up time.

4. Avoid caffeine the last eight hours before bedtime, alcohol the last three, and heavy meals, spicy foods and exercise late in the evening. Note that caffeine is found in coffee, tea, sodas and colas, diet pills, and chocolate. Be aware of any medications you're taking and their potential side effects.

5. Avoid naps. For most people who have a sleeping problem a nap in the day will make it harder to get sleep that night. If you do nap, put a short time limit on it.

6. Have a comfortable cool quiet dark place to sleep.

7. If you're having pain at night, take something for that well before bedtime: medication, hot soaks or whatever helps, except alcohol.

8. Have a pre-bedtime routine and use it every night before bed. This is a time for quieting down and the routine tells your brain that it's time to get ready to sleep.

Appendix 4. Medications

In naming medications I use the generic name, and where appropriate, give the brand name in parentheses. The generics are usually much cheaper; prices of some of the brand names are obscene. The generics usually work as well, and usually at the same dose, as the brand name, but not always. Occasionally the generic medications from two different companies are not the same.

Medications for sleep

I'm not a fan of sleep medications. They can cause problems and some of them are really bad. If you practice good sleep hygiene, medications are often not necessary. If someone really needs sleeping pills, it is best to just take them occasionally, on bad nights. This avoids the problems of tolerance, habituation, addiction, and the side effects from their gradually building up in the body. People who take them every night usually have psychological and maybe physical habituation; the pills often aren't truly helping with sleep but it's hard to get off of them. If the person would wean themself off, they might sleep just as well, or as poorly, without them as they do with them. This is another hard sell, though.

If someone is going to use a sleeping pill every night, it is much better if every fourth night they use a different type than usual, to reduce the problems. A better alternative is to take nothing every fourth night and just calmly accept they may not sleep much that night.

There are times when sleeping pills are necessary. I won't go into great detail, but here are the highlights:

trazadone (Desyrel)- an old antidepressant that is very sedating to most people, works pretty well as a sleeping pill, is not addictive and doesn't cause most of the other sleeping pill problems.

zolpidem (Ambien) - a sleeping pill, advertised as not causing addiction or habituation. Pretty effective for most people. It does have a few possible side effects and some people can't use it because of them. Even though it's said not to build up tolerance, I recommend that people skip it about every fourth night and use something else that night if they need to. Ambien is obscenely expensive but you can buy the generic.

zaleplon (Sonata) - like a short term Ambien, which you can take if you only have trouble falling asleep or if you wake up in the middle of the night and can't fall back to sleep. It only lasts a few hours and is also reported not to cause many problems.

antihistamines - like benadryl, or Tylenol PM, etc. For some people, these work pretty well for a while, but they tend to build up tolerance pretty fast.

Long term they can cause problems. I recommend them only for occasional use.

lorazapam (Ativan)- a benzodiazepine, a class of tranquilizers. It has the problems of the tranquilizers and sleeping pills. I recommend it only as a last resort or sometimes for the fourth night if you're skipping Ambien. It is not good to take it every night as it will build up tolerance and habituation and does have a risk, although low, of addiction.

Others - most other sleeping pills are bad and should be avoided; there probably are some exceptions though.

To be avoided at all times and for any condition and without exception is alprazolam (Xanax). This is a benzodiazepine, like lorazapam and a host of others in the benzodiazepine family (almost all of which end in "am" in the generic name). All of them are more or less the same, except for Xanax, which is quite effective, but no more so than the others, and which is extremely and severely addictive. With all the other benzodiazepines, in order to get into serious trouble you have to abuse them and for a long time. With Xanax, you can get into serious trouble from addiction and from withdrawal, even if you only use them for a short time and exactly the way the doctor ordered. I have seen many casualties from alprazolam (Xanax), and I strongly recommend that you avoid it altogether.

Medications for ADD

The book probably needs to have something about these medications, although it's basically about strategies. William W. Dodson, MD, in his article "Real-World Office Management of ADHD in Adults", Psychiatric Times, Nov. 2006, says that the real purpose of the medications is to help us focus enough that we will be able to use the strategies. That may overstate it a bit, but I agree that the strategies are the important thing. I will give you some of my ideas about these medications, but if you want to know more about them, try the other books.

atomoxetine (Straterra) - an antidepressant that is marketed as an ADD medication. Research show that it works. So does buproprion (Wellbutrin) and perhaps some of the other antidepressants which work on norepinephrine. I don't know how or why Strattera is any different from the other antidepressants. I've never prescribed it and I don't have much faith in it. It would be worth trying for someone who has a history of substance abuse where I wouldn't want to prescribe Ritalin or for someone who wanted to try something "gentler".

methylphenidate (Ritalin) - this is what I prescribe for my patients. It usually works. Sometimes we have to reach high doses to get a good effect. One of the nice things about Ritalin is that you can tell pretty quickly, in a day or two, if it's going to help or not, although you might need to try a higher dose. Another nice thing is that you can take it just when you want to use it; you don't have to stay on it daily for it to work. It can cause stomach upset, weight loss, jitteriness, and insomnia, but usually it doesn't at the right dose when taken properly. The brand name is very expensive; the generic form is cheap. However, some people do better with the extended release form which costs more. A few people genuinely do better with the brand name than the generic, if they can afford it. Most of my ADD patients who use it are on plain generic and it works fine.

dexmethylphenidate (Focalin) - this is similar to Ritalin but supposed to work a little better. It's very expensive and I rarely prescribe it. I haven't seen much written about it lately and actually don't know much about it.

Adderal and other amphetamines – these can be very helpful, especially if the Ritalin didn't work well enough. I don't prescribe them, for no very rational reason. If a patient needs these, I refer them to a colleague who is expert in ADD and in these medications. I don't prescribe amphetamines myself because I find them a little scary and because I have no experience with them since I don't prescribe them. In other words, I don't prescribe them because I have no experience with them because I don't prescribe them because I have no experience with them because--. There is nothing wrong with them.

With all of these ADD medications, you and your doctor need to be careful if you have any heart problems, high blood pressure, or other medical problems. Your doctor should ask you and should know all about this.

Appendix 5. Relaxation

Relaxation techniques

These are good when you're feeling tense, over-whelmed, anxious, stressed, or having insomnia:
1. Three deep breaths
   - Take a deep breath, as deep as you can, hold it as long as it's comfortable, and then s l o o o o o w l y let it out.
   - Repeat.
   - Repeat a third time.

Don't do this more then three times in a row or it can throw your blood chemistry off. If you want, you can repeat it in about three minutes. Most people find this very relaxing.

2. alternate nostril
   - Push your right nostril closed with your finger and breathe in normally through your left nostril.
   - Close your left nostril and breathe out normally through your right nostril.
   - Breathe in through your right nostril.
   - Close right nostril, out through left.
   - In through your left nostril.
   - Out through right.
   - And so on, for as long as you wish.

Now you can try this without using your finger at all; although it's anatomically impossible, I believe that I can do it.

3. Muscle Tensing.
   - Tense the muscles in your feet as tightly as you can, hold it a brief time (six seconds?), and let them slowly relax, paying close attention to the feeling of the relaxing muscles. Now your lower legs. Then thighs. Butt. Lower back and abdomen. Fists. Upper arms. Upper back, chest and shoulders. Neck. Face - clench everything as tight as you can, hold, slowly let go. Focus on the feeling of the relaxing muscles. That's it. You can repeat it

if you wish. This is particularly helpful for sleep.

4. Laugh
   • That's it. Just laugh. Try it. It can really change your mood, state of mind, and tension.

Find out which one or ones of these techniques work best for you and practice them. You can use them anywhere, especially the three deep breaths, which no one will notice. With practice, you'll get better at them and they will be more effective.

Appendix 6.   Meditation

Meditation – a different method?
Meditation is helpful for ADD, as well as for general health. I meditate every morning. I'm no good at it; it seems quite incompatible with ADD. I don't try to empty my mind; that seems impossible. I've learned to just notice my thoughts but let them pass through without getting involved in them. This is described as "The train comes into the station but you don't have to get on board." When I see that I've become involved in my thoughts, I say my mantra, "Shalom", and return to the meditating state. As I

said, I'm not good at this; I can meditate for about ten minutes, maybe fifteen on a good day.

There are different ways to begin. I have a quiet place where I won't be disturbed and the phone is turned off. I practice a spiritual meditation, which simply means that at the beginning I say a short prayer and think of this as a time that I'm particularly open to God. A non-spiritual approach just skips this part. It helps to use one of the relaxation techniques first and then begin the meditation. There's lots of material available on the internet on ADD and meditation. One site says that you can meditate standing or walking if sitting still is hard for you.

The main thing with meditation is to not become frustrated with it. You're probably not going to be very good at it. Just do what you can and you'll find it helpful.

Appendix 7. Therapy

Therapy, counseling and coaching

I'm a big fan of therapy. With hard work, people can make very significant changes in themselves and in their lives. Nobody had perfect parents nor grew up in a perfect world. We all carry childhood wounds which still cause us some trouble. We may or may not be having symptoms but we're not reaching our full potential. Dynamic therapy, which is what I generally mean when I say therapy, aims at understanding the relationship between whatever difficulties we may be having and their origins in childhood, and at processing the feelings. It's a process of learning and of healing. We can change patterns of thinking, of emotional response and of behavior. It is not about blaming parents or avoiding responsibility for our behavior; it's about understanding and processing.

Theoretically, everyone could benefit from therapy to improve their lives, no matter how well they are currently functioning. But therapy is hard work and requires time and commitment. There's a book by Johnson well titled (almost)– Therapy: The Hard Work Miracle. Most people will not invest the time and effort unless they're having significant problems. Therapy requires courage, honesty about oneself, and some ability to think psychologically. Not everyone is equipped to use it.

Cognitive therapy is another approach. It focuses on entrenched patterns of thinking which are not realistic nor helpful. It also looks at the ties to childhood experiences, but with less emphasis on that, and it deals less with emotions. There is significant overlap with dynamic therapy.

Counseling, as opposed to therapy, implies a supportive and encouraging relationship with some advice about dealing with current problems. Some significant change can result.

Coaching for ADD implies a supportive and encouraging relationship, educating about ADD and teaching strategies for coping. If someone handles their ADD better, there will be some change in psychological factors, such as self esteem and shame, for example.

All of these approaches involve some hard work and courage. While dynamic therapy is more extensive and ambitious, any of these approaches can lead to significant change and significant improvement in life.

I'm not suggesting at all that ADD is caused by poor parenting or by childhood experiences. It is largely genetic and has to do with brain wiring. But the reason many of us need therapy is to deal with the effects of having ADD: the shame, poor self image, and other issues. These effects usually begin in our childhood and then receive a lot of reinforcement through the rest of our lives. These effects need to be addressed and healed.

I assume that an ADD coach knows a lot about ADD. If you are looking for a therapist or a counselor, you want to make sure that they know a lot about ADD. They don't necessarily have to be like me and have ADD themself, but they need to knowledgeable or they won't understand.

Your life can be better just by using strategies. And even a small change (dare I mention the keys again?) can make a significant difference. Still, I hope you will also get some help with the other issues.

Appendix 8. List of lists

I like making lists and I find the lists and the making of them very helpful. I have discussed a lot of lists, so here's a summary:

1. to-do – the list of five things that are top priority now, on the red card, always with me. I won't necessarily get all five things done today.

2. the orange and yellow cards - for the things to do next (orange) and things that aren't so important or urgent (yellow). Always with me.

3. "the evolving working envelope list"– on my desk. Things I need to get to today or tomorrow. Includes the five top things, but I may not work right down that list; I likely will be doing other things too.

4. the Big List – the list of things I would like to do today or this week or this month. I can pull things off here to put onto the other lists. On my desk on a yellow legal pad. I may check it once a week or once a month.

5. the Really Big Far Off list – things I will probably eventually get to. This summer? Next year? Clean the garage, organize my file cabinets, buy new rug for the office. On a yellow legal pad. I may check this every three months or so.
6. the list of three – in my head. What I'm doing right now and what comes next.
7. the "list" of one – I try to focus only on what I'm doing right now and not be thinking of all the other lists and other tasks; that's part of the reason for making lists in the first place.

Appendix 9.   Follow up

1. Tom- when I asked Tom about interviewing him about strategies, he told me that he didn't have any. That was strange; how can someone with ADD survive without strategies? Then in the interview he told me of two strategies he has, and I put them in the book.

Months later, Tom's girlfriend brought up that when he's supposed to bring some food to her house, he puts his car keys in his refrigerator so he can remember. Strategy! Then Tom recalled that when he goes somewhere and takes his coat off, he always puts his keys in his coat pocket so that he can't leave without his coat. Strategy also.

Months after that, I was in Tom's house, and he showed me the counter top near the door to his garage. He always empties his pockets onto the counter - billfold, notes, everything - as soon as he comes in the house. He also puts there anything that he is going to need when he goes somewhere (like Richard's green bag). Strategy. Next to the counter is a hook to hang his keys on. Tom says he hasn't totally achieved the habit of hanging them there immediately; sometimes when he comes in his hands are full, but if he puts them somewhere else he will eventually move them to the hook (if he made it an inflexible rule, it would eventually become a habit and he would put them there before he did anything else, and then they would always be there).

Then Tom showed me the checklist taped to the counter. It says:

1. lock door
2. set alarm
3. get briefcase (if needed)
4. Take water (this is Santa Fe)

Tom says he's made a habit of going through the checklist every time he goes out, like a pilot before taking off in a plane. The checklist is a great strategy, but it might not work for me because once I was used to seeing it I probably wouldn't notice it. However, if I made it a rule, and especially if I made a mind game of imagining myself a pilot, it might work.

Since the counter is by the door where he goes out, and since he can't go anywhere without his keys, this system (or may I say, these strategies?) works pretty well for him.

When we talked about all this, Tom explained that he had never thought of these various things as strategies; they were just things he did to make his life better. But I was writing the book, and I couldn't keep revising it every time Tom revealed a new strategy, so I just left his chapter as it was and have the latest update, as of the moment, here in this appendix.

I don't want to say I told you so (yes, I do), but it was hard to imagine how someone with ADD could get by without strategies. Tom has made a number of comments about the book and the strategies. He says he doesn't like rules, even rules he has made for himself. He will not follow them. He does have a hook for his keys, but he doesn't always use it. This is not a problem for him.

This illustrates again that everyone is different, and what works for one person won't necessarily work for another. It also shows that a problem has to bother you enough before you will make the effort to work on it. Tom found the idea of changing "I have to" into "I need to" helpful, because he doesn't like being told what to do.

Tom says the steps idea is not very helpful because he has a lot of large projects and he doesn't know what the steps will be until he gets into the job. I refrained from suggesting that at that point he could make steps. Instead, his strategy is to plan, "Today I will work two hours on this project," and then stop for the day. That's a different way to do small steps; pretty clever.

Tom says that rewards won't work for him, because he'll cheat and just take the reward without doing the work first. I refrained from suggesting that he make the rewards big and something he would not ordinarily do for himself. Tom says that "the urgent overwhelms the important." This makes sense to me. Something may be less important but still has to be done today, so something more important may have to wait until tomorrow. But the way he operates, urgent things may come up in Tom's life more than for most of us. Tom sorts things into "tasks", which are things that will take some time, and "quick to-do's" like a phone call, that can be done in a moment and don't have to go on a to-do list. These sometimes can just be done as they pop up without listing them at all, like using the small bits of time to do small tasks. Sometimes Tom lists a bunch of short phone calls he needs to make and considers that one task. But he points out that sometimes the small to-do's can be used as a distraction, to avoid some other task. The strategy would be to be aware of doing that, and maybe set a time limit or limit the number of small tasks.

You remember that if Tom thinks he can finish something by the fifteenth of this month, he'll tell them it will be ready by the tenth of next month. Later he commented on this, saying, "But I still might not get started on it 'til the ninth."

Tom recognizes that he has ADD and that it causes him some problems. He has some strategies, but from my viewpoint his life looks more difficult than it needs to be. I've speculated on some possible reasons that he doesn't use more strategies to make his life better, but that's just my speculating. I came up with more speculation after I read this section. Maybe Tom is basically a rebel? Maybe he doesn't accept rules or deadlines, or schedules or anything that feels constricting or restrictive to him. Maybe he's not going to do things the regular way. Maybe he isn't going to let himself be controlled by pop-ups and alarms. Maybe he doesn't want to acknowledge that he uses strategies. Maybe his position that "I'm going to be a real goof-off." really means that he is going to be a rebel. And maybe he really is easy-going enough that things like paying penalties on his bills and other hassles really don't bother him.

I don't know. But it's possible that maintaining the rebel position is more important to him than making his life easier.

2. Ms. J

Ms. J, the lady with the bad job who never does good enough, can't finish anything, procrastinates, is angry and plays solitaire, suddenly had a break through. I don't know why. She talks about "the new me." She is asserting herself, setting boundaries, much less angry, and is getting things done. She is much happier and is feeling good about herself.

3. Balance

I have been brushing my teeth balancing on one foot for well over six months now. My ADD may be have improved slightly, not enough to be sure of it, and if it is, how do I know it's due to the balancing? But it doesn't cost anything, so I plan to keep it up.

Appendix 10. Mr. L

This is the story I left out because although Mr. L and Mr. C are different individuals with their own unique personalities, their stories sound nearly identical. Still, you might find Mr. L's story interesting and useful.

Mr. L is a 30 year old single man, very intelligent and a good athlete who is finally finding himself. He has a very accomplished, highly educated father, perhaps one could even say over-accomplished, if there is such a thing. How many degrees does one person need, and how many fields does a person need to master? Mr. L did alright in school but I think that he spent a lot of time daydreaming and could have done better-or he could have if he didn't have ADD. He has the ability to stick with things and to complete them, if he's interested in the task. In high school he was on a sports team where he was in a minority and was subjected to lots of harassment and abuse. Even so, he stuck with it and did well, although he remembers being miserable. Then he went to a difficult technical school and he completed that. Then he couldn't find a job in his field and he got discouraged and depressed.

Mr. L then decided to do a triathlon, the sports ordeal of doing a swimming race, a bike race, and running a marathon all in one event, which to me is incredible. For most good athletes simply running a marathon is quite an accomplishment. A marathon was, past tense, one of my life goals that I never accomplished (remember that Ms. M's husband also did a triathlon?). Mr. L set the goal of completing the triathlon. He felt good while he was training. He did well in the triathlon. Then he became depressed again, having accomplished his goal and having no idea what to do next. He bounced around from one menial job to another, having some problems with the bosses. He was pretty dissatisfied and was having depressions off and on. His parents, who were partly supporting him much of the time, were understandably concerned and frustrated. His father was giving him big doses of good advice and constructive criticism, as well as just plain criticism. His mother also had many suggestions; those didn't bother him as much as the input from his father, the very accomplished man.

Mr. L also had a long standing habit of second guessing himself over minor errors or lapses he made. He would get preoccupied with this second guessing. This was more depressing. Sometimes what he considered errors weren't actually errors, but just the idea that he could have done something better than he had. Do you remember we talked about perfectionism? Do you remember it perfectly?

At the urging of his parents, Mr. L came to see me for help. He himself didn't see the need for it and didn't think it would do any good. But unlike Mr. C, he was quite willing to talk about himself and his problems. The first thing he focused on was having no goal, no idea of what he wanted to do. He had a couple of ideas for business projects, which didn't sound very realistic to me, although I didn't say so. Maybe they were great creative ideas; they were certainly outside the box. Or maybe these ideas were similar to the daydreaming he'd done in school. Understandably he couldn't find funding for the projects. At our first meeting this overall picture, particularly the occupational difficulties, immediately made me think of ADD. As I heard more of his story it supported the diagnosis. So he took the ADD test, which pretty well confirmed it. He started Ritalin and found that it helped him focus and think more clearly. The Ritalin made it easier to be motivated and easier to start to do things instead of letting them slide. So he functioned somewhat better, and felt somewhat better, but he still had his basic problems. He didn't know what he wanted to do. He still had the preoccupation with perceived errors, which seemed a combination of perfectionism and compulsiveness. He was still somewhat depressed off and on. And, like Mr. C, he wasn't able to stand up to his father.

Mr. L had been to technical school but never to college. I suggested that he try a number of different college courses to see if he found a field that he truly liked. He didn't like that suggestion. Another suggestion was that we meet together with his father. He really didn't like that suggestion. He liked the Ritalin, but he still didn't see the point to therapy and he stopped coming.

Mr. L knocked around for a while and then came back to see me, this time as his own idea. He'd enrolled in a different type of technical school and was enjoying it and doing well. It's in a field where he's pretty well guaranteed a job when he graduates. It sounds like this will work for him this time. He uses the Ritalin and finds it very helpful for his studies. He has stood up to his parents in an appropriate and constructive fashion, and things are better between them. He doesn't seem to have much trouble with the depression now, but still is troubled with the preoccupations with perceived errors. He decided that therapy might be helpful after all.

However, he got busy and we had scheduling difficulties, and he stopped for a while. He started having some trouble in his classes. Unfortunately, I haven't heard from him lately. It's possible that the old ADD thing came up again, and he started school in a blaze of enthusiasm and then his focus center fizzled out as it was no longer novel and he was less challenged by it. I hope not. Still, Mr. L now understands that he has ADD. He has Ritalin, is not getting depressed like he was, and is doing much better with his father, so he has a much better chance of coping with the ADD and making this work this time. I hope so.

Final update: Mr. L just came back to see me. He had a rocky patch in school after the initial enthusiasm wore off. He had trouble focusing on his studies. He'd stopped using the Ritalin because he wanted to do it 'on his own'. He'd never gotten around to reading the studying helps I had sent him. He got kind of down. But he stuck it out and managed to get through the year. He is back on the Ritalin and finds it helpful, and is doing better now.

Glossary of the way terms are used in this book

acronym - a word, or pseudo-word, made from the initial letters of something, often an agency: ex: Nafta, Hippa, Yalpa

ADD - attention deficit disorder. Technically should be ADHD, attention deficit hyperactivity disorder, with subtypes: hyperactive, inattentive, mixed. I use ADD because the hyperactivity is not a major issue for me.

ADHD - see ADD

assay – verb, transitive: to examine or analyze: to assay a situation; to assay an event; noun : determination of the amount of metal, especially gold or silver, in an ore, alloy, etc.; a detailed report of the findings in assaying a substance.

conditioning - a significant part of the sleeping issue, and other issues. In the famous experiment of Pavlov's dogs, Pavlov rang the bell and then gave the dogs meat, over and over. Then he just rang the bell without meat, but the dogs salivated just as though they were getting the meat. They had been conditioned to salivate at the bell. In the same way, we have conditioning going on, so that we unconsciously produce conditioned, or automatic, responses. We want to condition our brain that bed means sleep and avoid conditioning it that the bed means something else. For example, some experts advise not to put your clock in the bedroom where you can see it. If you start waking up at 3 a.m. every night and check the clock and see that's its 3 a.m., your brain will be getting conditioned to wake up at 3 a.m., and the pattern will keep going.

dead end project – this is a big project, like writing a book, or researching a topic, that in the end, has no real payoff, doesn't move us towards any of our goals. It's a waste of time. Wasting time in general means frittering away time, like watching meaning-less TV, playing a computer game, or arguing in a chat room; it isn't a project, with an end point, but just a waste of time. Relaxing means making a conscious decision to take a break, for the explicit purpose of relaxing, and has a time limit.

demoralization - loss of morale; to lose hope, to feel that you can never do anything right or good enough; defeated, deflated, hopeless and helpless; 'Why bother trying?'

depression- a medical illness with an imbalance of neurochemicals in the brain, which needs treatment. Sometimes people confuse depression and other states, such as sad, down, unhappy, miserable, frustrated, angry, dissatisfied, demoralized, grieving, and so on, which are all normal human experiences. It can sometimes be useful to get help with some of those states, but they are not an illness. Depression is.

DSM - diagnostic and statistical manual of the American Psychiatric Association. Current version is DSM IV; they are working on V as we speak. DSM gives all the official psychiatric diagnoses and criteria, that is, lists of symptoms that must be present to make the diagnosis by the book. It is fairly good, was designed by a committee, and has strengths and weaknesses. We are still lacking good scientific basis for some of the diagnoses.

habit-when something is a habit, you automatically do it without having to think about it or make a decision.

intention, intentional, intentionality - doing something intentionally, on purpose, because you decided to do it, rather than because you somehow just drifted into it.

mnemonic - a type of memory device; a word, phrase or longer piece, that encodes information that we want to remember. For example, "Roy G Biv" helps us remember the colors of the rainbow.

power of one - the powerful strategy of focusing on just one thing you need to do and forgetting about all the rest until that one is done.

power of five – the powerful strategy of limiting a to-do list to five things. This prevent feeling over-whelmed and getting paralyzed.

repetitive script -see script

rule-a commitment you have made to yourself to always do a certain thing.

script-we are often not aware of the scripts that we follow, over and over, like a bad habit. These generally involve another person, which could be our partner, our parent, or our boss for example. It could be an argument:
A. "Why are you so X"?! (X= lazy, nasty, clumsy, etc)
B. "I'm not X!!"
A. "There you go, using denial again."

B. "Well, Mr. Perfect, like you always admit your flaws."

A. "Now you're sounding just like your mother."

B. "Why do you always pick on my family?!!
And so on.

If you can recognize the repetitive pattern, the script, you can change it, at any point. Instead of saying, "I'm not X" you could try "How do you mean?" or "I was born that way" or "Spaghetti and meatballs" or anything else that isn't in the script. Try it and see what happens.

self esteem - how we feel about ourselves, especially our sense of worth.

self image – the picture of ourselves we carry in our head; who we think we are, what we think we're like.

self-talk - the things we are saying to ourselves in our heads. It can be positive, "Hey, you can do this. Stick with it." or negative, "You're really stupid. You did it again." Sometimes we're aware of our self talk, sometimes not.

shame – the emotion we feel when we aren't measuring up to our standards, or those of others, and we feel exposed, feeling that others can or soon will see our failure and our flaws. A deep seated basic internal feeling. A common result of having ADD.

slogans - like mottos, some saying that gives you a guideline or a nudge in the right direction, helps you stay on track. Can be a memory aid and sometimes a morale booster.

spotting - the process of paying attention, noticing, and noting to ourselves, without judging, whenever we do something that we are trying to change. It is the first step in the process of changing a habit. It helps us become more aware of our doing it, and also can weaken the power of the habit. For example, "Oh, I know what that is; that's just my old 'stupid me' tape playing again."

therapy - see appendix 7

tool - something that you can use to help you do something.

woo woo - a Santa Fe term referring to therapies and concepts which are new agey, left field, outer space, etc. and not supported by valid research. Santa Fe may be the woo woo capital of the world, with myriad offerings of crystal therapy, aroma therapy, color therapy, pyramid therapy, reflexology, iridology, past life regression therapy, channeling therapy, and high colonic irrigation to clean out the

toxins. Some of those therapies may be very helpful for all I know, but they still qualify as woo woo.
Acupuncture used to be woo woo, but now has scientific validation.

Kind of a Bibliography

BOOKS:
Adler – Scattered Minds
Greenbaum – Finding Your Focus
Grossberg – Making ADD Work
Hallowell – Delivered from Distraction
Johnson – Characterlogical Transformation: the Hard Work Miracle
Kolberg – ADD-Friendly Ways To Organize Your Life
Lamott - Traveling Mercies : Some Thoughts on Faith.
Lerner - The Dance of Anger;   explains relationships
Lerner - The Dance of Intimacy ; even more
Orlov - The ADHD Effect On Marriage
Pirsig - Zen and the Art of Motorcycle Maintenence
Real - I Don't Want To Talk About It; explains about men
Sarkis - 10 simple solutions to adult ADD

Safren – <u>Mastering Your Adult ADD</u>
Tanner - <u>You Just Don't Understand</u>;   about men and women

ARTICLE:
William W. Dodson, MD, in his article "Real-World Office Management of ADHD in Adults", <u>Psychiatric</u> <u>Times</u>, Nov. 2006,

INTERNET:
Attention Deficit Disorder Association - http://www.add.org/
FOFA - http://www.findonefindall.com/
Mincu - http://www.thrivewithadd.com/
NIMH - http://www.nimh.nih.gov/health/topics/attention-deficit-hyperactivity-disorder-adhd/index.shtml
Orlov - http://www.adhdmarriage.com
Puryear - addadultstrategies.wordpress.com
Quily - http://adultaddstrengths.com/;
http://www.addcoach4u.com/

Douglas A. Puryear MD has been practicing psychiatry for over forty years. He was sixty-four years old before he realized that he has ADD. He lives in Santa Fe, New Mexico, with his wife and near his grandson Michael. His previous book is <u>Helping People in Crisis</u>.

CPSIA information can be obtained at www.ICGtesting.com
Printed in the USA
LVOW121548020513

332035LV00014B/581/P